Urban Soundscapes

Sound and listening are intrinsically linked to how we experience and engage with places and communities. This guide puts forward a new conceptual framework of embodied affectivity that emphasises listening in urban research and design and advances new ways of knowing and making. The guide invites landscape architects and urban designers to become *soundscape architects* and offers practical advice on sound and listening applicable to each stage of a design project: from reading the environment to intervening on it.

Urban Soundscapes foregrounds listening as an affective mediator between subjects and multispecies environments, and a vehicle to think and conceptualise environmental research and design beyond prevailing visual and human-centred modes. The guide expands landscape architects' and urban designers' tools and skills to assess existing soundscapes, predict how those soundscapes will be altered through their designs, consider sound as a creative and active part of the design process and envisage how users might perceive and be affected by those soundscapes as they evolve in time. The volume sits in the interface of research and practice and interweaves theoretical, methodological and creative contributions from acoustic ecology, ecoacoustics, bioacoustics and sound art. Each of the design stages is illustrated through project examples that demonstrate the many advantages of incorporating attentive listening and sound into Landscape Architecture and Urban Design Practice. This book shows how incorporating listening and sounding as part of the design process promotes slow and subtle ways of practice, adds social and ecological value through the reduction of noise pollution and by monitoring the health of habitats, and enables the design of soundscapes that complement the character and design intent of a scheme and elicit joy and wonder.

The book will be of interest to practitioners and academics in landscape architecture, and other design and spatial fields such as urban design, architecture, geography sound art and engineering, who play a primary role in the composition of the soundscape.

Dr Usue Ruiz Arana is a chartered landscape architect, researcher and educator. Usue is the Degree Programme Director for the *Master of Landscape Architecture* at Newcastle University and teaches across design studios, professional practice and design thesis modules. Her research is focused on two interrelated strands: more-than-human conceptualisations and listening and sounding in Landscape Architecture practice. Through her research, Usue seeks to affirm non-humans as designers, and design and art as forms of research, drawing from her experimental arts methods that include soundwalks, photography and temporary installations, and her 20-year career in practice. Her keen interest in design and art as forms of research informs her role as *Thinking Eye* editor of the peer reviewed *Journal of Landscape Architecture*.

Urban Soundscapes

A Guide to Listening for Landscape Architecture and Urban Design

Usue Ruiz Arana

Routledge
Taylor & Francis Group

NEW YORK AND LONDON

Designed cover image: Usue Ruiz Arana, Hai Anh Nguyen, Alison Unsworth, Kazusa Hayashi, Mian Han, Victoria Hole, iStock.com/lscatel57

First published 2024
by Routledge
605 Third Avenue, New York, NY 10158

and by Routledge
4 Park Square, Milton Park, Abingdon, Oxon, OX14 4RN

Routledge is an imprint of the Taylor & Francis Group, an informa business

Library of Congress Cataloging-in-Publication Data
Names: Ruiz Arana, Usue, author.
Title: Urban soundscapes: a guide to listening for landscape architecture and urban design / Usue Ruiz Arana.
Description: New York, NY: Routledge, 2024. | Includes index. |
Identifiers: LCCN 2023041089 | ISBN 9781032065960 (hardback) | ISBN 9781032065946 (paperback) |
ISBN 9781003202981 (ebook)
Subjects: LCSH: Sound (Philosophy) | Listening (Philosophy) | Sound in design. | Human ecology. | Landscape architecture. | City planning.
Classification: LCC B105.S59 R85 2024 | DDC 712—dc23/eng/20231122
LC record available at https://lccn.loc.gov/2023041089

ISBN: 978-1-032-06596-0 (hbk)
ISBN: 978-1-032-06594-6 (pbk)
ISBN: 978-1-003-20298-1 (ebk)
ISBN: 978-1-032-72590-1 (eBook+)

DOI: 10.4324/9781003202981

Typeset in Bembo
by codeMantra

Access the Support Material: www.routledge.com/9781032065960

Ena, Miguel eta Lili-rentzat (To Ena, Miguel, and Lili)

Contents

Contents

Figures

Soundtracks

Please note that these can be found embedded in the ebook+ version of the book for ebook+ readers, or by accessing the Support Material at www.routledge.com/9781032065960 for all other formats.

Acknowledgements

With thanks to,

Catherine Dee, for many inspiring conversations over lunch.

Dan Hill, for lending his ears, creativity and words to the Old Pottery.

Armelle Tardiveau, for helping me navigate academia alongside my writing.

Charlotte Veal, for her attentive reading and insightful comments on the introductory chapter that helped steer following ones.

Stef Leach, Lotte Dijkstra, Rudi van Etteger and Clive Davies for bringing to my attention books, works, artists and events that have permeated these pages.

Maggie Roe, for reminding me that theory should be foregrounded.

Ian Thompson and Matt Ozga-Lawn, for their encouragement as Ph.D. supervisors and to Ian thereafter for proofreading key chapters of the book, chopping my long sentences and prompting me to clarify ideas.

Tim Waterman and Prue Chiles, who not so long ago examined my PhD thesis with care and generosity, giving me the confidence to write this book.

Jacek Smolicki, Tim Shaw, Antonella Radicchi, Richard Bentley, Sarah Jones-Morris, Jack Harvie-Clark and David de la Haye, who enthusiastically agreed to be interviewed for this book, and whose words are contained in case studies.

All my Newcastle University landscape architecture and urban planning students for embracing with eagerness listening and sounding exercises and contributing insights and drawings to these pages.

Matthew Margetts, from EDable Architecture, and H + N + S Landschapsarchitecten for enabling me to include their drawings and photographs.

Editors, Kate Schell, for embracing the idea of this book and support thereafter, and Nick Craggs, for his guidance during the production stages and editorial team

Evie Evans, Megha Patel, Jake Millicheap, and Selena Hostetler for their prompt replies to all my queries and professional guidance.

My parents, Eugenia and Manuel, and my sisters, Inge-Lore and Aiala, for following the making of the book from the distance, accompanying me in walks and field recording sessions, and for their support throughout.

My kids, Ena, Miguel and Lili, who have patiently endured the writing of this book straight after the completion of my Ph.D., and whose bedtime stories are yet to fully recover from my night-time writing.

Alan, for reminding me of life beyond work and books.

The blackbirds, the seagulls, the pigeons, the sparrows, the crows, the robins, the blue tits and the long tits that, unknowingly, have followed my writing from outside the window.

Introduction

> sound ... is not the object but the medium of our perception.
>
> (Ingold, 2007, p. 11)

One of my happiest childhood memories is of being underwater and listening to the force of the sea as a strong wave passed over me. As a kid, I spent hours jumping the waves of the Atlantic Ocean in Hendaye, a French village on the border with Spain. Two summers ago, I returned to that beach and taught my eldest daughter how to jump the waves. As a wave approaches, you assess its size to decide whether to jump over it or whether it is wiser to duck under it. Immersed in the water, sensing those waves and feeling the strong thump in my ears as they passed over, I was instantly transported to my childhood and all those hours spent in the sea.

Sound and listening, through ears and bodies, are intrinsically linked to how we experience and engage with places and communities, and this forms the central premise of this book. There are many other listening experiences that I link to my childhood from afar, and to Hondarribia, a Basque village, close to the border with France, where my parents live: the rhythm of the church bells that punctuates the day reminding residents of key events; traditional Basque songs that move me and transport me home; the breaking of the waves against the shore and the sizzling of the foam as the sea takes them back (Soundtrack 0.1); the cacophony of the lively streets in the marine town; the multitude of languages mixed in street conversations at any one time – Basque, Spanish and French; footsteps on the cobbles of the old town, echoing along narrow streets; sounds filtering from adjacent streets and inviting pedestrians to explore what is happening; boats flapping their sails as they

DOI: 10.4324/9781003202981-1

navigate the strong winds at the mouth of the River Bidasoa; seabirds calling along both shores of the estuary; heavy rain thumping on pavements; or the tunes and thunderous blasts of the canons that accompany the annual town parade.

🎵 Soundtrack 0.1 Sizzling of sea foam.

Sounds are also a source of ongoing conflict for the residents of Hondarribia, however. The summer brings with it seasonal residents and a multitude of positive listening experiences, as described above. The summer also brings months of sleepless nights for town centre residents. In the summer of 2016, the town council installed signs bearing the words *Jaitsi bolumena mesedez* (turn the volume down, please) in the Marina neighbourhood and surrounding areas requesting noise abatement (Figure 0.1). These signs were mainly targeted toward bar and restaurant owners and their customers to remind them of residents' rights to sleep. At that time, the Marina neighbourhood was suffering from excessive noise from nightlife, and the windows were adorned with handwritten posters bearing words such as *Lo egin nahi dugu* (we want to sleep). The excessive noise that residents complained about that summer is not captured in noise maps, where Hondarribia appears as a relatively quiet city (Hondarribiko Udala, 2017). This noise, however, continues to be many residents' daily nightmare.

Figure 0.1 Signs installed by Hondarribia's municipality to encourage quieter uses in town.

The annoyance and sleep disturbances that the residents of Hondarribia experience are not unique to this neighbourhood. Exposure to environmental noise is a growing concern as it can adversely impact the health and well-being of both human and non-human communities (such as birds and bats), an impact that for humans goes beyond hearing loss and encompasses physiological and psychological effects. A report by the WHO Regional Office for Europe and the European Commission Joint Research Centre quantified the public health burden of environmental noise and estimated that 'at least one million healthy life years are lost every year from traffic-related noise in the western part of Europe' (2011, p. V). Sleep disturbance and annoyance are mainly responsible for this loss, followed by cardiovascular disease, cognitive impairment in children and tinnitus (ibid.). In non-human communities, exposure to environmental noise can interfere with animals' 'foraging behaviour, shifted temporal activity patterns, decreased abundance, reduced condition, and altered reproductive success' (Levenhagen *et al.*, 2021, p. 177).

Soundscape architects

Sound and listening are yet to permeate everyday landscape architecture and urban design practice. However, integrating sound and listening into built environment professions is essential to avoid the conflicts and health and well-being impacts that soundscapes can trigger, as highlighted by scholars and artists. Composer and accordionist Pauline Oliveros, for example, proposed that urban designers and planners should become *deep listeners* to engage with the soundscape and shape it (2015). Oliveros' *deep listening* is an improvisation and meditation practice that she developed over a lifetime to integrate hearing (involuntary) with listening (selective) (The Center for Deep Listening, 2021). For Oliveros, *deep listening* involves listening in 'as many ways as possible to everything that can possibly be heard all of the time as a way to connect listeners with the environment and its inhabitants' (ibid). Similarly, composers and sound artists Bruce Odland and Sam Auinger critiqued the lack of listening in urban design (2010). In an aptly titled article *Hearing Perspectives (Think with Ears),* Odland and Auinger likened the soundscape of MOMA's sculpture garden to 'any taxi rank in midtown NYC' and lamented a culture that prioritises the visual in decision-making and does not *think with ears* (ibid.).

Thinking with ears was also advocated by Canadian composer and educator Raymond Murray Schafer (1977). In *The Soundscape: Our Sonic Environment and the Tuning of the World*, a publication that emerged from the *World Soundscape Project,*

Schafer proposed that we are all soundscape composers (ibid.). Schafer's work is not devoid of criticism and limitations, as discussed in this volume. Nevertheless, it highlights the primary role that landscape architects and urban designers play in that composition. All landscape architecture and urban design interventions, no matter how small, sound. Everything vibrates, sounds, or can be heard or sensed through bodies. Through our design and management interventions, we play a part in composing the *geophony* (geophysical sounds), *biophony* (biological sounds), and *anthrophony* (anthropogenic sounds) of the environment (Krause, 1987). However, how many of us think of ourselves as *soundscape architects*?

In the last 20 years, landscape architects' and urban designers' visualisation, modelling and simulating tools and skills have developed immensely, reflecting the visual modes of thinking, knowing and doing that prevail in the profession. During that period, soundscape research has advanced considerably in urban planning, geography, acoustics, bio and ecoacoustics, acoustic ecology and sound art, amongst others, to improve our acoustic environments and consider sound more than mere noise to be mitigated. With application to urban soundscapes and human health, this wave of research was initiated by the Environmental Noise Directive (END, Directive 2002/49/EC) (European Parliament and Council, 2002). The END was not only concerned with noise and its detrimental effect on human health and well-being but also sought to protect positive environmental soundscapes in the form of quiet areas. The technical guide for identifying quiet areas that followed the END included the *soundscape approach* as a suitable methodology (European Environment Agency, 2014). The *soundscape approach* conceptualises the soundscape as a perceptual construct and accordingly prioritises human perception over acoustic measurements, as detailed throughout this volume. With application also to urban soundscapes and landscape planning, design and management, considerable research has been carried out in other disciplines that study sound and the environment, including bioacoustics and ecoacoustics, sound studies and sound art. Despite the breadth of research on soundscapes, listening and active consideration of sound is yet to permeate everyday landscape architecture and urban design practice. We lack the knowledge and skills, including attentive listening, to assess existing soundscapes, predict how soundscapes will be altered through our designs, consider sound as an active part of the design process, or envisage what projected environments would sound like (Ruiz Arana, 2020). Caught up in visual modes of thinking and doing, we are yet to fully embrace the possibilities of *thinking with our ears* as *soundscape architects*.

Many professionals do *think with their ears* and *train their listening*. Doctors, for example, *train their listening* to detect abnormal sounds in patients' internal organs.

Similarly, engineers and car mechanics *attune their listening* to detect sound changes in motors (Ruiz Arana, 2021). Despite the crucial role that landscape architects and urban designers play in shaping the soundscapes surrounding us, listening does not play a primary role in our training or practice. In our training, drawing, sketching and manipulating visual space are key skills to develop and master, yet little attention is paid to listening, auralisations or aural space. In our practice, designs are conceptualised and presented through drawings and images, and landscape assessments largely focus on visual assessments to the detriment of aural assessments and aural ways of thinking and doing.

In my landscape architecture career in practice, spanning 14 years before I started paying attention to listening in 2014, I thought of sound seldom, usually just as noise that needed mitigation in certain sites or in the creation of sensory gardens for health settings or educational environments that sought to target all the senses. Training my listening, engaging with existing research and creative practices from all those fields introduced above, and developing a portfolio of creative practice research focused on sound made me realise the advantages that listening can bring to build environment professions and research. Building on my research and creative practice, this volume puts forward a new conceptual framework of embodied affectivity that foregrounds listening in urban research and design to enable multispecies soundscapes for the health and well-being of human and non-human communities, to promote slow and subtle ways of doing landscape architecture and to de-centre humans in urban design. This volume also provides the reader with creative and practical tools and techniques for incorporating listening and sounding as part of the design process, advancing new ways of knowing, learning and making through listening that supplement prevailing visual modes.

From sound as a material object to listening as the medium of our perception

Landscape architects and urban designers are soundscape composers and, more importantly, soundscape performers and audiences. Understanding the interaction between those different roles is key to becoming soundscape architects. Architect, author and educator Klaske Havik reminds us that 'in literature, the user appears twice, not only as a character whose activities unfold in time and space, but also as the reader who, in a sense, co-produces the story by his or her own imagination' (2012, p. 17). Similarly, in the design of the environment, the designer appears twice. First and foremost, as an active user of the space, reading and co-producing the landscape by their presence in it. Second, as the designer, using their imagination and expertise to transform the space, conceptualising and envisaging new futures for it. Accordingly, this volume emphasises first the role of listening as an affective mediator of the interaction between people and place and, by extension, designers as audience and performers. Second, this volume conceptualises sound as a material and creative object in the design process and, by extension, designers as composers.

Barry Truax, in his influential book *Acoustic Communication*, advocates a communication model of sound to understand better the interrelationships between sound(s), listener(s) and environment(s) (1984). He proposes that 'a sound means something partly because of what produces it, but mainly because of the circumstances under which it is heard' (ibid, p. xii). His thinking aligns with constructivist understandings of landscape as an interactive relationship between people and place (Council of Europe, 2000). We are an integral part of the landscape, performers and audience, and sound (through listening) mediates our relationship with the landscape and its communities. Sound, as mediation between listener and environment, operates at different spatial and temporal scales, as the opening vignette demonstrates. It mediates the relation between the listener and the environment at a particular moment and place (e.g., sounds filtering from an adjacent street and inviting me to explore what is happening), between the listener and the memories of the environment that the sound elicits (the waves that awaken childhood memories), between listener(s) and soundmaker(s) (the many street conversations of the town), between communities and their environment (the church bells reminding residents of key events), between the environment and its history (the footsteps in the old town, echoing through thick stone walls and narrow streets) and between environments (the calls of the seabirds along both shores of the Bidasoa). If sound, as anthropologist Tim Ingold succinctly says, is 'the medium of our perception' (2007, p. 11), then by extension, listening becomes a 'way of knowing', as musician and sound scholar Gascia Ouzounian proposes through her concept of *auditology (2021)*.

The perceptual and relational understanding of sound introduced above is central to the concept of the soundscape advanced by the International Organization for Standardization as the '*acoustic environment as perceived or experienced and/or understood by a person or people, in context*' (BSI, 2014, p. 1). Different disciplines adjust the understanding of the soundscape according to their focus of study. Within soundscape ecology, for example, the soundscape is 'the collection of biological, geophysical and anthropogenic sounds that emanate from a landscape and which vary over space and time reflecting important ecosystem processes and human activities'

(Pijanowski *et al.*, 2011, p. 1214). This second definition of soundscape shifts the focus from a human-centred perceptual construct towards a de-centred enquiry that foregrounds all communities in the making and perceiving of the soundscape. Historian Emily Thompson interlinks these two conceptualisations when she proposes that a soundscape, akin to a landscape, 'is simultaneously a physical environment and a way of perceiving that environment; it is both a world and a culture to make sense of that world' (2012, p. 117). The soundscape is the aural expression of the physical environment, including its communities. It is the medium to perceive and interact with that environment, which depends on individual, social and cultural aspects and characteristics (ibid.).

As well as mediating a relation, a sound or soundscape can be evaluated as a material, aesthetic and affective object: we can ask whether it is perceived as positive or not, whether it is appropriate to a place or not. Thompson's intertwined definition of soundscape encompasses these different facets of sound, which are relevant to the work of built environment professionals and scholars, as the soundscape expresses the culture, character and identity of a place as perceived by its inhabitants, mediates the relation between human and non-human communities and their environment and informs de-centred ways of practising landscape architecture and urban design. Sound is also a material, creative and affective object with applications to all project stages.

If we envisage sound as both a material object and mediator of a relation, listening, in turn, can have many interrelated functions and be employed in interrelated modes. In the first part of this book on *attunement*, I put forward a conceptual framework that encompasses three interrelated modes of listening which expand visual modes of thinking, knowing and doing in landscape architecture and urban design: (1) *listening as communication*, (2) *aesthetic listening* and (3) *affective listening* (Figure 0.2).

1. First, listening, as discussed, can help us understand a place, and its communities, providing information about the character of a place and what is happening around it.
2. Second, listening is an aesthetic pursuit and can contribute to how a space is used and valued.
3. Last, listening is a source of affective engagement with the environment, a relationship that occurs regardless of whether communication occurs (Gallagher, 2013, p. 41).

Figure 0.2 The three modes of listening in landscape architecture and urban design.

Drawing upon embodied affectivity theory (Fuchs and Koch, 2014), I argue that in our interaction with the environment through listening, we are affected by the sounds and silences of the environment, an affection that conditions our actions within the environment. Emotions are bodily reactions and actions that result from affections and feedback to them (ibid.). Emotions drive our actions in the environment, help us connect with the environment and determine our priorities (ibid.). Thus, affective listening is the most ordinary and essential mode of environmental listening, as it mediates our interaction with the environment.

Affective listening is the umbrella that can (but does not have to) encompass *aesthetic listening* and *listening as communication*. This is the case, for example, for the thump of the strong waves passing over me while immersed in the water, which awaken memories and invite me to stay, regardless of whether the vibrations themselves provide information about the sea's force or the waves' height. This is also true for the loud music that prevents residents from sleeping. Annoyance, in this case, is independent of whether the music is fully heard or understood, yet it is contextual.

Affective listening enables researchers and designers to disrupt visual modes of doing. First and foremost, it embeds researches and designers in an environment as part of fieldwork, interweaving experiential and objective site inquiries, thus interlinking their role of as active listeners and co-producers of a place and as planners, designers and researchers. *Affective listening* also helps researchers and designers uncover the specificity of a place, its inhabitants and its aural affordances, which might contrast with visual affordances and invite other forms of practice (including more-than-human). *Affective listening* also helps designers relate to how current and future human and non-human communities might be affected by interventions and how they might interact with prospective spaces, refining conceptual designs.

Listening in those three interrelated modes can be threaded through all the stages of the life of a landscape architecture and urban design project, from site investigation to post-occupancy studies, as attested by the methodological tools and techniques put forward in this book. Besides the many uses and benefits that should become apparent as the reader progresses through the volume, now is a critical time to start listening to respond to emerging policies, the climate and biodiversity emergency, and urbanisation rates. Emerging policies, such as the Noise and Soundscape Action Plan for Wales, require the planning of positive soundscapes as well as providing noise mitigation or reduction (Welsh Government, 2018). The climate and biodiversity emergency demands new forms of practice attuned to non-humans and environments, and listening can be an integral part of these. Finally, increasing urbanisation requires positive soundscapes for the health and well-being of urban communities.

Now is also a crucial time to listen as the recent COVID-19 pandemic has, in many ways, opened our ears and bodies to sound. With the reduction of traffic noise and mandates to stay local, we started to attune to the sounds of our immediate environment, whether welcome sounds, such as birdsong, or unwelcome ones, such as the noise from ventilation systems. We have an opportunity now to decide whether we return to pre-COVID soundscapes or take this opportunity to change how we sound radically and to leave meaningful space for all the non-human voices that we have started to hear.

Structure of the book

This book is structured into three parts and an annex which, taken together, encompass the interrelated tenets of this book: (1) to foreground listening as an affective mediator between subjects and multispecies environments, (2) to foreground listening as a vehicle to think and conceptualise environmental design beyond prevailing visual and human-centred modes, and (3) to conceptualise and design multispecies soundscapes (and, by extension, landscapes) through the integration of human and non-human centred soundscape research and approaches.

The first tenet is addressed and advanced in the opening part, *Attunement*. Chapter 1 starts by contextualising this book within sound and soundscape research and practice in disciplines concerned with the study of the environment, including acoustic ecology, sound studies, bioacoustics and ecoacoustics, acoustics and sound art, to develop a working definition of soundscape to guide the work (Chapter 1). Chapter 2 advances a conceptual framework for listening as affective mediator between subject and environment, drawing from embodied affectivity theory. The chapter foregrounds emotion as the driver of action in the environment, which is central to environmental design. Chapter 3 discusses the effects of non-listening on human and non-human health and well-being. The chapter concludes with practices and exercises geared towards tuning into the environment, from *deep listening* to soundwalking, as starting points for becoming *soundscape architects*. Chapter 4 showcases case studies and practitioners attuned to the environment.

The second tenet is addressed in the central part, *Composition*. The work of landscape architects and urban designers is concerned with reading, transforming and representing the environment (Jørgensen *et al.*, 2020). Accordingly, this part follows these three stages in the design process. It provides a theoretical, methodological and pedagogical contribution to landscape architecture and urban design by providing tools and techniques for listening and sounding as part of those three stages. This part is organised into theoretical and methodological chapters (5 and 7) and case study chapters (6 and 8) that put those theories and methods into practice. Chapters 5 and 6 are concerned with reading the landscape through listening. Chapters 7 and 8 concern soundscape composition: transforming and representing the landscape through listening and sounding.

The third and last tenet is addressed in the last part, *Performance*. The work of landscape architects and urban designers is also concerned with monitoring sites post-completion, as landscapes are never finished and are constantly evolving.

Non-humans are central to that evolution, so Chapters 9 and 10 in this part focus on non-human theories and methods for soundscape monitoring and design and how these can be integrated with human-centred approaches.

The concluding annex provides an abridged version of the tenets of this book and the theoretical, methodological and creative contributions for listening and sounding as part of the design process. The annex is intended as a manual for practice to provide practitioners with a concise guide on integrating listening and sounding within their projects.

Some of the case studies featured in this book are my work: landscape architecture schemes, creative research experiments and academic design studio projects I have developed along my listening journey. Other case studies feature artists, researchers and practitioners from various fields whom I have met along the way and whose work has imprinted on my own. These take the form of interviews inspired by the books on field recording and sound art edited by Cathy Lane and Angus Carlyle (2013, 2021). The aim is for the interviewee to guide the narrative of the case study and invite different readings of the material. As well as these main case studies, examples by others are threaded throughout the book to give an overall picture of the breadth of ongoing soundscape projects and practice.

In a single volume, it is impossible to contain all there is to say about listening and sounding and all the research and practice relevant to urban soundscapes. These pages, however, give the reader a robust theoretical and practical introduction to the subject and provide many references and case studies for follow-up study.

As the reader will have guessed by now, listening has been integral to the development of this book. The reader is invited to listen to the many sounds embedded in this work in the midst of reading or in between readings and to put into practice the exercises threaded within. Sounds are embedded as descriptive narratives for readers to co-create through their imagination and as sound files in the ebook to listen to.[1]

Note

1. This book draws from my Ph.D. Thesis, in particular Chapters 1 and the Annex (Ruiz Arana, 2020).

References

BSI (The British Standards Institution) (2014) 'ISO 12913-1: 2014 Acoustics — Soundscape Part 1 : Definition and conceptual framework'.

Council of Europe (2000) *European Landscape Convention, Florence 20.10.2000,* European Treaty Series, No. 176, 7p. Available at: https://rm.coe.int/1680080621.

European Environment Agency (2014) *Good practice guide on quiet areas.* Copenhagen.

European Parliament and Council (2002) 'Directive 2002/49/EC of the European Parliament and of the Council of the 25th June 2002, relating to the assessment and management of environmental noise', *Official Journal of the European Communities*, L189, pp. 12–25.

Fuchs, T. and Koch, S. C. (2014) 'Embodied affectivity: On moving and being moved', *Frontiers in Psychology*, 5(June), pp. 1–12. doi: 10.3389/fpsyg.2014.00508.

Gallagher, M. (2013) 'Listening, meaning and power', in Carlyle, A. and Lane, C. (eds) *On listening.* Devon: Uniformbooks, pp. 41–44.

Havik, K. M. (2012) *Urban literacy: A scriptive approach to the experience, use and imagination of place.* Technische Universiteit Delft. Available at: http://resolver.tudelft.nl/uuid:6eb74e99-29aa-41fa-bba9-c5ae887999f7.

Hondarribiko Udala. (2017) *Mapa de ruido y zonificacion acustica del municipio de Hondarribia (Gipuzkoa).* Available at: https://www.cali.gov.co/documentos/529/mapa-ruido-dagma/.

Ingold, T. (2007) 'Against soundscape', in Carlyle, A. (ed.) *Autumn leaves.* Paris: Double Entendre, pp. 10–13.

Jørgensen, K., *et al.* (2020) 'Teaching landscape architecture: A discipline comes of age', *Landscape Research*, 00(00), pp. 1–12. doi: 10.1080/01426397.2020.1849588.

Krause, B. (1987) 'Bioacoustics, habitat ambience in ecological balance', *Whole Earth Review*, 57(Winter), pp. 14–18.

Lane, C. and Carlyle, A. (2013) *In the field: The art of field recording.* Devon: Uniformbooks.

Lane, C. and Carlyle, A. (2021) *Sound arts now.* Devon: Uniformbooks.

Levenhagen, M. J. *et al.* (2021) 'Ecosystem services enhanced through soundscape management link people and wildlife', *People and Nature*, 3(1), pp. 176–189. doi: 10.1002/pan3.10156.

Odland, B. and Auinger, S. (2010) *Hearing perspective (Think with Your Ear), O + A.* Available at: http://www.o-a.info/background/hearperspec.htm (Accessed: 21 July 2015).

Oliveros, P. (2015) *The difference between hearing and listening, TEDx talks.* Available at: https://www.youtube.com/watch?v=_QHfOuRrJB8 (Accessed: 27 March 2023).

Ouzounian, G. (2021) 'The Sonic rewilding of cities: Listening after lockdown', paper presented at *Crafting a sonic urbanism: Listening to non-human life.* Paris. https://

www.gaite-lyrique.net/plein-ecran/contenu/realiser-un-urbanisme-sonique-a-lecoute-de-la-vie-non-humaine.

Pijanowski, B. C. *et al.* (2011) 'What is soundscape ecology? An introduction and overview of an emerging new science', *Landscape Ecology*, 26(9), pp. 1213–1232. doi: 10.1007/s10980-011-9600-8.

Ruiz Arana, U. (2020) *The enchantment of the wild: A journey into wildness through listening*. Newcastle University, Available at: http://theses.ncl.ac.uk/jspui/handle/10443/5178.

Ruiz Arana, U. (2021) 'Thinking with my ears', *Landscape Journal*, 21(2), pp. 29–32.

Schafer, R. M. (1977) *The soundscape: Our Sonic environment and the tuning of the world*. Rochester, VT: Destiny Books.

The Center for Deep Listening (2021) *About deep listening, the center for deep listening*. Available at: https://www.deeplistening.rpi.edu/deep-listening/.

Thompson, E. (2012) 'Sound, modernity and history', in Sterne, J. (ed.) *The sound studies reader*. Oxon and New York: Routledge, pp. 117–129.

Truax, B. (1984) *Acoustic communication, Springer handbook of ocean engineering*. Norwood, NJ: Ablex Publishing Corporation. doi: 10.1007/978-3-319-16649-0_15.

Welsh Governemnt (2018) *Noise and soundscape action plan*. Available at: https://www.gov.wales/sites/default/files/publications/2019-04/noise-and-soundscape-action-plan.pdf.

WHO Regional Office for Europe (2011) *Burden of disease from environmental noise*, World Health Organization.

PART I
_____

Attunement

Chapter One

Landscape, soundscape

Listening disciplines and inter-disciplinary projects

Several existing and emerging environmental fields of study and disciplines *think with their ears*, and their scope of study sometimes overlaps. These include:

- *Acoustic ecology,* which is concerned with how we perceive and design our acoustic environment and with using environmental sounds for sound composition (Schafer, 1977). Acoustic ecology seeks to 'integrate the listener within the soundscape' with the understanding that we are responsible for the design of it (Truax, 1984, p. Xv).
- *Acoustics,* which is an interdisciplinary field concerned with the study of 'the generation, transmission and reception of energy in the form of vibrational waves in matter' and its impact on everyday (human) life (Institute of Acoustics, 2022). The parallel field of *psychoacoustics* is concerned with the perceptual study of vibrational waves. Acoustics studies 'objective acoustic parameters, such as intensity, frequency and waveform', while psychoacoustics is interested in their subjective equivalents: 'loudness, pitch and timber' (Truax, 1984, p. 5).
- *Bioacoustics and ecoacoustics,* which are centred on the study of sound for animal communication, including 'behaviour, life-history theory, and the physics of sound production by animals' (Pijanowski, Villanueva-Rivera *et al.*, 2011, p. 204).
- *Soundscape ecology,* which places itself alongside landscape ecology, as it studies 'all sounds emanating from a given landscape, including biological, geophysical and human sounds, which together reflect the ecological processes of that landscape' (Pijanowski, Farina *et al.*, 2011).

DOI: 10.4324/9781003202981-3

- *Sound art,* which encompasses a wide variety of artists who use sound (listening and sounding) in many forms. Among these, a growing number of environmental sound artists actively engage with and integrate the environment within their artwork (Bianchi and Manzo, 2016).
- *Sound studies,* which is an interdisciplinary framework concerned with studying sound from a humanities and social sciences perspective. It studies 'what sound does in the human world, and what humans do in the sonic world' (Sterne, 2012, p. 2).
- Finally, *acoustemology,* which is a term coined by anthropologist Steve Feld in the 1990s to describe a way of 'knowing-with and knowing through' sound. This emerged from his fieldwork in Papua New Guinea with the Kaluli, a culture deeply attuned to their acoustic environment (Feld, 2015, p. 12). Many practitioners and researchers have adopted the concept as it foregrounds sound as a medium for relating and knowing, which is one of the emphases of this book.

The role that aesthetics and human perception play within the above disciplines can differentiate them (Barclay and Gifford, 2018) and group them. Thus, acoustics, acoustic ecology, sound studies and sound art would be human-centred inquiries. In contrast, soundscape ecology, bioacoustics and ecoacoustics would seek to de-centre or remove human subjectivity. Our work as landscape architects and urban designers concerns humans, non-humans, and more-than-humans (understood as the myriad of entanglements between humans and non-humans) as we plan, design and manage spaces and places for all communities. Accordingly, the theoretical, creative and practical tools and techniques for incorporating listening and sounding put forward over subsequent chapters draw from both phenomenological, human-centred sound inquiries and de-centred disciplines. This volume also aims to foster interdisciplinary collaborations in projects by highlighting these disciplines, projects and theories.

Following this short overview of disciplines, the coming pages introduce the reader to relevant theories, research and projects.

Acoustic ecology and the world soundscape project

The field of acoustic ecology originated at the Simon Fraser University in Vancouver. Here, in the late 1960s, Canadian composer and educator Raymond Murray Schafer set up the *World Soundscape Project* (WSP) research group. The group aimed to study and respond to Vancouver's rapidly changing soundscape, which Schafer felt was getting increasingly noisier, and to get people listening to their acoustic environment. The scope of their first project, Vancouver, was later extended to Canada and five European villages (Truax, 2018). The group developed the notion that the sounds of a particular locality reflect the identity of that community.

In *The Soundscape: Our Environment and the Tuning of the World,* Schafer proposed that we all play a role as composers of the soundscape, understood as 'any portion of the sonic environment regarded as a field for study' (1977, p. 274). In Schafer's conceptualisation, the soundscape was a 'huge musical composition unfolding around us' that we simultaneously listen to, perform and compose (ibid., p. 271). Thus, it was a perceptual and aesthetic field of study.

Aptly, Schafer introduced a musical terminology for the soundscape, which is still relevant today. A soundscape comprises 'keynote sounds, signals, and soundmark sounds' (1977). *Keynotes* in music define the tonality of a piece, and in the soundscape, they are the background sounds, not consciously heard. Examples include sounds resulting from a place's geography and climate: 'water, wind, forests, plains, birds and animals' (ibid., p. 10). *Signals* are 'foreground sounds … listened to consciously' (ibid.). Therefore, any sound could become a signal through conscious listening. Included here are 'acoustic warning' signals such as bells, whistles, horns, and sirens (ibid.). Finally, *soundmarks*, equivalent to landmarks, are those unique sounds that form part of a community's identity (ibid.).

Schafer also introduced the terms *hi-fi* and *lo-fi* to assess the soundscape and describe the move from a rural to an urban one, with the connotation that it was a move from a positive to a negative soundscape (1977, p. 43). In a *hi-fi* soundscape, there is little ambient noise, and sounds can be distinguished clearly; it has a 'favourable signal-to-noise ratio … and there is perspective – foreground and background' (ibid.). In a *lo-fi* soundscape, the perspective is lost, and individual sounds can no longer be distinguished amongst many sounds (ibid.). Appropriately, Schafer defined a human-scale space in relation to the 'human ear and human voice' as one where background sound does not mask the human voice (Schafer, 1967, p. 23).

In Schafer and WSP's *lo-fi/hi-fi* classification of the soundscape, the likening of modern culture to noise has been a focus of critique as it is deemed incompatible with current urban soundscapes (Lacey, 2016). The work has also been criticised for considering the soundscape as an aesthetic composition akin to music, to the detriment of sound as communication (Truax, 2012) and for its Western cultural focus, which, it is argued, has left out and ignored indigenous voices (Akiyama, 2015).

Despite that criticism, some of WSP's concepts and guidance are still highly relevant to urban planning, design and management, such as:

- WSP's original aim to get people listening to their acoustic environment and to make them question what cities sound like.
- The idea is that the sounds of a particular place reflect the identity of that community and therefore contribute to the landscape character and identity of a place.
- That we are all soundscape composers, and as landscape architects and urban designers, we should strive to be conscious soundscape composers. The musical terminology and *hi-fi, lo-fi* concepts introduced above can help design comfortable and rich soundscapes for all communities.

Acoustic communication

Barry Truax, an original member of the WSP, expanded on its findings to shift focus from a perceptual, aesthetic understanding of the soundscape to a 'communicational model' that bridged the objectivity of acousticians and the subjectivity of aesthetic-human perception models of soundscape studies (Truax, 2012, p. 194).

Truax's communicational approach to acoustics considers sound as information exchange and listening, correspondingly, as the medium of the exchange between individuals and their environment (1984). Sound, Truax argues, 'is capable of creating relationships between listeners and their environment in a dynamic process of embodied cognition' (ibid., p. 194). Accordingly, Truax employs the term soundscape to describe 'how the individual and society as a whole understand the acoustic environment through listening' (ibid., p. xii). Truax's communicational model emphasises the importance of context to sound and listening, as the meaning of sound depends on who or what makes that sound (the source of the sound) and the 'circumstances under which it is heard' (ibid., p. xii).

Truax's understanding of the soundscape relates to contemporary, constructivist, understandings of landscape as a dynamic relation, an interaction of people and place and not only as a physical field of study (Council of Europe, 2000). A landscape is understood as an area whose character results from the interaction of human and non-human factors, while sound and soundscape are an expression and medium of that interaction. The soundscape is, therefore, perceptual and contextual. This understanding of soundscape is useful in two ways. First, it reminds us as designers that we are listeners and soundmakers. Therefore, we are integral parts of the soundscape, both subjects and objects. Second, it enables change (through design) to happen at any point in this dynamic relationship between sound source, listener and context (Truax, 1984).

Truax has also provided useful reflections on the findings of the WSP's *Five Villages Soundscapes* project, which documented the soundscape of various villages in Scotland, France, Italy, Germany and Sweden. The purpose of the study was to find out the role that sounds played in community life. It introduced the concept of *acoustic community* to describe the prevalent (and mostly positive) role the soundscape of the community had in everyday life (Truax, 2021). The concept of *acoustic community* reinforces Schafer's idea of a human-scale or human-centred soundscape, where human sounds are not masked by technological sounds (ibid.). Truax advances the need to maintain and develop 'soundscapes on a human scale' where communities feel that they belong to their environment and where adverse health and well-being effects (of noise) are minimised (ibid., p. 125). This idea of healthy soundscapes is also transportable to non-human scales, as discussed later in this chapter.

Before we leave the WSP, we must remember the work of another member, Hildegard Westerkamp. Westerkamp's approach to listening has had a big influence on my work and contributed to this book's premises. Her work is discussed in Chapter 2 when discussing *affective listening* and in Chapter 8 as part of the case studies.

The WSP, together with Schafer, Truax and Westerkamp's subsequent work, developed the field of acoustic ecology. Two consequent approaches are relevant to this book: the *Positive Soundscape Project* (PSP) and the *soundscape approach*. Both approaches prioritise human perception over acoustic measurements and expand the study of urban soundscapes beyond noise.

Positive Soundscape Project an inter-disciplinary approach

The *PSP* was a UK-based inter-disciplinary soundscape study that sought to develop a theoretical model for understanding and classifying soundscape perception beyond good or bad (Davies *et al.*, 2013). The project used various quantitative and qualitative methods, including soundwalks, and concluded that the 'distinction between sound and noise is essentially an emotional one' (ibid., p. 230). The study developed a model for soundscape perception based on two dimensions of the emotional response: calmness and vibrancy (ibid.). *Calmness* is strongly

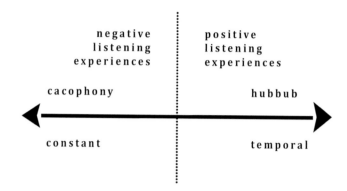

Figure 1.1 Vibrancy soundscape model adapted from (Davies *et al.*, 2013).

linked to pleasantness, and *vibrancy* depends on two registers: *cacophony-hubbub* and *constant-temporal* (Figure 1.1).

Cacophony-hubbub relates to the number of sound sources and how they mix, harmoniously or not, while *constant-temporal* relates to the degree of monotony and rhythm. *Calmness, hubbub* and *temporal* categories are related to positive listening experiences, whereas *cacophony* and *constant* relate mainly to negative ones (ibid.). As discussed in Chapter 7, this and subsequent models are a useful resource for developing aural strategies for a site.

Soundscape approach

The *soundscape approach* was proposed as a suitable methodology to help identify quiet areas in the technical guide (European Environment Agency, 2014), which followed the European Environmental Noise Directive 2002/49/EC (European Parliament and Council, 2002). The *soundscape approach* encompasses research and projects guided by three recent publications from the International Organization for Standardization: ISO 12913 Parts 1, 2, and 3, with Part 4 currently under development. Part 1 provides a conceptual framework for the term soundscape; Part 2 describes the requirements for data collection and reporting for soundscape studies focused on the key components of the soundscape: 'people, acoustic environment and context' (BSI, 2018, p. 2); and Part 3 guides how to analyse the qualitative and quantitative data collected through the methods introduced in Part 2. Given their relevance to urban soundscape research and practice, a brief introduction to each of the parts and key terms is provided below:

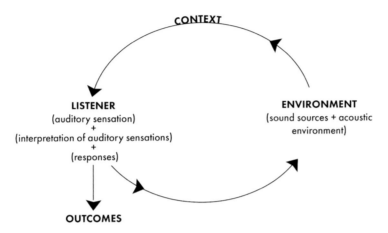

CONTEXT

LISTENER
(auditory sensation)
+
(interpretation of auditory sensations)
+
(responses)

ENVIRONMENT
(sound sources + acoustic
environment)

OUTCOMES

Figure 1.2 Elements in the perceptual construct of the soundscape adapted from (BSI, 2014, Figure 01).

Part 1

Part 1 defines the variables that affect the perception of the environment through sound: 'context, sound sources, acoustic environment, auditory sensation, interpretation of auditory sensation, responses, and outcomes' (BSI, 2014, p. 1) (Figure 1.2).

Context includes the interactions between people, places and activities in time and space (ibid., p. 1). It, therefore, is affected by personal and environmental variables that influence the auditory sensation, its interpretation and consequent responses. Examples of contextual variables are weather, lighting, other sensorial information, an individual's attitude to the sound source, emotions, perceived control over sound and activities engaged in (ibid.).

Sound sources are all the things that produce sounds and are thus the origin of the acoustic environment. The *acoustic environment* is the collection of sounds that reach the listener, having travelled through the environment (ibid.). The acoustic environment differs from the soundscape in that the latter is the acoustic environment as perceived by the listener.

Auditory sensation is the neurological process triggered by auditory stimuli, and *interpretation* is the processing of the auditory signals leading to understanding the acoustic environment.

Finally, *responses* are immediate reactions and actions, which might affect the context, and *outcomes* are long-term effects of those responses (BSI, 2014). Examples of a response could be leaving a space due to annoyance caused by sounds, while examples of an outcome might be a change of habits (ibid.).

Part 2

Part 2 proposes a methodology aimed at bridging the gap between the soundscape as 'measured by people' (through soundscape *descriptors* that capture the perception of the acoustic environment) and the soundscape as 'measured by instruments' (through acoustic *indicators* that anticipate a *descriptor*) (BSI, 2018, p. 4). The methodology for data collection includes soundwalks aimed at measuring the soundscape through human perception. During soundwalks, participants fill in questionnaires or participate in interviews to report on soundscape *descriptors*. The methodology for data collection also includes binaural acoustic measurements aimed at extracting acoustic *indicators* (i.e., sound pressure level) and psychoacoustic *indicators* (i.e., sharpness, tonality, roughness and fluctuation strengths). The aim is to study people, context and the acoustic environment by integrating different methods.

The terminology of sounds introduced in Part 2 follows that which Schafer originally proposed, with *background sounds* (equivalent to *keynotes*) and *foreground sounds* (equivalent to *signals*). The soundscape literature adds a further term, *salient sounds*, equivalent to *soundmarks,* which are listened to attentively (Kang *et al.*, 2016).

Part 3

Part 3 provides the methods and tools to analyse the wide range of data collected in Part 2, understanding that one method might take precedence over others, depending on the project's scope and the data collected. Analysis methods include statistical analysis for quantitative perceptual data and systematic text analysis for qualitative perceptual data. Analysis for binaural sound measurements is linked to the psychoacoustic metrics described in Part 2 and correlated to the perceptual data analysis. The binaural data analysis can form the basis for mapping psychoacoustic data (BSI, 2019).

The *soundscape approach* proposes three steps towards soundscape planning and design: (1) *acoustic characterisation*, (2) *planning* and (3) *design and optimisation* (Kang *et al.*, 2016).

1. *Acoustic characterisation* requires the characterisation of a place through physical and perceptual data using the methodology detailed earlier.

2. *Planning* includes identifying *acoustic goals* that might be based on current or future functions of the place or its history and local culture. Planning also includes anticipating how those *acoustic goals* might be perceived.
3. *Design and optimisation* include identifying design solutions for current soundscape problems, such as reducing unwanted sounds and applying masking techniques (ibid.).

Many recent studies have been, and are currently, carried out under the umbrella of the *soundscape approach*. Examples of the *soundscape approach* applied to planning and design are few but include Nauener Platz in Berlin (ibid.) and Valley Gardens in Brighton (Aletta *et al.*, 2015), which the reader is invited to review further.

Key takeaways from the *soundscape approach*, applicable to everyday practice, are introduced in the next chapters as they are applied to the site inventory and assessment and aural strategies stages of projects.

A new trajectory for soundscape research?

The *soundscape approach* results in quantitative data that relates to the physical and perceived characteristics of soundscapes (Aletta, Kang and Axelsson, 2016). Creative practitioner and sonic researcher Jordan Lacey proposes that, in doing so, the *soundscape approach* has bifurcated from the humanities and artistic approach, which was the original direction of soundscape research (2019). Lacey advocates a new trajectory for soundscape researchers, bringing artists and designers together with urban planners and scientists (ibid.). In keeping with this new trajectory, this volume emphasises perceptual and creative findings and how they might be applied to everyday practice while drawing from the *soundscape approach*.

A listening and sounding approach for landscape architecture and urban design

We can add a set of disciplines to the ones advocated by Lacey for a new integrated approach to soundscape planning, design and management. These consider the soundscape beyond human perception to include the many organisms with which we share our environment.

A further definition of the soundscape is required here to encompass the scope of these disciplines as 'the collection of biological, geophysical and anthropogenic sounds that emanate from a landscape and which vary over space and time reflecting important ecosystem processes and human activities' (Pijanowski *et al.*,

2011, p. 1214). Sound, here, is still relational, as an integral part of animal behaviour and communication (including humans).

Several findings from ecological perspectives are essential to interdisciplinary soundscape approaches. The first is the *Acoustic Niche Hypothesis* (ANH), developed by musician and soundscape ecologist Bernie Krause (1993). Krause observed that in a wide variety of complex soundscapes, the vocalisations of animals did not overlap, proposing that organisms adapt their calls to avoid frequency and temporal overlaps with other species that share their habitat, thus finding their acoustic niches. This results in a tuned animal orchestra (ibid.). Therefore, the tuning of the animal orchestra can be a sign of the ecosystem's health, as species need time to find their acoustic niches. Consequently, a recently disturbed ecosystem, where the species makeup has been altered, would have an out-of-tune orchestra and require time to recover and retune (Krause and Hoffman, 2012).

Two additional ecological hypotheses complement the ANH in describing how animals change their signals according to their habitat: The *Morphological Adaptation Hypothesis* and the *Acoustic Adaptation Hypothesis* (Pijanowski, Villanueva-Rivera *et al.*, 2011). The *Morphological Adaptation Hypothesis* proposes that animal morphology evolves according to habitat, as morphological changes such as the length of a trachea influence the calls that those animals produce. The *Acoustic Adaptation Hypothesis* proposes that certain animals can amend their calls to maximise their reach within the habitat that they are in (ibid.). Together with the ANH, these hypotheses substantiated the idea of an *acoustic community* introduced earlier, where both human and non-human beings adapt and develop to communicate and thrive (Truax, 2021).

As a counterpart to Lacey's interdisciplinary proposition and to encompass the fields of bio and ecoacoustics, we can look at sound artist and researcher Leah Barclay's understanding of acoustic ecology today. At the beginning of this chapter, we talked about acoustic ecology as a discipline separate from others. For Barclay, however, acoustic ecology today is truly interdisciplinary and the umbrella for all other disciplines and fields, including 'deep listening, acoustemology, psychoacoustics, field recording, soundscape ecology, bioacoustics and ecoacoustics' (Barclay, 2022)

Whether we call it acoustic ecology or not, this interrelated umbrella of disciplines and fields combines scientific and artistic methods and human, non-human, and more-than-human interests. It provides the foundation – knowledge, skills and tools – for disrupting visual modes of thinking and knowing and becoming *soundscape architects* (Figure 1.3).

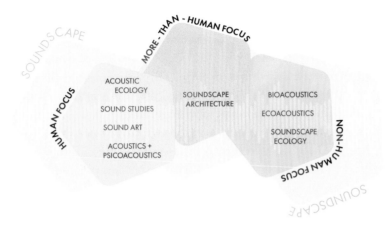

Figure 1.3 Interrelated umbrella of disciplines that feed into soundscape architecture.

Having reviewed relevant disciplines and approaches to soundscape research and practice, we return next to the concept of soundscape and how it is conceptualised within the aims of this work.

On soundscape

The word soundscape, as an analogue to landscape, connects people and place through sound and listening. It is the interaction between all sounds emanating and travelling through a place at any one time and the inhabitants engaging and making sense of the landscape and making sound in the process. This understanding of soundscape is akin to Thompson's conceptualising of it, advanced in the introduction, as 'simultaneously a physical environment and a way of perceiving that environment; it is both a world and a culture to make sense of that world' (Thompson, 2012, p. 117). The soundscape is, therefore, experiential and relational and a physical environment to assess and design with. In this conceptualisation, listening and soundmaking are the mediators between soundscape as a material object and physical environment and soundscape as an intersubjective set of relations.

The concept of soundscape has limitations. Ingold stresses two limitations in his essay *Against soundscape* that are worth keeping in mind as the reader progresses through this volume (2007). The first is that the soundscape, as an object of study, can shift our focus from sound as mediation to sound as a material object. Studying a soundscape in isolation is akin to studying the symptoms of a disease without studying the root and mechanism of that disease. Sound is relation and communication, and we should not focus on the perceptual assessment of the object alone. The second, which is deeply intertwined with the first, is the compartmentalisation of the landscape in line with the divisions between our different senses (Ingold, 2007). Landscapes are experienced with and through all the senses simultaneously, and it is difficult, or rather impossible, to isolate one sensorial experience from the rest. We process information about the environment through the interplay of all our sensory systems – vision, audition, olfaction and somatosensation (touch, proprioception and haptic perception). Each system collects and decodes information differently but in a coordinated manner. For example, to navigate space, the body rapidly analyses a large amount of visual, auditory and somatosensory information. The goal is to determine the body's position relative to the external spatial arrangement and any moving object through a multi-sensorial interpretation of the information gathered (Bremmer, 2005). The senses are, therefore, fully integrated, and it is difficult to isolate each sensory experience, as there are complex associations and interplays between the different sensorial systems. In saying that we need to become *soundscape architects,* this volume emphasizes an underdeveloped area of our work and how it might invite different forms of practice without forgetting that the soundscape is an expression of the landscape, to be perceived and experienced with the totality of our senses.[1]

The first step towards becoming a *soundscape architect* is to listen and attune to the environment, which is the premise of the next chapter.

Note

1. An earlier version of this chapter was included in my Ph.D. Thesis (Ruiz Arana, 2020).

References

Akiyama, M. (2015) *Unsetting the word soundscape project: Soundscapes of Canada and the politics of self-recognition, sounding out!* Available at: https://soundstudiesblog.com/2015/08/20/unsettling-the-world-soundscape-project-soundscapes-of-canada-and-the-politics-of-self-recognition/.

Aletta, F., et al. (2015) 'Characterization of the soundscape in Valley Gardens, Brighton, by a soundwalk prior to an urban design intervention', *Proceedings of Euronoise 2015, C. Glorieux, Ed.,* Maastricht, pp. 1547–1552.

Aletta, F., Kang, J. and Axelsson, Ö. (2016) 'Soundscape descriptors and a conceptual framework for developing predictive soundscape models', *Landscape and Urban Planning*, 149, pp. 65–74. doi: 10.1016/j.landurbplan.2016.02.001.

Barclay, L. (2022) 'Acoustic ecology research in Australia', paper presented at *R. Murray Schafer's ecologies of music and sound re-examined*. Carleton University: Research Centre for Music, Sound, and Society in Canada. Available at: https://youtu.be/J-cXu4DVVCo?si=NaLjvH_gU0-LlWuH

Barclay, L. and Gifford, T. (2018) 'The art and science of recording the environment', *Leonardo*, 41(2), p. 184. doi: 10.1162/Leon.

Bianchi, F. W. and Manzo, V. (2016) *Environmental sound artists: In their own words*. Oxford: Oxford University Press.

Bremmer, F. (2005) 'Navigation in space – The role of the macaque ventral intraparietal area', *The Journal of Physiology*, 566(1), pp. 29–35.

BSI (The British Standards Institution) (2014) 'BS ISO 12913-1: 2014 Acoustics — Soundscape Part 1 : Definition and conceptual framework'.

BSI (The British Standards Institution) (2018) 'PD ISO / TS 12913 - 2 : 2018 BSI Standards Publication Acoustics — Soundscape', BSI Standards Publication.

BSI (The British Standards Institution) (2019) 'PD ISO / TS 12913 - 3:2019 BSI Standards Publication Acoustics — Soundscape - Part 3: Data analysis', pp. 1–30.

Council of Europe (2000) '*European Landscape Convention, Florence 20.10.2000*', European Treaty Series, No. 176, 7p. Available at: https://rm.coe.int/1680080621.

Davies, W. J., *et al.* (2013) 'Perception of soundscapes: An interdisciplinary approach', *Applied Acoustics*, 74(2), pp. 224–231. doi: 10.1016/j.apacoust.2012.05.010.

European Environment Agency (2014) *Good practice guide on quiet areas*. Copenhagen.

European Parliament and Council (2002) 'Directive 2002/49/EC of the European Parliament and of the Council of the 25th June 2002, relating to the assessment and management of environmental noise', *Official Journal of the European Communities*, L189.

Feld, S. (2015) 'Acoustemology', in Novak, D. and Sakakeeny, M. (eds.) *Keywords in sound*. Durham, NC and London: Duke University Press, pp. 12–21.

Ingold, T. (2007) 'Against soundscape', in Carlyle, A. (ed.) *Autumn leaves*. Paris: Double Entendre, pp. 10–13.

Institute of Acoustics (2022) *What is acoustics?* Institute of Acoustics. Available at: https://www.ioa.org.uk/careers/what-acoustics.

Kang, J., *et al.* (2016) 'Ten questions on the soundscapes of the built environment', *Building and Environment*, 108(2016), pp. 284–294. doi: 10.1016/j.buildenv.2016.08.011.

Krause, B. (1993) 'The Niche hypothesis', *Soundscape Newsletter*, 6, pp. 6–10.

Krause, B. L. and Hoffman, J. (2012) 'Q & A Bernie Krause soundscape explorer', *Nature*, 485(May), p. 308. doi: 10.1038/485308a.

Lacey, J. (2016) *Sonic rupture: A practice-led approach to urban soundscape design.* New York: Bloomsbury Academic.

Lacey, J. (2019) 'Thoughts towards a fourth phase of soundscape research: (Re) merging quantitative and artistic practice', *Inter.noise and Noise-Con Congress and Conference Proceedings, Internoise 19,* Madrid, Spain, pp. 698–706.

Pijanowski, B. C., Farina, A., *et al.* (2011) 'What is soundscape ecology? An introduction and overview of an emerging new science', *Landscape Ecology*, 26(9), pp. 1213–1232. doi: 10.1007/s10980-011-9600-8.

Pijanowski, B. C., Villanueva-Rivera, L. J., *et al.* (2011) 'Soundscape ecology: The science of sound in the landscape', *BioScience*, 61(3), pp. 203–216. doi: 10.1525/bio.2011.61.3.6.

Ruiz Arana, U. (2020) *The enchantment of the wild: A journey into wildness through listening.* Newcastle University. Available at: http://theses.ncl.ac.uk/jspui/handle/10443/5178

Schafer, R. M. (1967) *The book of noise.* Wellington, New Zealand: Price Milburn & Co.

Schafer, R. M. (1977) *The soundscape: Our Sonic environment and the tuning of the world.* Rochester, Vermont: Destiny Books.

Sterne, J. (2012) 'Sonic imaginations', in Sterne, J. (ed.) *The sound studies reader.* Oxon and New York: Routledge, pp. 1–17.

Thompson, E. (2012) 'Sound, modernity and history', in Sterne, J. (ed.) *The sound studies reader.* Oxon and New York: Routledge, pp. 117–129.

Truax, B. (1984) *Acoustic communication, Springer handbook of Ocean engineering.* Norwood, NJ: Ablex Publishing Corporation. doi: 10.1007/978-3-319-16649-0_15.

Truax, B. (2012) 'Sound, listening and place: The aesthetic dilemma', *Organised Sound* 17(3), pp. 193–201. doi: 10.1017/S1355771811000380.

Truax, B. (2018) *The world soundscape project, Barry Truax.* Available at: https://www.sfu.ca/~truax/wsp.html (Accessed: 2 November 2018).

Truax, B. (2021) 'Acoustic sustainability in urban design: Lessons from the world soundscape project', *Cities & Health*, 5(1–2), pp. 122–126. doi: 10.1080/23748834.2019.1585133.

Chapter Two

Affective listening

The ear hears, the brain listens, the body senses vibrations…
to hear is the physical means that enables perception,
to listen is to give attention to what is perceived both acoustically and
psychologically.

(Oliveros, 2015)

In the spring of 2020, at the start of the COVID-19 pandemic, I set up an office in my home attic, a room with slanted ceilings and large roof windows. As we swapped in-person meetings for endless Zoom calls, I started to notice, through listening, that I was not alone. Working from home, isolated, the chimney birds became my constant companions, alerting me through their singing and calling. My listening attention drifted throughout the day. At times the birdcalls moved to the background of my attention. At times I would open the window to engage with them actively. I could not understand what they were saying, yet I was party to many conversations. Blackbirds, pigeons, seagulls. Communicating from one chimney to the next. From one row of terraced houses to the next. In a constant unintelligible chatter. Listening to their chatter was comforting – knowing that they were there, oblivious to the pandemic and its consequences (Soundtrack 2.1).

🎵 Soundtrack 2.1 Chimney birds.

Electronic music producer, researcher, and educator Michael Gallagher challenges the 'assumption … that listening is primarily about the transmission of meaning' (2013, p. 41). Meaning is not only transmitted but also made through listening, and

DOI: 10.4324/9781003202981-4

acquiring meaning is not the only role of listening. Meaning, through listening, is shaped by the context, the way in which words are transmitted, and the bodily expressions of that transmission; thus, an affective relation can be established through that interaction, independently of meaning (ibid.). Truax also emphasises context as essential to give meaning to sound (1984), yet Gallagher foregrounds the role of the listener (and soundmaker) in meaning-making and relating (2013). We can term this mode of listening that seeks to relate as *affective listening*. *Affective listening* does not require that we strip sound of meaning. At the same time, it does not rest on the meaning of the sound (ibid.). The purpose of this kind of listening is not to assess sound as a 'purely aesthetic experience' (ibid., p. 43), which is the purpose of *acousmatic* listening (Chion, 1994) and recommended by ISO 12913 norms for sound-walk participants (BSI, 2018). Rather, the purpose of *affective listening* is to engage us with our surroundings and is thus 'the most simple, everyday form [of listening], and perhaps its most vital' (Gallagher, 2013, p. 43). The comfort of the birds singing outside my attic window was precipitated by this kind of listening. Listening was a vehicle to develop an affective engagement with the birds, being reassured by their daily presence. Their singing conveyed something to me through listening, even though I could not understand what they were saying. Listening, lastly, gave me joy – it was an aesthetic pursuit.

The value of listening for landscape architects and urban designers stems from the interweaving of these three modes of listening: listening as an aesthetic and creative practice, listening as communication and listening as affective engagement, as they all play a role in how we read and experience the environment, assess it and transform it. This volume emphasises listening as *affect*, as this is the most simple, mundane and vital for the experience of the environment and can encompass all other modes. Listening as *affect* invites modes of practice that work with what is already there, waiting to be discovered or valued through listening, subtle interventions aligned with current planetary concerns and goals. Listening as *affect* is central to our everyday practice, as the reader will discover through this and subsequent chapters.

Hearing and listening

To hear and to listen are not interchangeable terms, as composer and accordionist Pauline Oliveros remind us (2015). To hear is to perceive sound through body and mind (involuntary action), whereas to listen is to pay attention to those sounds that our body perceives (intentional action) (ibid.). This chapter is primarily concerned with listening as a conscious act, as something which can be trained in our research and practice. As a first step to training our listening and understanding its many facets, this section introduces the reader first to hearing as an unconscious physiological and psychological act and second to listening as a conscious act.

Hearing: physiology, psychology, and multi-sensoriality

Our hearing system is binaural, as we each have two ears, one on each side of our head. Information regarding a sound is gathered through both ears and transported to the auditory cortex, where it converges to create a binaural representation of sound. Each ear is composed of an outer, a middle and an inner section. The outer ear gathers sound waves through the ear flap and funnels them through the ear canal to the middle ear. Here, the sound waves make the eardrum and associated three ossicles vibrate, amplifying the signal. These vibrations are transmitted to the cochlea or inner ear, where the sensory hair cells amplify and transform vibrations into nerve impulses transmitted to the brain via the auditory nerve (WHO, 2015). The auditory nervous system is connected with the limbic and paralimbic structures of the brain involved in the storing of memories (Welsh Government with the Noise Abatement Society, 2022) and the processing of emotions (Koelsch, Skouras and Lohman, 2018).

Through hearing, we can detect subjective sound parameters, including loudness, pitch, and timbre, which are the psychoacoustic counterparts of the objective acoustic parameters of intensity, frequency, and waveform (Truax, 1984). Thus, loudness is the perceived intensity of sound, which is measured in decibels (dB or dBA, when adjusted to human hearing); pitch is the perceived frequency of sound, which is measured in hertz (Hz); and timbre is the perceived quality of sound, which depends on the waveform (ibid.). Human hearing usually ranges from 20 to 20,000 Hz and from 0 dBA to 140 dBA.

These hearing ranges are typical, as we do not all hear equally. Hearing differences depend on culture, species, context and individual physiological and psychological variations. The *Aural Diversity* project, led by Andrew Hugill and John Drever, provides an overview of the range of differences in hearing and their consequences for different fields of study, including architecture and design, that the reader might want to explore further (2023).

Environmental hearing enables us to be alert to our surroundings. Through hearing, our ancestors could detect and locate the calls and movements of predators and prey 24 hours a day (Blesser and Salter, 2009). This alertness in hearing serves an evolutionary purpose; as we cannot close our ears, we were always alert to any warning signs, even in the dark (Feld, 1996). Today, hearing still keeps us alert day and night: it is the sound of my crying baby that wakes me up in the night and demands my attention or a loud siren that alerts me to an oncoming ambulance in the middle of the road. However, the possibilities of hearing and listening are much greater than this warning role.

Before I conclude this brief introduction to hearing, it is worth highlighting some fundamental differences between hearing and sight, which have implications for landscape and urban research and practice:

- Hearing puts us at the centre of the aural field, as we hear 360 degrees. Looking puts us at the edge of the visual field, as we see 180 degrees (Ruiz Arana, 2020).
- Depending on many variables, hearing can provide much information or none. For example, one can get a sense of space on a stormy day as thunder is reflected from adjacent surfaces. On a fine day, however, in the same space, there might be no sound at all. In any case, the information unfolds over time (Hull, 2013). With sight, however, we can grasp images in an instant (Ruiz Arana, 2020).
- We have less control over our hearing than we do over our looking, as we cannot close our ears the same way we can close our eyes, and we are, therefore, always subjected to sound.
- As discussed later in Chapter 4, aural space and visual space do not always correspond. For example, we can hear sound events hidden from sight or far into the distance, and sound can cross physical and visual boundaries.

Modes of listening

The perception of the environment through hearing and listening depends on many contextual variables, as previously discussed and summarised in Figure 1.2 (Chapter 1). Individual variables affect our hearing (auditory sensation). Cultural variables, expectations and sensory factors affect our listening (interpretation of auditory sensation). Environmental, situational and personal variables affect how we engage with and act in the environment (responses and outcomes) (BSI, 2014).

Listening, therefore, enables us to gather information about the environment as we interact with it and act within it. Listening can take many forms in the process, depending on attention and purpose.

Degree of attention

Truax identifies three modes of listening linked to depth of attention: *listening-in-search, listening in readiness* and *background listening* (1984). *Listening-in-search* encompasses searching for prompts or affordances in the environment and is the most attentive of the three modes. This mode of listening enables the extraction of in-depth detail about the environment and can be focused on a specific sound 'to the exclusion of other sounds' or 'may be global' (ibid., p. 19). *Listening-in-readiness* encompasses a midway attentiveness that enables the extraction of important detail about the environment, while 'the focus of one's attention is probably directed elsewhere' (ibid.,). It has a midway focus whereby the listener is ready to find and assess new information in the environment without taking over everything else. For this mode of listening, Truax provides an example of a mother who awakes in the night to her baby's cries but not to other salient noises. This listening mode requires a hi-fi environment that enables interacting with the environment to extract meaningful information without too much effort (ibid.). Lastly, *background listening* is the least attentive of all modes and encompasses being aware of sounds without extracting any relevant information from them. It is termed background as sounds listened to stand 'in the background of our attention', yet we can turn our attention to them if needed (ibid., p. 20).

Intentionality

Composer Michel Chion, building on the work of another composer, Pierre Schaeffer, identifies three modes of listening according to their purpose: *causal, semantic* and *reduced* (1994). Through *causal* listening, the most common mode, we gain information about the source of the sound, whether visible or invisible. Through *semantic* listening, we interpret the message the sound transmits (in a code or language). Finally, through *reduced* listening, a term originally coined by Pierre Schaeffer, we focus on the characteristics of a sound without searching for its cause or meaning (ibid.). Schaeffer coined another term related to reduced listening: *acousmatic* listening or listening to a sound without seeing its cause. Sound, in this case, is the main object of perception, which encourages *reduced* listening or *causal* listening if one tries to locate the source of the sound (ibid.). Reduced listening requires sounds to be constant to be listened to repeatedly. *Causal* and *semantic* listening are contextual and help to extract meaning from the everyday environment, whereas reduced listening seeks to isolate sound from its context (Tuuri and Eerola, 2012).

Building on Chion and Schaeffer's taxonomy, Kai Tuuri and Tuomas Eerola have developed their own taxonomy of listening modes to reflect different elements and levels that contribute to creating meaning through listening (2012). Based on intentionality and a theoretical model of embodied cognition, their taxonomy encompasses nine modes of listening, organised into three hierarchical levels: *experiential, denotative* and *reflective* listening. In their theoretical framework of embodied cognition, perception and action are intrinsically linked, as meaning is extracted and created from the environment through the subject's embodied interaction (ibid.). At the *experiential* level, listening is pre-attentive and, therefore, the most basic mode of subject–environment interaction and meaning-making through listening. At the *denotative* level, listening seeks to extract meaning from the sources of sound and context. Finally, at the *reflective* level, listening concentrates on the sound quality (reduced listening) and the appropriateness of the sound to the context (critical listening). The reader is invited to turn to Tuuri and Eerola's work for an in-depth description of the different modes within each listening level (2012).

Three modes of listening

The three modes of attentiveness that Truax introduced four decades ago are still valid, and the reader will find themselves moving from one to another in their own journey to listening. On a soundwalk, for example, the reader might *listen-in-search*, seeking to gather as much information as possible through listening as they interact with the environment. Equally, on a site visit as designer, the reader will seek to read and evaluate the environment through listening. Walking on a daily commute, on the other hand, the reader might *listen-in-readiness*, accustomed to familiar sounds, yet paying attention to new information as it is gathered through listening. Finally, on a day out in the park, the reader might find themselves *background listening* without paying attention to any sounds in particular. As planners, designers, managers and researchers, we should also be aware that the degree of attentiveness through which our schemes are experienced will vary.

The three modes of intentionality put forward in this volume are *listening as affect* (or affective listening), *listening as communication* (or communicative listening) and *listening as aesthetic pursuit* (or aesthetic listening). These three listening modes are interrelated and build on the above-mentioned taxonomies. *Listening as affect* equates to *experiential* listening. *Listening as communication* equates to *denotative* listening and encompasses *causal* and *semantic* listening. Finally, *aesthetic listening* equates to *reflective* listening and includes *critical* and *reduced* listening.

Tuuri and Eerola's listening taxonomy is focused on hierarchical levels of embodied cognition. While acknowledging that different modes of listening derive from different levels of cognition, the theoretical model of listening that I put forward foregrounds the role of the body in the affective interaction of subjects and their environment drawing on a theoretical model originally developed by psychiatrist and philosopher Thomas Fuchs (2013). As the reader will uncover, *affective listening* is the primary, most ordinary and essential mode of environmental listening, as well as the umbrella that can encompass – though it does not have to – *communicational listening* and *aesthetic listening*, which in turn involve different levels of cognition.

Listening as affect

Embodied affectivity

Thomas Fuchs and Sabine Koch define *affection* and *emotion* as two inseparable and mutually interactive aspects that modulate the subject's engagement with the environment. In this model, *affect* is understood in psychological terms as 'something's ability to influence your mind in a way that is linked to your body' (Barrett and Bliss-Moreau, 2009, p. 1). In turn, *emotion* is understood as the bodily reaction and action that results from affection. Fuchs and Koch draw attention to the Latin origin of the word 'emotion', which is '*emovere*, to move out' (2014, p. 3) when proposing that 'in affectivity we are moved by movement [affect] and moved to move [emotion]' (ibid., p. 4). That is, we are affected by 'salient features of a situation' (*affective affordances*) that trigger 'a specific bodily resonance (*affection*) which in turn influences the emotional perception and evaluation of a situation and implies a corresponding action readiness (*e-motion*)' (ibid., p. 2). Let us look at this model in more detail.

To be affected is to be moved by something, by *the affective affordances* of the environment that we attend to intentionally (ibid., p. 2). Emotions are the *bodily resonances* that emerge from that *affective intentionality*, which involves attending to *affective affordances,* appraising them and 'giving them a significance and weight they would not have without emotion' (ibid.). *Affective intentionality* involves a basic cognitive-emotional process gained through previous 'affect-inducing experiences', which explains why young children, for example, feel emotions (ibid.). Even when emotions involve abstract thought, the affective significance of a situation is mediated first and foremost through the embodied response to it (ibid.). Therefore, *bodily resonances* are how emotions are experienced through the body and include bodily reactions such as 'autonomic nervous activity' (e.g., raised heartbeat) and 'sensations, postures and movements' that feed back into those emotions (ibid.). For example, if my voice starts trembling due to nervousness, becoming aware of that trembling increases my nervousness. *Bodily resonances* move us to act, as they encompass *action resonance*, which is the 'potential for movement' embedded in emotion (ibid., p. 3). For example, when we are scared, we are moved to escape, which we might or might not end up doing, but the potential for action is always there.

Emotion is therefore always embodied, always relational, as in each situation, I attend to something that is outside of me – a thing or object in the environment – through my own body (ibid., p. 3). This model of affectivity, relational and embodied, builds on Merleau-Ponty's reversibility of perception (1968) which proposes that perception has its 'own perspective' (ibid., p. 10), as what I sense I always sense through my bodily senses (Figure 2.1).

Interaffectivity

From Fuchs and Koch's circular model of embodied affectivity, we conclude that *affects* and *emotions* are always relational and dependent on a particular environment, its affective qualities and the subject's embodied reaction and interaction with these. They are located within the subject and, most importantly, between the subject and the environment. This circular interactivity also applies to social interactions or

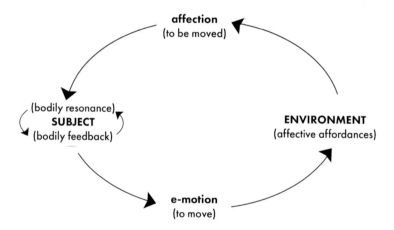

Figure 2.1 Embodied affectivity model, adapted from (Fuchs and Koch, 2014, Figure 1).

interaffectivity. In the context of this book, social interactions are understood in their broadest terms to include human–non-human interactions. In a social interaction, there is 'dynamic mutual feedback between bodies' (2014, p. 5). We express our emotions through our *bodily resonances* and behaviour, which affect the emotions of others through their own *bodily resonance*, which feeds back into our emotions. This dynamic feedback is an interbodily resonance that connects both bodies. In a social interaction, my embodied affectivity cycle interacts with another, altering and conditioning each other's *affective affordances* and *bodily resonances*. (ibid.). Our bodies are thus the *medium of interaffectivity* (ibid., p. 9).

Interaffectivity operates at two levels: primary and cognitive empathy (Fuchs, 2017). Primary empathy is pre-reflective, intercorporeal and the 'basis of social cognition' as it implies 'an intuitive understanding of others' emotions in our embodied engagement with them' (ibid., pp. 3–4). This primary empathy can then be extended to 'higher-level cognitive capacities such as perspective-taking'; however, pre-reflective interaffectivity remains the basis of social cognition (ibid.).

This distinction between primary and higher empathy was clearly described by Merleau-Ponty when he proposed that

> Faced with an angry or threatening gesture, I have no need, in order to understand it, to recall the feelings which I experienced when I used these gestures…the gesture does not make me think of anger, it is anger itself.
>
> (1945/2005, p. 214)

In *interaffectivity*, we sense and react intuitively first and think and reflect afterwards. Primary empathy is central to how we relate to the environment and human and non-human others (Figure 2.2).

Embodied affectivity in listening: listening as relation

Hearing is an involuntary activity, and listening is an intentional one. Listening, therefore, encompasses *affective intentionality*. Through listening, we pay attention and are affected by the sounds and silences of a particular setting that trigger certain *bodily resonances* that modulate how we appraise and perceive the setting and respond to it. Through listening and drawing on Fuchs and Koch's model, we are moved by the silences and sounds of the environment, and we act as a response (2014). Listening to sounds and silences of an environment, including those of our own making,

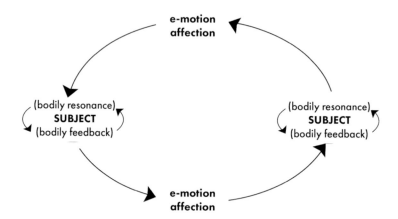

Figure 2.2 Interaffectivity model, adapted from (Fuchs and Koch, 2014, Figure 2).

modulates our emotive response to the environment and, thus, our behaviour within it. Our emotive response is independent of the meaning of those sounds, as it is first the result of basic cognitive-emotional processes, as the opening vignette of the rooftop bird demonstrated. Higher-level cognitive-emotional processes, such as communication and aesthetic appraisal, can follow but do not have to. Our emotive response, triggered by listening as an embodied contextual response, is not only a response to the soundscape but, more importantly, mediates our interaction with the landscape and its communities (Figure 2.3).

The model of embodied *affective listening* that I put forward can be situated within recent studies that have sought to apply emotion theory to soundscape research. Fiebig *et al.*, for example, have developed a conceptual framework for soundscape perception that builds on the ISO conceptual framework (Figure 2.1) to incorporate emotion theory concepts (2020). Their framework differentiates between *basic emotions* and *appraisals*. *Basic emotions* provoked by a soundscape are pre-reflective and influence the 'individuals' behaviour, well-being and health without one being aware of it' (ibid., p. 9). *Appraisals* lead to 'short-term behavioural responses' in the first instance that, in time, lead to outcomes and influence moods, attitudes, and knowledge, which then feed back into appraisals. The study makes a case for expanding beyond the physical acoustic indicators currently used to predict soundscape within the ISO norms, as they strip sound of real context and meaning. Thus, they would only be valid for basic emotions and cannot predict emotional outcomes (ibid.). Indicators, they argue, should also include non-acoustic indicators, and a consensus is required on the 'descriptors to be predicted' in the first place

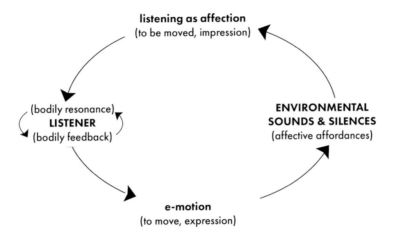

listening as affection
(to be moved, impression)

(bodily resonance)
LISTENER
(bodily feedback)

**ENVIRONMENTAL
SOUNDS & SILENCES**
(affective affordances)

e-motion
(to move, expression)

Figure 2.3 Affective listening model, developed from (Fuchs and Koch, 2014, Figure 1).

(ibid., p. 10). The emphasis on affective engagement in listening in the model also concurs with soundscape research that follows a *valence* and *arousal* model of affect and proposes that the affective response to a soundscape is the most important factor for classifying a soundscape as positive or negative (Axelsson, 2015; Aletta, Kang and Axelsson, 2016).

With the model introduced in these pages, I emphasize the value of basic embodied emotions as inseparable from more abstract appraisals of the environment and affection and emotion as a circular process. The intensity of emotions is always felt through *bodily resonances* that feed back to those emotions in a circular process, as 'cognitions … do not differ in intensity'; bodily emotions do (Fuchs and Koch, 2014, p. 1). Whereas Fiebig *et al.* set out to study the *soundscape* through a model of affect, I set out to study *listening* as affective mediator of the interaction between subject and environment. Let us have a look at some environmental listening examples.

In 2015, I spent a year living in Toronto and researched a particular landscape, Leslie Street Spit (also known as Tommy Thompson Park), a man-made peninsula and accidental wilderness on Toronto's lakeshore. I visited the Spit many times throughout the year. On one of my visits, a hot Saturday in mid-July, I turned to the pioneer woodland in the older part of the Spit for some shelter. As I walked towards the shore, I listened to the many sounds hidden in the woodland that took me away from the buzz of the city: the rustling of the leaves, the chirping of the crickets in the tall meadow, the song of the American robins amongst the tree canopies and finally the soothing sound of waves breaking against the shore. By the shore, I took

Figure 2.4 Walking towards the shore at Leslie Street Spit, Toronto.

my sound recorder out and started recording. Soon enough, I was frustrated by the music coming from a nearby boat that I could hear but not see. My body was tensing, my heartbeat racing. The music interrupted my enjoyment (and recording) of the natural environment, and I walked away. The meaning of the song, in this case, did not matter. I was affected by the music, its rhythm and bass. I could feel myself getting angry and frustrated, which made me more frustrated, and finally, I walked away (Figure 2.4).

On one of my later visits to the Spit, a Saturday early afternoon, the day was cooler, with a mild breeze and choppy water conditions at the lake. The Spit was also calmer, with fewer visitors. Two salient sounds caught my attention and accompanied me throughout the walk: that of the waves breaking at the shore and the stridulation of the crickets. Halfway through the walk, I noticed that the rhythmic stridulation of the crickets had become the metronome for my feet and even my heartbeat. I was overcome by a calmness that lasted the duration of the walk. The environment's rhythm modulated my bodily rhythm, inviting me to slow down and enjoy the moment. My *bodily resonances* – the pace of my walking and my heartbeat – responded to the sounds of the environment and, in turn, modulated my emotion (calmness), my response to the setting and what I did within it. The frustration with the music in the first example, and the stridulation of the crickets in the latter, moved me to move without my searching for meaning in the actual sounds.

It is not only the sounds of the environment (including its inhabitants) that affect us but also its silences and our own soundmaking when we are in the environment. For example, in the winter of 2016–2017, I spent months researching a different landscape, Northumberland National Park in the UK, identified as one of the tranquil areas of the country in the current tranquillity map of England (Campaign to Protect Rural England (CPRE), 2007). In one of my walks in the Upper Coquetdale Valley, I arrived at a closely planted conifer forest halfway up a hill. The forest was quiet and dark, the dense canopies muting the calls of the birds above. In this quietness, my bodily sounds seemed to amplify, occupying all acoustic space, which was unnerving, and prompted me to exit the forest as fast as I could (Ruiz Arana, 2019). In this case, the *affective affordances* were the quietness in the environment and my own sound-making, which triggered *bodily resonances*, an emotive response and action – to walk as fast as I could.

The examples above demonstrate how listening is always embodied, situated and affective. Although these examples are not explicit when it comes to *interaffectivity*, the reader will be able to draw on their own experience of lived situations. A child tensing in the presence of a loud voice, for example, without necessarily understanding what is being said and hiding or moving away. Or the many times that we smile involuntarily when hearing someone laughing. *Interaffectivity*, through listening, applies to all social interactions, which can include more than humans. Animals running away from loud noises of our making (heavy footsteps, for example), or humans being alerted to a non-human presence through the crackling of leaves in planting (Ruiz Arana, 2023).

As I have previously introduced, communication and aesthetic evaluation can be suspended in affective listening. Geographer and sound artist AM Kanngieser terms this suspension as a 'belief in being with', as we relate through listening to unseen or unknown others (2020). Another suspension is embedded in *affective listening*: the suspension between 'our inner and outer sound worlds'; between subject and environment (Westerkamp, 2017, p. 30). This suspension is 'both highly personal and at the same time universal' as when we listen, we relate to the 'current conditions of the acoustic environment, and those of our innermost sound world, our thoughts and emotions' (ibid.). Westerkamp describes this suspension and the implied movement between the outside and the inside as 'that rather hard to grasp, ephemeral in-between moment of perception' (ibid.). Let us return to the example of the walk through the conifer forest introduced above to further explore the suspension between subject and environment.

In the quietness of the forest, I was both a subject experiencing the soundscape and an object in the environment for others (and myself) to experience. This and other walks along the most tranquil areas of Northumberland National Park made me aware of my soundmaking, as well as the many sounds of the environment: sitting by a small brook after a long walk, for example, becoming aware of the many sounds of the running water, distant calls of birds, brushing branches at the edge of the forest, my breathing and heartbeat slowing down and finally the sounds of my breathing and gurgling stomach mingling with those of the water. In this instance, I attended to *affective affordances* through listening (i.e., the running water calming me down) and sensing and appraising my *bodily resonance* (i.e., my breathing) that modulated my response. In this instance, through my presence and soundmaking, I provided *affective affordances* for others.

This mingling of interior and exterior sounds, more acute in the quiet, relates to what Salome Voegelin has termed the *beginning of listening* (2010). At this *beginning of listening*, we become entangled in a dialogue of internal and external sounds (Ruiz Arana, 2019), alternating between sensing and being sensed, but never at the same time, in a suspension between one and the other that corresponds with Merleau Ponty's reflexibility of perception (1945/2005). The *beginning of listening* and the affective engagement triggered through it is always situated in the subject-environment relation and embodied in the hinge between subject and object, between 'inner and outer sound worlds' (Westerkamp, 2017).

Affective listening: the power of emotion for design

'Emotions serve a purpose' (Fiebig, Jordan and Moshona, 2020, p. 2). Through emotions, we assess environmental situations and act accordingly. Emotions, as we have discussed, as well as being embodied, are always relational and shared, as in each situation, we are affected by something or someone outside of us through our own bodies (Fuchs and Koch, 2014, p. 3). Thus, emotions are our bodies telling us what matters in our world. Emotions 'interrupt the ongoing course of life to inform us, warn us, tell us what is important and what we have to react upon' (ibid., p. 4). In this manner, emotions help us to determine our actions and values.

Jane Bennett also brings attention to the power of emotion in helping us define what matters, establish a kinship with the world and then develop a set of ethical values that stem from that kinship (2001). Emotions connect us 'in an affirmative way to existence … [they] remind us that it is good to be alive … [which] encourages the finite human animal, in turn, to give away some of its own time and effort on behalf of other creatures' (ibid., p. 156). In Bennett's proposition, emotion and reason complement one another in pursuing the ultimate goal: an enacted ethic of generosity towards others (Ruiz Arana, 2020).

Affective engagement intertwines environment and subject through perception and action. Through listening, affective engagement exposes us as an integral part of the landscape, sensing and being sensed. Reflecting on this engagement, we develop a care for others that stems from having sensed this relation with others, enabling us to shape our actions accordingly. Emotion, in embodied affectivity, is the trigger to enact a code of ethics developed through reason.

What is the value then of *affective listening* for knowing and making in landscape architecture and urban design? In the introduction, we discussed how, in the environment, the designer appears twice. First, as an inhabitant of the space, reading and co-producing landscapes by their presence within them, and second as the designer, using their imagination and knowledge to conceptualise and envisage new futures for them. We can relate this now to *affective listening*. First, through listening, the designer is an integral part of the environment, alternating between subject (experiencing) and object (for others to experience). It is in this interaction that affective bodily engagement is established. Then, the designer envisages alternative futures for the site from that established engagement. Here, a focus on *affective listening* might help us develop practices attuned to the environment. As Bennett suggests, from the kinship developed through affective engagement, we can develop an ethical framework that considers living beings other than humans. Feeling that connection with non-human or more-than-human beings is no guarantee that practices of care will follow; however, it does make it more likely to happen, encouraging us to de-centre humans in the design process. A focus on listening also encourages alternative aesthetic valuations. For example, this might be the case in post-industrial wild landscapes that might not be visually appealing, as they are regarded as un-tidy, yet not 'genuinely natural' (Plumwood, 1993, p. 162). Nevertheless, these post-industrial landscapes might be aurally rich as an expression of their biodiversity. Thus, listening might encourage us – and others – to value what is already there, making wilder aesthetics acceptable in the public realm.

Throughout this chapter, I have developed a theoretical model of *affective listening* and introduced key values of applying it to expand prevailing visual ways of knowing and making. In short, affective engagement is the primal and most important bodily response that listening to sounds elicits, as it mediates the relation between subjects and their environment and conditions the subject's behaviour within the environment. *Affective listening*, in turn, can encompass both communicational and aesthetic listening, as the listener searches for meaning and relates the listening experience to memories and past events. The affective engagement established moves us to act; in the case of designers, it moves us to act through practices that are attuned to the environment.

Having discussed the value of *affective listening*, Chapter 3 takes us through the consequences of not listening for the health and well-being of human and non-human communities, making a case for tuning in urban design.

References

Aletta, F., Kang, J. and Axelsson, Ö. (2016) 'Soundscape descriptors and a conceptual framework for developing predictive soundscape models', *Landscape and Urban Planning*, 149, pp. 65–74. doi: 10.1016/j.landurbplan.2016.02.001.

Axelsson, Ö. (2015) 'How to measure soundscape quality', *Euronoise 2015*, pp. 1477–1481. Available at: https://www.conforg.fr/euronoise2015/proceedings/data/articles/000067.pdf.

Barrett, L. F. and Bliss-Moreau, E. (2009) 'Affect as a psychological primative', *Advances in Experimental Social Psychology*, 41(08), pp. 167–218. doi: 10.1016/S0065-2601(08)00404-8.Affect.

Bennett, J. (2001) *The enchantment of modern life: Attachments, crossings and ethics*. Princeton, NJ: Princeton University Press.

Blesser, B. and Salter, L. (2009) 'The other half of the soundscape: Aural architecture', in *World Federation Acoustic Ecology Conference*. Mexico City.

BSI (The British Standards Institution) (2014) 'ISO 12913-1: 2014 Acoustics — Soundscape Part 1 : Definition and conceptual framework'.

BSI (The British Standards Institution) (2018) 'ISO / TS 12913 - 2 : 2018 BSI Standards Publication Acoustics — Soundscape', BSI Standards Publication.

Campaign to Protect Rural England (CPRE) (2007) *Tranquillity map: England*. Available at: https://www.cpre.org.uk/resources/countryside/tranquil-places/item/1839?gclid=EAIaIQobChMIxYuys8eE3wIVirztCh0-2A9pEAAYASAAEgJvW_D_BwE.

Chion, M. (1994) *Audio-vision: Sound on screen*. New York: Columbia University Press. doi: 10.1007/978-1-60327-219-3.

Feld, S. (1996) 'Waterfalls of song: An acoustemology of place resounding in Bosavi, Papua New Guinea', in Feld, S. and Basso, K. (eds) *Senses of place*. New Mexico: School of American Research Press, pp. 91–135.

Fiebig, A., Jordan, P. and Moshona, C. C. (2020) 'Assessments of acoustic environments by emotions – The application of emotion theory in soundscape', *Frontiers in Psychology*, 11(November), pp. 1–13. doi: 10.3389/fpsyg.2020.573041.

Fuchs, T. (2013) 'The phenomenology of affectivity', in Fuldford, K. W. M. et al. (eds) *The Oxford handbook of philosophy and psychiatry*. online edi. Oxford Academic. Available at: https://doi.org/10.1093/oxfordhb/9780199579563.001.0001.

Fuchs, T. (2017) 'Intercorporeality and interaffectivity', in Meyer, C., et al. (eds) *Intercorporeality: Emerging Socialities in Interaction*. New York: Oxford University Press, pp. 3–23. doi: 10.1093/acprof:oso/9780190210465.003.0001.

Fuchs, T. and Koch, S. C. (2014) 'Embodied affectivity: On moving and being moved', *Frontiers in Psychology*, 5(June), pp. 1–12. doi: 10.3389/fpsyg.2014.00508.

Gallagher, M. (2013) 'Listening, meaning and power', in Carlyle, A. and Lane, C. (eds) *On listening*. Devon: Uniformbooks, pp. 41–44.

Hugill, A. and Drever, J. L. (2023) *Aural diversity, aural diversity*. Available at: https://auraldiversity.org/index.html (Accessed: 30 May 2023).

Hull, J. (2013) *Touching the rock: An experience of blindness*. New York: SPCK.

Kanngieser, A. (2020) *To tend for, to care with: Three pieces on listening as method. Part 1*, *The Seedbox*. Available at: https://theseedbox.se/blog/to-tend-for-to-care-with-three-pieces-on-listening-as-method/ (Accessed: 25 April 2022).

Koelsch, S., Skouras, S. and Lohman, G. (2018) 'The auditory cortex hosts network nodes influential for emotion processing: An fMRI study on music-evoked fear and joy', *PLoS ONE*, 13(1): e0190057. doi: 10.1371/journal.pone.0190057.

Merleau-Ponty, M. (1945/2005) *Phenomenology of perception*. online ed. London and New York: Routledge.

Merleau-Ponty, M. (1968) *The visible and the invisible*. Edited by C. Lefort. Evanston: Northwestern University Press.

Oliveros, P. (2015) *The difference between hearing and listening, TEDx talks*. Available at: https://www.youtube.com/watch?v=_QHfOuRrJB8 (Accessed: 27 March 2023).

Plumwood, V. (1993) *Feminism and the mastery of nature, feminism and the mastery of nature*. London and New York: Routledge.

Ruiz Arana, U. (2019) 'The wild in silence', *Interference Journal*, (7 Sound & Environment: Sense of Place). Available at: http://www.interferencejournal.org/wp-content/uploads/pdf/Interference Journal - Issue 7 - The Wild in Silence.pdf.

Ruiz Arana, U. (2020) *The enchantment of the wild: A journey into wildness through listening*. Newcastle University. Available at: http://theses.ncl.ac.uk/jspui/handle/10443/5178

Ruiz Arana, U. (2023) 'Soundwalking in the phonocene: Walking, listening, wilding', in Smolicki, J. (ed.) *Soundwalking: Through time, space, and technologies*. New York: Focal Press, pp. 18–33. doi: 10.4324/9781003193135-2.

Truax, B. (1984) *Acoustic communication, Springer handbook of Ocean engineering*. Norwood, NJ: Ablex Publishing Corporation. doi: 10.1007/978-3-319-16649-0_15.

Tuuri, K. and Eerola, T. (2012) 'Formulating a revised taxonomy for modes of listening', *Journal of New Music Research*, 41(2), pp. 137–152. doi: 10.1080/09298215.2011.614951.

Voegelin, S. (2010) *Listening to noise and silence: Towards a philosophy of sound art*. New York, London: Continuum.

Welsh Government with the Noise Abatement Society (2022) *Technical Advice Note (TAN) 11: Air Quality, Noise and Soundscape. Supporting document 1: soundscape design*.

Westerkamp, H. (2017) 'The practice of listening in unsettled times', *Invisible places: Sound, urbanism and sense of place Conference Proceedings*. Sao Miguel Island, Azores, Portugal, pp. 29–45.

World Health Organization (2015) *Hearing loss due to recreational exposure to loud sounds: A review*. Geneva: WHO Press.

Chapter Three

Tuning in

Environmental noise

Human health and well-being

Exposure to environmental noise is a growing concern as it can adversely impact our health and well-being, an impact that encompasses auditory and non-auditory effects. The word *noise* in the following environmental legislation is employed to denote sound that becomes harmful above a certain legal limit measured in decibels, and this connotation is used throughout this chapter. Noise has other interrelated meanings, from unpleasant sounds (OED online, 2023) to interference in a communication system (Truax, 1999). Beyond this chapter, the word *noise* is avoided as much as possible. This is because of its subjective nature in perception and variability in hearing and listening amongst individuals and species, which relates to health and well-being effects. In humans, genetics, age and certain conditions, including hypertension and diabetes, can 'increase the risk of acquiring noise induced hearing loss' (WHO, 2015, p. 4). In humans, what is music for some might be noise for others.

Noise-induced auditory effects, such as hearing loss and tinnitus, are caused by damage to our hearing system (WHO, 2015). Hair cells in the inner ear can be damaged through one single exposure to extreme noise levels or sustained exposure to high noise levels. This damage ranges from cell fatigue that causes temporary hearing loss or tinnitus to irreversible damage or death of the hair cells that brings permanent hearing loss. This last is a loss of hearing sensitivity that happens gradually

DOI: 10.4324/9781003202981-5

and affects both ears. First, the ability to hear high-frequency sounds is lost, which might be difficult to detect as it does not affect daily life. Progressively, however, other frequencies are affected, which hinders communication and comprehension. Even though hearing loss is irreversible, it can be paused when the exposure to noise is removed. Hearing loss and tinnitus lead to poorer quality of life as they can cause sleeping problems, anxiety, depression, reduced motivation and inability to concentrate, and in children, learning disabilities and impaired language acquisition (ibid.).

Noise-induced non-auditory effects, in turn, are caused by psychological and physiological stress responses and sleep disturbance and include annoyance, cardiovascular disease, metabolic effects and cognitive disorders (WHO, 2018). Environmental noise, therefore, can greatly impact our daily life and activities (ibid.), highlighting the need to understand what constitutes safe listening in the composition of our urban soundscapes.

Safe listening outdoors

In 2018, the World Health Organization published recommendations for safe listening outdoors to protect citizens' health and well-being from environmental noise damage (2018). The guiding principles of the recommendations were developed to reduce exposure to harmful sound levels from road traffic, aircraft, railways, wind turbines and leisure activities and to keep communities informed of potential changes in noise exposure (ibid.).

Safe listening depends on sound intensity (measured in decibels) and duration (WHO, 2015). The threshold for causing hearing effects is identified as sound intensity of 85 dB(A) or above over an 8-hour period (ibid.), yet the targets for safe listening are much lower (WHO, 2018). For example, for exposure to road traffic noise, the WHO recommends 'reducing noise levels produced ... below 53 decibels (DB) L_{den} (2018, p. xvi), where L_{den} refers to the 'day-evening-night weighted sound pressure level' (ibid., p. x). For exposure to leisure noise (see below), the recommendation is to reduce the 'yearly average from all leisure noise sources combined to 70 dB L_{Aeq24h}' (ibid., p. xviii), where L_{Aeq24h} refers to 'A-weighted, equivalent continuous sound pressure level' over a 24-hour period (ibid., p. x). These recommendations have been developed for Europe, supported by evidence gathered from research worldwide, and thus recommendations are applicable globally (ibid.).

Of note is the inclusion of leisure noise within WHO recommendations. Leisure noise during night hours, as discussed in the introduction for the town of

Hondarribia, is a growing concern for residents of many cities globally. In Spanish cities, for example, leisure noise is the source of most complaints in the urban environment to the country's ombudsman (Kassam, 2023). In Barcelona, where 57% of the population is exposed to noise levels above recommended WHO limits, night noise is mostly attributed to nightlife. It has led to implementation of awareness campaigns and sound limiters (Ajuntament de Barcelona, 2021). Italy suffers a similar fate, with a recent landmark court case resulting in Brescia city council having to compensate €50,000 to a couple living in the town for 'failing to safeguard them against [nightlife] noise' (Giuffrida, 2023) (Figure 3.1).

The effects of environmental sounds on human health and well-being can also be beneficial. Sound is 'a source of pleasure, contributes to creating a sense of place, and maintains and reinforces cultural heritage and well-being' (Farina, 2018, p. 2). Natural sounds, for example, have demonstrated 'cognitive and emotional benefits' (Levenhagen *et al.*, 2021). Benefits include attention restoration and cognitive recovery (Zhang, Kang and Kang, 2017; Shu and Ma, 2019), stress recovery and perceived health and well-being (Cerwén, 2016; Aletta, Oberman and Kang, 2018).

Figure 3.1 Signs in Vienna's public realm reminding residents to be quiet during hours of night rest (10 pm–6 am).

These benefits are linked to sounds perceived as appropriate to their setting and not to the absence of all sound (Levenhagen *et al.*, 2021). The biophilia hypothesis is one theory of why natural sounds are conducive to relaxation and recovery (Ruiz Arana, 2019). According to the biophilia hypothesis, humans have a natural connection and appreciation for nature and other living things, dating back to our hunter-gatherer ancestors (Wilson, 1984). For instance, the sound of water flowing would have indicated a healthy and thriving environment, while birds singing would have signalled a safe and predator-free area (Nayar, 2017).

Non-human health and well-being

Sound affects not only us but also the many organisms with which we share our environment, as attested by the breadth of research investigating the effect of anthropogenic noise on both animals and plants.

Effects of anthropogenic noise in animals are well documented and range from changes in 'individual behaviours to changes in ecological communities' (Shannon *et al.*, 2016, p. 982), as noise can interfere with animals' 'foraging behaviour, shifted temporal activity patterns, decreased abundance, reduced condition, and altered reproductive success' (Levenhagen *et al.*, 2021).

Animals respond to temporal changes in the soundscape, as demonstrated during the COVID-19 pandemic when animals seized the opportunity to occupy new-found (human) silences. For example, white-crowned sparrows in the San Francisco Bay 'altered their acoustic signalling in response to reduced noise pollution' during the COVID-19 lockdown (Derryberry *et al.*, 2020, p. 575). Sparrows responded to this newfound silence by producing songs of greater quality and lower amplitudes to improve the extent of their communication and the prominence of their song (ibid.). This example and many other studies carried out in terrestrial and marine environments demonstrate the benefits that a more sustained quieting could bring for biodiversity recovery in urban environments (Kunc and Schmidt, 2019).

Animals not only occupy silences but also adapt to prevailing environmental sounds. Birds close to airports, for example, start their calls earlier in the morning or abstain from singing while planes take off (Dominoni *et al.*, 2016). Embryos of many species listen to and learn from exterior sounds and adapt their development as a response to the perceived world (Mariette, Clayton and Buchanan, 2021, p. 722). Oyster larvae follow marine soundscapes 'in search of a suitable habitat', and enriching soundscapes (underwater) can aid with oyster reef restorations

(McAfee *et al.*, 2022). Frogs increase vocalisation when exposed to rain and chorus acoustic playbacks in the environment (Muñoz *et al.*, 2020). Moreover, a wide range of animals is attracted to vocalisations of their own species, with acoustic playbacks used for various purposes in wildlife management – from leading animals to habitats away from humans to guiding birds to bird boxes (Putman and Blumstein, 2019).

Animals also adapt their calls to avoid frequency and temporary overlaps with other species in their ecosystem, thus finding their acoustic niches and being able to communicate, as discussed in Chapter 1 through the *Acoustic Niche Hypothesis* (Krause, 1993). Therefore, the soundscape's effect should not always be thought of as negative, as it can be key to animal development and survival, and interventions upon the landscape that enrich the soundscape can also positively impact ecological restoration.

Plants also respond to changes in the soundscape. Plant roots follow acoustic vibrations first and soil moisture later to locate water, a process that can be disturbed by noise (Gagliano *et al.*, 2017). plant root structure is also compromised by noise (Solé *et al.*, 2021). Recruitment of seeds and species diversity can be affected by exposure to noise, an outcome attributed to the effect of noise in the animals that disseminate the seeds, suggesting that noise causes 'cascading ecological effects' (Phillips, Termondt and Francis, 2021). Plants are not only affected by sound but also communicate through sound. Plants emit sound as a consequence of 'physiological processes' (Gagliano, 2013), weather conditions, such as wind and rain (Sueur, Krause and Farina, 2019), and communication (Dalal, 2021). For example, plants under stress (dehydrated or injured) emit ultrasonic 'airborne sounds' that can be detected and responded to by nearby plants and other organisms (Khait *et al.*, 2023).

Policies and guidance

The physiological and psychological effects of hearing and listening (in humans and non-humans) depend on decibels and on how those sounds are perceived and interpreted. Although decibel measurements and environmental noise legislation are useful for reducing overall sound levels and halting physiological damage, these measures cannot be the only consideration given to environmental sound. Environmental sounds are always perceived and experienced in context through our bodies. Thus, the physiological and psychological effects triggered by listening mediate the interaction with the environment and can be both detrimental and beneficial for that interaction.

The realisation that sound is more than noise is also permeating current guidance and policy. For example, the previously introduced Environmental Noise Directive (END) of 2002 required EU member countries to produce noise maps and management plans and to protect positive soundscapes in the form of quiet areas (European Parliament and Council, 2002). The END led to a technical guide for identifying quiet areas (European Environment Agency, 2014) and to the ISO 12913 soundscape norms that prioritise human perception in assessing the acoustic environment. As another example, the tranquillity maps for England were developed using a participatory appraisal methodology which identified positive and negative factors (visual and acoustic) that people associated with tranquillity (MacFarlane, Haggett and Fuller, 2005). The tranquillity maps for England aimed to protect tranquillity and continue to inform landscape management (e.g., Northumberland National Park Authority, 2022). A last and recent example is Wales' *Noise and Soundscape Action Plan (2018–2023),* which seeks to move away from traditional approaches to noise control based on acoustic measurements towards developing soundscapes appropriate to each place (Welsh Government, 2018). When drafting this chapter (Spring, 2023), the Welsh government was consulting on changes to their planning guidance concerning air quality, noise and soundscape through the development of a *Technical Advice Note (TAN) 11: Air Quality, Noise, and Soundscape* (2022). This consultation on planning policy guidance included, for the first time, a supporting document on *Soundscape Design* that foregrounded good soundscape design as a key component of the multisensorial consideration of the overall design for a scheme. The supporting document provided a vehicle to help achieve the aims of a project and better placemaking (Welsh Government with the Noise Abatement Society, 2022). TAN11 will require certain planning applications to include a *Noise and Soundscape Design Statement* and will detail when a *soundscape design approach* might be more appropriate or required alongside traditional noise management (ibid.). In the context of this policy, a *soundscape design approach* is defined as a 'participatory … approach to design-led or facilitated by a soundscape specialist' that considers how users experience the soundscape in context and how it influences their behaviour and actions (ibid., p. 5).

These emerging policies, guidance and concerns for soundscapes open creative avenues for landscape architects and urban designers to apply aural strategies focused on health and well-being. We will consider some of these in later chapters. These policies and guidance, however, remain human-centric, despite the breadth of research on the effect of noise on animals and plants. Thus, guidelines on safe listening for non-humans are yet to be published. As we move to life-centred or bio-centred – as an alternative to human-centred – approaches to landscape and urban planning, design and management, we need to understand non-human listening and communication better to integrate non-human and human approaches to sound and noise management. The methods and tools discussed in Chapters 9 and 10 provide avenues for integration.

Understanding how sound impacts human and non-human communities has many implications for the planning, design and management of urban environments. Chapter 1 introduced the concept of *acoustic communities* where human and non-human beings can communicate and thrive, which relates to human-scale and non-human-scale design and health and well-being. I return to this concept in later chapters. Chapter 2 argued for the value of listening as a mediator of our embodied, affective relation with the environment and an invaluable tool for planning and designing environments conducive to health and well-being. We now turn to exercises geared towards tuning into the environment as the start of a journey towards cultivating our listening and becoming soundscape audience, performers and composers.

Tuning in

At this point, the reader might still wonder what there is to cultivate about listening. Is listening not integral to our everyday functioning and practice, something we do by default? In trying to answer this question, it is useful to pose counterpart questions:

If we, landscape architects and urban designers, were already listening, would our cities and landscapes sound the way they currently do, impacting daily lives and activities?

If we were engaging with sites and communities through affective listening, would we still prioritise humans in design and visual modes of aesthetic appreciation over others?

Oliveros posed similar questions when proposing that we turn into *deep listeners* to become aware of the soundscape to be then able to shape it (2015). All our planning, design and management interventions are aural interventions after all, no matter how small. Our aural interventions are perceived and experienced by different communities and individuals as part of the multisensorial experience of place, and they condition how those communities interact with a particular space and with one another. Our aural interventions physically and psychologically move users prompting them into action and developing an ethics of care towards the environment and others. As Oliveros proposes, our thinking and interventions (aural or otherwise) should start from designers' and communities' *deep listening* and engagement with place to encourage practices that start from established kinships with the human and non-human communities of a place. In this way, we can avoid the detrimental effects of non-listening on health and well-being in the planning, design and management of environments. The following exercises will help the reader in their journey towards *affective listening*.

The beginning of listening

Ear cleaning and *ear opening* are terms coined by Murray Schafer to describe how ears must be cleaned as a pre-requisite to developing a sensibility to the environment through sound (Schafer, 1967). Schafer carried out several *ear cleaning* exercises with his experimental music students at Simon Fraser University. *Ear cleaning* exercises included being silent for a day to focus on the sounds of others, finding an interesting sound to bring to class or keeping a soundscape diary for sounds encountered (ibid.). As Oliveros rightly pointed out, however, our ears cannot be cleaned or trained; our listening, as a conscious activity, can be trained (2015). Listening is a 'lifetime practice that depends on accumulated experiences with sound'; as such, it is a practice that we can actively develop, as the more we listen, the more we train our listening (ibid.). *Deep listening* encompasses two interconnected 'modes of listening – focal and global' (Oliveros, 1999, p. 1). *Focal listening* involves listening attentively to specific sounds and their detail, while *global listening* encompasses opening our listening to all sounds (ibid.). The result is a practice that seeks to listen 'in every possible way to everything possible to hear no matter what you are doing' and encompasses listening to 'the sounds of daily life, of nature, or one's own thoughts as well as musical sounds' (ibid., p. 1).

The model of affective listening proposed in this book draws from Oliveros' deep listening (1999) and Voegelin's beginning of listening (2010), introduced earlier, as listening is always embodied and situated. As listeners (and designers), we are affected by what we hear, and we affect the environment through our soundmaking that provides *affective affordances* for others to sense. This embodied affection is part of our daily experience of the environment and is integral to fieldwork at the start of a project. The reader is therefore encouraged to turn to Oliveros's *deep listening* exercises (e.g., Oliveros, 2013) and Schafer's *ear cleaning* exercises (1967). The latter, better termed *listening* rather than *ear cleaning* exercises are a starting point to cultivate listening and develop a sensibility towards the environment through sound. I will return to Oliveros' *deep listening* when discussing aural space in Chapter 5 and the Sounding Bodies, Sounding Space case study in Chapter 6.

Soundwalking

Participating in or organising soundwalks is another useful exercise for tuning into the environment. In a guided soundwalk, participants are taken through varied environments in silence and might come together at key points of the walk or at the end to gather experiences. Artists and researchers use soundwalks for different purposes. Soundwalks can be a way of engaging with our immediate surroundings and being present. Soundwalks can also be used to evaluate the soundscape functionally and aesthetically: the acoustic properties of different spaces and the background, foreground and unique sounds of a place. Both purposes feed into our work, as we need to engage with an environment to assess and transform it. Let us have a look at both purposes in more detail.

Soundwalks for engagement

Soundwalks were part of the exercises Schafer originally proposed for *ear cleaning*, understood as 'explorations of the soundscape of a given area using a score as a guide' (Schafer, 1977, p. 213). These *ear cleaning* soundwalks were aesthetic pursuits carried out in silence, with perceptions of the soundscape discussed at the end. Hildegard Westerkamp expanded the focus of the soundscape as a material object when she proposed that a soundwalk is 'an ear-environment relationship … it is an exploration of what the naked ear hears and how we relate and react to it' (1974). Thus, it is a way of being present and engaging with the environment traversed. Westerkamp's understanding aligns with walking practices that relate to the environment and accords with those landscape architecture scholars who propose that a landscape cannot be evaluated without it first being experienced (van Etteger, 2013; Ruiz Arana, 2023). When we conceptualise landscape as a dynamic relation between people and place, walking develops into an act of becoming landscape as we read and write the landscape while we move through it (Ruiz Arana, 2023). With a focus on listening, walking acquires an immediacy, which triggers an affective engagement. Inner and outer sounds vary in time and space, demanding our attention and mediating how we relate to the environment, as exemplified, for example, by the experiences of walking along Leslie Street Spit or Northumberland National Park described in Chapter 2. Today soundwalks can take many forms and bring attention to the soundscape through active listening and to the inhabitants, spaces and relations of the places traversed and can form an essential part of any landscape assessment and engagement.

Soundwalks that engage us with our surroundings can also be mediated. In mediated soundwalks, participants might listen to pre-recorded soundtracks on headphones while walking through a specific environment, thus transforming their usual engagement and experience (e.g., Cardiff and Miller, 2019).

Soundwalks for soundscape (affective) assessment

Within the *soundscape approach*, guided soundwalks are the methodology for data collection. Participants fill in questionnaires or carry out interviews at key points along the walks, and binaural acoustic measurements are also taken to extract acoustic indicators (e.g., sound pressure level) and psychoacoustic indicators (i.e., sharpness, tonality, roughness and fluctuation strengths). These soundwalks are discussed in further detail in Chapter 5 as they relate to the early stages of a project.

Soundwalks, regardless of their purpose, come with limitations that emerge from being guided, as participants cannot alter the route or comment as they go along (Paquette and McCartney, 2012, p. 139). By not being able to alter the route, participants cannot explore environments that might catch their attention along the walk. By not being able to comment along the walk, certain observations might be missed.

I have carried out soundwalks for various purposes with various participants, including the general public, qualified landscape architects and students of landscape architecture and planning, using methods adapted to participants and the walk's purpose. Examples are included in the listening and sounding exercises in Chapter 6 and Annex, with instructions for calibrating listening that the reader might find useful for their own soundwalking. I have also participated in soundwalks led by other disciplines that have deeply enriched my own work. The case studies in Chapter 4 showcase approaches to soundwalking and researchers and practitioners that have imprinted on my soundwalking practice and might prompt the reader to explore collaborations with other disciplines for their work. The case studies also include a short design studio carried out with Master of Landscape Architecture students at Newcastle University at the beginning of their course, designed to engage them in their immediate environment and start to expand their modes of thinking beyond visual and physical considerations (FIgure 3.2).

Figure 3.2 Soundwalking with landscape architecture students, September 2022, Exhibition Park, Newcastle upon Tyne.

Part I on *Attunement* has developed a theory of affective listening and has made a case for starting to listen in landscape architecture and urban design research, teaching, and practice. Following the case studies of Chapter 4, parts II and III on *Composition* and *Performance* show how affective listening and aural practices can permeate the different stages of a project, providing a counterpart to the dominant visual modes of thinking and making. The stages described in Chapters 5–10 are common to those detailed in the Landscape Institute's publication *The Landscape Consultant's Scope of Services* (2018) and the stages of work published by the Canadian Society of Landscape Architects, American Society of Landscape Architects, Australian Institute of Landscape Architects and Asociación Española de Paisajista's, which are also common to the work stages of other landscape architecture professional bodies and many other built environment professional bodies across the world.

References

Ajuntament de Barcelona (2021) *Cutting noise pollution improves health*, Ajuntament de Barcelona. Available at: https://www.barcelona.cat/infobarcelona/en/tema/health-and-safety/cutting-noise-pollution-improves-health_1044868.html.

Aletta, F., Oberman, T. and Kang, J. (2018) 'Associations between positive health-related effects and soundscapes perceptual constructs: A systematic review', *International Journal of Environmental Research and Public Health*, 15(11), pp. 1–15. doi: 10.3390/ijerph15112392.

Cardiff, J. and Miller, G. B. (2019) *Walks, Janet Cardiff George Bures Miller*. Available at: http://cardiffmiller.com/artworks/walks/# (Accessed: 14 September 2019).

Cerwén, G. (2016) 'Urban soundscapes: A quasi-experiment in landscape architecture', *Landscape Research*, 41(5), pp. 481–494. doi: 10.1080/01426397.2015.1117062.

Dalal, V. K. (2021) 'Understanding acoustic communication in plants', *Journal of Biomedical Research & Environmental Sciences*, 2(9), pp. 815–820. doi: 10.37871/jbres1314.

Derryberry, E. P., *et al.* (2020) 'Singing in a silent spring: Birds respond to a half-century soundscape reversion during the COVID-19 shutdown', *Science*, 370(6516), pp. 575–579. doi: 10.1126/SCIENCE.ABD5777.

Dominoni, D. M., *et al.* (2016) 'Airport noise predicts song timing of European birds', *Ecology and Evolution*, 6(17), pp. 6151–6159. doi: 10.1002/ece3.2357.

European Environment Agency (2014) *Good practice guide on quiet areas*. Copenhagen.

European Parliament and Council (2002) 'Directive 2002/49/EC of the European Parliament and of the Council of the 25th June 2002, relating to the assessment and management of environmental noise', *Official Journal of the European Communities*, L189.

Farina, A. (2018) 'Ecoacoustics: A quantitative approach to investigate the ecological role of environmental sounds', *Mathematics*, 7(1), pp. 1–16. doi: 10.3390/math7010021.

Gagliano, M. (2013) 'Green symphonies: A call for studies on acoustic communication in plants', *Behavioral Ecology*, 24(4), pp. 789–796. doi: 10.1093/beheco/ars206.

Gagliano, M., *et al.* (2017) 'Tuned in: plant roots use sound to locate water', *Oecologia*, 184(1), pp. 151–160.

Giuffrida, A. (2023) 'Italy's top court orders city to pay €50,000 to couple over nightlife noise', *The Guardian*. Available at: https://www.theguardian.com/world/2023/jun/05/italy-top-court-orders-city-to-pay-euro-50000-couple-noisy-nightlife-brescia-residents.

Kassam, A. (2023) '"Like a vacuum cleaner running all day": noisy nightlife making Spanish streets"uninhabitable"', *The Guardian*. Available at: https://www.theguardian.com/world/2023/mar/25/spain-noisy-nightlife-tensions.

Khait, I. *et al.* (2023) 'Sounds emitted by plants under stress are airborne and informative', *Cell*, 186(7), pp. 1328–1336.e10. doi: 10.1016/j.cell.2023.03.009.

Krause, B. (1993) 'The Niche hypothesis', *Soundscape Newsletter*, 6, pp. 6–10.

Kunc, H. P. and Schmidt, R. (2019) 'The effects of anthropogenic noise on animals: A meta-analysis', *Biology Letters*, 15(11), pp. 1–5. doi: 10.1098/rsbl.2019.0649.

Landscape Institute (2018) *Landscape consultant's scope of services S1: Landscape design & administrative/post contract services*. Landscape Institute.

Levenhagen, M. J., *et al.* (2021) 'Ecosystem services enhanced through soundscape management link people and wildlife', *People and Nature*, 3(1), pp. 176–189. doi: 10.1002/pan3.10156.

MacFarlane, R., Haggett, C. and Fuller, D. (2005) *Mapping tranquillity: Defining and assessing a valuable resource*. Available at: http://www.cpre.org.uk/resources.

Mariette, M. M., Clayton, D. F. and Buchanan, K. L. (2021) 'Acoustic developmental programming: a mechanistic and evolutionary framework', *Trends in Ecology and Evolution*, 36(8), pp. 722–736. doi: 10.1016/j.tree.2021.04.007.

McAfee, D., *et al.* (2022) 'Soundscape enrichment enhances recruitment and habitat building on new oyster reef restorations', *Journal of Applied Ecology*, (July), pp. 1–10. doi: 10.1111/1365-2664.14307.

Muñoz, M. I., *et al.* (2020) 'Biotic and abiotic sounds affect calling activity but not plasma testosterone levels in male frogs (Batrachyla taeniata) in the field and in captivity', *Hormones and Behavior*, 118(November 2018), p. 104605. doi: 10.1016/j.yhbeh.2019.104605.

Nayar, A. (2017) *Millions of people in cities rely on recorded nature sounds to manage sleep and stress and scientists are slowly understanding why it works*, Motherboard. Available at: https://motherboard.vice.com/en_us/article/wjzepx/sonic-tonic-stress-week2017 (Accessed: 3 July 2018).

Northumberland National Park Authority (2022) *Northumberland National Park management plan 2022*.

OED online (2023) *noise, n.*, Oxford University Press. Available at: https://www.oed.com/view/Entry/127655?rskey=jWQ8Ge&result=1#eid.

Oliveros, P. (1999) 'Quantum listening: From practice to theory (To practice practice).', *Sound Art Archive*, pp. 1–22. Available at: https://s3.amazonaws.com/arena-attachments/736945/19af465bc3fcf3c8d5249713cd586b28.pdf.

Oliveros, P. (2013) *Anthology of text scores, women & music*. Edited by S. Golter and L. Hall. Kingston, NY: Deep Listening Publications.

Oliveros, P. (2015) *The difference between hearing and listening, TEDx talks*. Available at: https://www.youtube.com/watch?v=_QHfOuRrJB8 (Accessed: 27 March 2023).

Paquette, D. and McCartney, A. (2012) 'Soundwalking and the bodily exploration of places', *Canadian Journal of Communication*, 37(1), pp. 135–145.

Phillips, J. N., Termondt, S. E. and Francis, C. D. (2021) 'Long-term noise pollution affects seedling recruitment and community composition, with negative effects persisting after removal', *Proceedings of the Royal Society B: Biological Sciences*, 288(1948), pp. 1–9. doi: 10.1098/rspb.2020.2906.

Putman, B. J. and Blumstein, D. T. (2019) 'What is the effectiveness of using conspecific or heterospecific acoustic playbacks for the attraction of animals for wildlife management? A systematic review protocol', *Environmental Evidence*, 8(1), pp. 1–9. doi: 10.1186/s13750-019-0149-3.

Ruiz Arana, U. (2019) 'The wild in silence', *Interference Journal* (7 Sound & Environment: Sense of Place). Available at: http://www.interferencejournal.org/wp-content/uploads/pdf/Interference Journal - Issue 7 - The Wild in Silence.pdf.

Ruiz Arana, U. (2023) 'Soundwalking in the phonocene: Walking, listening, wilding', in Smolicki, J. (ed.) *Soundwalking: Through time, space, and technologies*. New York: Focal Press, pp. 18–33. doi: 10.4324/9781003193135-2.

Schafer, R. M. (1967) *Ear cleaning*. Toronto: Berandol Music Limited.

Schafer, R. M. (1977) *The soundscape: Our sonic environment and the tuning of the world*. New York: Knopf.

Shannon, G., *et al.* (2016) 'A synthesis of two decades of research documenting the effects of noise on wildlife', *Biological Reviews*, 91(4), pp. 982–1005. doi: 10.1111/brv.12207.

Shu, S. and Ma, H. (2019) 'Restorative effects of classroom soundscapes on children's cognitive performance', *International Journal of Environmental Research and Public Health*, 16(2), pp. 1–15. doi: 10.3390/ijerph16020293.

Solé, M., *et al.* (2021) 'Seagrass Posidonia is impaired by human-generated noise', *Communications Biology*, 4(1), pp. 1–11. doi: 10.1038/s42003-021-02165-3.

Sueur, J., Krause, B. and Farina, A. (2019) 'Climate change is breaking earth's beat', *Trends in Ecology and Evolution*, 34(11), pp. 971–973. doi: 10.1016/j.tree.2019.07.014.

Truax, B. (ed.) (1999) *Handbook for acoustic ecology*. 2nd ed. Cambridge Street Publishing. Available at: http://www.sfu.ca/sonic-studio-webdav/handbook/index.html.

van Etteger, R. (2013) 'Wish you were here walking with me: Walking as a tool for the aesthetic evaluation of designed landscapes', in Heather H. Yeung (ed.), *Selected Essays from the On-Walking Conference*. Sunderland: Art Editions North, pp. 322–332.

Voegelin, S. (2010) *Listening to noise and silence: Towards a philosophy of sound art*. New York, London: Continuum.

Welsh Governemnt (2018) *Noise and soundscape action plan*.

Welsh Government with the Noise Abatement Society (2022) *Technical Advice Note (TAN) 11: Air Quality, Noise and Soundscape. Supporting document 1: soundscape design*.

Westerkamp, H. (1974) 'Soundwalking', *Sound Heritage*, III(4), pp. 18–27.

WHO (2018) *WHO Environmental Noise Guidelines for the European Region*.

Wilson, E. (1984) *Biophilia*. Cambridge, MA; London: Harvard University Press.

World Health Organization (2015) *Hearing loss due to recreational exposure to loud sounds: A review*. World Health Organization.

Zhang, Y., Kang, J. and Kang, J. (2017) 'Effects of soundscape on the environmental restoration in urban natural environments', *Noise & Health*, 19(87), pp. 65–72. doi: 10.4103/nah.NAH_73_16.

Chapter Four

Tuning in practice

Walking Festival of Sound with Jacek Smolicki and Tim Shaw

In the autumn of 2019, I was invited by Tim Shaw and Jacek Smolicki, founders of the *Walking Festival of Sound*, to lead an event for the Newcastle edition. The festival, now in its third instalment, brings together a myriad of practitioners to investigate a city through walking and listening, and in the process, 'augment and challenge the way we perceive, navigate through, and care for our shared environments' (Smolicki and Shaw, 2023).

That October, I led an evening soundwalk along Newcastle's mediaeval Quayside through low frequented paths and uneven stairs sporadically maintained in search of the folklore creatures that once animated Newcastle's Quayside. Through walking and listening, we sought to bring those creatures, and the sentiments they elicit, back to life.

That October, I also participated in many other festival events, expanding my ears to creative ways of relating to the environment and others through sound. The festival has been home to various practitioners that invite us to think of space differently through listening. In mid-April 2022, I met up (virtually) with Tim Shaw and Jacek Smolicki to learn more about the festival's origins, some of the festival events and practices, and future developments.

How did the walking festival of sound start?

Tim Shaw (TS). It is important to mention how we met because we met on a soundwalk, in Vancouver, as part of ISEA (*International Symposium for Electronic Arts*)

DOI: 10.4324/9781003202981-6

in 2015. We realised that we had a lot of common interests and started performing collaborative soundwalks together. In soundwalks and other experimental sound practices, the audience is often also the practitioners. There is often a close link between the people leading soundwalks and those participating in them. So, we met on this walk and started to correspond afterwards.

Jacek Smolicki (JS). That walk was led by Jean Routhier, one of the members of the Soundwalk Collective in Vancouver, continuing the legacy of the *World Sound-scape Project*. He and Hildegard Westerkamp were involved in ISEA and invited to do a couple of events. ISEA is usually a very busy event with a lot going on. Often, it concentrates on technological applications within arts: lots of screens, blinking lights and interactive pieces. In this very dense programme, I spotted an unmediated soundwalk. I approached it as a break from all this overstimulation. Through the soundwalk, Routhier led a very simple exercise of attentive listening to the surroundings with no technology. After the soundwalk, a group of participants, including Tim and myself, decided to go for a drink to discuss the experience, our practices and potential ideas for doing something collaboratively back in Europe. And then, we applied for a residency in Switzerland, which was a great format for us to continue our discussion.

(TS) Yes, we applied for an ARC residency in Switzerland called *Walk and Talk*, intended for artists to form new collaborations. We didn't think about a festival at first; it all came through practising soundwalking as a method for listening and performing. We realised a project called *Returning the Ear*, which was about taking an audience on a soundwalk and ending the walk in a space where we would perform with materials collected from the spaces walked. It is not an original idea, others have done it before (i.e., Max Neuhaus' *Listen,* 1966), but we were experimenting with different ways of presenting our work. And then, Jacek, I think you said that you would love to organise a festival of happenings in public space, where different soundwalking practitioners come together to present work in different sites; a city-wide festival with different starting points, different artists invited to share their work in diverse contexts. That's how it began as a concept.

How has the festival developed since that initial concept? In part, you have had to adapt to a global pandemic and change the format of events.

(JS) I had been thinking about a walking festival for quite some time, a festival that would investigate a network of places through walking, as opposed to a festival held in a single venue. We decided to start by involving two places connected to some extent, the places we knew best, our cities of residence at the time.

The initial events were highly physical, in person, in both Stockholm and New-castle-upon-Tyne, funded by the Newcastle University Institute for Creative Arts Practice. The following year we applied for a grant from the European Cultural Foundation to explore new forms and modalities of solidarity in the context of different crises the European Union has been going through. We came up with the idea of linking Edinburgh and Kraków, two cities already connected by twin city partnership. This concept emerged after WWII as a form of bilateral collaboration between European cities beyond the constraints of national borders. This approach aligns with our ideas of thinking beyond national borders and exploring local activi-ties already happening in these places while trying to cross-feed them. But then, the pandemic took hold, and we had to move most of the activities online.

Moving online posed challenges but simultaneously opened the possibility of reaching audiences far beyond the boundaries of the planned events. For example, we had 300 people attending some of the online events.

(TS) Yes, exactly. Before the pandemic, I would have never thought of running a soundwalking festival online. It seemed the antithesis of bodily, situated perception and walking experience. Mediation through network technology intensified during the pandemic. Some positive things came from this forced way of working, such as engaging with an international audience and making the festival accessible. Even though this technology is not accessible to everyone, it widened the possibilities of what we were doing. We still have work to do here to make it an accessible format for more people.

Let's talk about audiences. Soundwalks attract people working with sound already or interested in it. Did the audience broaden as well with the move online? Or was it dependent on the participating artists and the nature of their work?

(TS) It partly depended on the artist, but in general, during the pandemic, sound-walks became better known and more popular as we listened to our environment differently.

(JS) I would also add that with the second edition, we moved beyond the arts and opened the festival to contributors who work with interesting subjects related to space but do not necessarily consider sound or soundscapes as important dimensions. We wanted to explore how existing research or spatial practices could benefit from being presented as soundwalks.

One example was the work of Lisa Williams, head of the Caribbean Association, who runs guided walks that revisit the history of Edinburgh (UK) and its implica-tion in the slave trade. She has curated a walk on Malvina Wells, who was born and died a slave. The walk is mostly a narration of Malvina, tracing her history. The walk takes you from Malvina's graveyard to the places where she lived and the people she worked for. Lisa and I had several exchanges online, and it was initially challenging for her to focus on the sonic aspect of her research.

In one of our conversations, however, Lisa described how, once, as she stood in the graveyard and about to start telling the story of Malvina, the bells started to ring, taking over her voice. Lisa suddenly realised that Malvina was buried in a tradition foreign to her ancestors. The bells ringing became a dissonant element of the walk, and she started to follow this idea, to think of how those places along the walk sounded and how they dissonated with Malvina's story. This is an example of how, in the future, we might broaden the festival's scope by inviting people who do not work with sound and are not sound artists. These practitioners can engage with sound as a medium that can reveal something additional about their work while offering those concerned with sound a new perspective or gateway into the subject of concern (Figure 4.1).

Figure 4.1 Travelling Rhythms with Lisa Williams, Credit: Jacek Smolicki.

Have any events or artists stood out for you since the festival started?

(TS) As you were talking about Lisa's work, Jacek, you reminded me of a similar experience that I had in the Newcastle edition of the festival. We invited the *Newcastle Modernist Society* to do a walk on T. Dan Smith's (Thomas Daniel Smith's) development of the city. T. Dan Smith was a controversial politician and leader of Newcastle City Council in the early 1960s who aspired to transform the city into the *Brasilia of the North*. Under his vision, road networks intensified through the city, and concrete modernist structures were built, replacing the neoclassical architecture of John Dobson. Car tunnels and elevated walkways for people formed the core of this utopian modernist city. *Newcastle Modernist Society's* practice focuses on the historical analysis of space through walking, akin to a tourist tour of a city. They used the WFoS as an opportunity to think about how sound and space related. This opened interesting questions about how this modernist development changed the sounds of the city: what the sounds of the city might have been before and what they were like afterwards. It also questioned the consequences of those developments today, with the leftovers of that utopic vision. For example, development then was based around the automobile as a way of entering and leaving the city. Now that is different from what many people want. We experienced this utopic vision in the present day and its remnants through the walk. And we experienced it sonically, through listening, which was super interesting. I had not thought about this modernist development in that way before. It is a good example of how soundwalks can be used by a wide range of practitioners and the possibilities it opens for both practitioners and participants (Figure 4.2).

(JS) It is a great example. During that walk, we were led to unfinished architectural spots that felt about to spill over in an uncontrolled way. And the same seemed to happen with the sounds that felt as if they had never been planned or controlled. We ended the walk on a balcony – a concrete gallery of sorts – built for modernist architecture enthusiasts. At the time, it was presented as a monument, a piece of art, where people would observe the novel traffic phenomenon while listening to its soundscapes. We stopped on this balcony and listened for an extended period of time.

(TS) What was magical about those balconies was the coming together of sound, light and movement, as the balconies overlook five or six different layers of intersecting roads, all going in different directions.

(JS) Almost a theatrical experience.

(TS) Exactly. When built, those balconies would have brought awe and wonder viewers. It still does to me now, even though I have lived in the city for a long time and never knew about them.

Figure 4.2 The Road to Holy City, Newcastle upon Tyne Modernist Society, Credit: Jacek Smolicki.

(JS) That makes me think of changing the title of our festival to *festival of the senses*. After many soundwalks we have curated or helped organise, we realised that they are multi-sensorial experiences. Another example we didn't participate in directly but helped facilitate in Kraków was a soundwalk by activist and artist Cecylia Malik. Cecylia is deeply committed to protecting neglected environments and local communities. Recently, she has been working with rivers, especially those vulnerable to the impact of heavy industries and real estate developers. Being from Krakow, I wasn't aware that the city has so many unknown rivers besides the main one that crosses through the city. Cecylia spent several years exploring those rivers, building rafts and documenting them differently. When I spoke to her about soundscapes, she realised she hadn't thought of sound when exploring them. For the festival, she created a soundwalk along one of the rivers, explicitly focusing on how human interactions, such as pouring concrete to control the current of the rivers and reinforce their banks, change the habitats and, in turn, the soundscapes. She worked with ornithologist Kazimierz Walasz to create a walk focused on sound. Again, opening possibilities for artists, researchers and activists, such as Cecylia, to use the festival

69

Figure 4.3 Siostry Rzeki walk by Cecylia Malik, Credit: Malgorzata Grygierczyk.

to reconfigure what they are working on and thinking about is important to us (Figure 4.3).

(TS) The festival is a very nice format to be experimental. Aspects such as equipment, exact duration, and specific activities do not have to be fixed before the event. Obviously, we need to know what time and where it will start, but that is pretty much the only constraints we give. We try to encourage participants to experiment with something new.

What about your work? What drew you to soundwalking?

(TS) I accidentally walked into it through a musical practice. I was always interested in electronic music and strange sounds. I began experimenting with electroacoustic music, a practice that often involves recording your own sounds. I was going out with my microphones and collecting sounds from my everyday environment to use in my compositions. I started to think of different ways to share the recordings and listening experience within soundscape composition. A classic way of doing that is by recording something in one space and playing it back in a different one, through a performance or installation, for example. I was interested in how the act of recording, and sound collecting, could be a performance within itself, disrupting this process a little. I started inviting people to come to do soundscape recordings with me and discovered that this might be interesting as a performance-walk. I developed a system where I could walk with people, record the environment and play it back in various ways, improvising directly with the soundscape. I developed a soundwalk without really knowing what soundwalking was and then realised that a wide range of people were working with soundwalking in many different fields. It was an established approach to a particular way of being in the world or experiencing a particular space. Then, I started to review the work of people like Hildegard Westerkamp and compositions such as *Kits Beach Soundwalk*, for example, which is not a soundwalk but a fixed media composition that engages with ideas of environmental listening and the sounds of the city. And then, with other people, I have been developing various walking performances and using walking to get to know a place and respond it. Now it is an integral part of my practice and approach. Everything begins with a walk.

(JS) I have always been interested in sound and music, on the one hand. On the other, my education was in design and arts. To some extent, my design studies and practice revolved around public spaces instead of indoor places. We have been trained to think of designers as producers or creators of objects. You design a beautiful object to be placed in a beautiful indoor environment. I was always trying to break out from this way of thinking and to think more broadly about design as a form of engagement with the public space and environment. A natural way to combine my music and design background was to work with sound and public space in some way.

However, my way into soundwalking was through my interest in documentation and amateur archiving practices of people who pay attention and consistently document different aspects of their surroundings, a subject of my practice-based doctoral studies. I have been conducting several practices that seek to record different peripheral aspects of our everyday lives in the public space. Some of these practices have been concerned with sound, such as *Minuting*, a one-minute soundscape recording I have pursued daily since July 2010.

Some of the inspirations also come from experimental theatre makers like Victor Turner and Jerzy Grotowski, who were trying to take theatre outside of the institutional context and bring it back to the environment.

Recently, my work has started to question the idea of soundwalking as an aesthetic framework by asking what happens when the soundwalk, the performance of it, is finished. What is the difference between me listening to the place as a soundwalker and me listening to it as a walking human? I have been trying to link research aspects of my practice and practices of others to ask whether we can conceive of soundwalking or walking and listening more broadly, not just as an artistic medium limited to a specific time and place, but also as an ethico-onto-epistemology, a way of being.

That also relates to my approach to listening as a way of being in the world or a window to notice things that we might miss otherwise.

(JS) Linking back to this idea, an interesting commonality between some of those amateur practitioners, those people passionately documenting one or several aspects of their surrounding world throughout their life, is that they do not frame their activities as art. It is just part of their life, everyday life. I am trying to think the same with soundwalks and how we can make them an integral element of our existence instead of a short-term aesthetic framework that we enter and then leave.

We have touched on many aspects of your work. To conclude, is there anything that you would like to discuss?

(TS) How do you, Usue (URA), understand soundwalking as someone from an architectural or urban design context? What's happening at the moment that interests you, and how do you see things changing?

(URA) Much work is being done from an acoustic perspective to amend or improve the actual soundscape, guided by the ISO 12913 publications, starting from assessing the soundscape from a human perspective, bottom-up and then by acoustic measurements. This wave of research and practice builds from the acoustic ecology tradition. The goal is acoustic to improve the soundscape and related to health and well-being because of the impact of noise on it. I am more interested in sound as a relation rather than a material product, although both are interrelated, and the ISO12913 publications also acknowledge this. With a focus on relation, what can listening help us discover, and can this listening help us think of design as relational?

(JS) It is an important shift, the move to listening (and design) as relational in how we don't only listen to but always *with*. I haven't encountered any writing of that kind in the context of design or architecture.

(TS) The ISO methodology also seems to assume a single way of listening that everyone listens to the same, an objective and quantifiable soundscape. We should invite someone from the ISO tradition to do a soundwalk and book-end it with somebody else who does something different.

(JS) At the ARC residency in 2018, I went to a noise festival, which I think you, Tim, performed at a couple of years later, called…

(TS) LUFF, *Lausanne Underground Film & Music Festival.*

(JS) Yes. It was KILL's concert there, one of the most intense noise performances I have ever attended. I spoke to one of my local friends who said that every year there is a section of police coming to the festival, the so-called noise police. They come with decibel metres, measure the level of noise, and if it crosses a certain threshold, they shut down the party. I thought of them as soundwalkers, particularly oriented, because they walk from one venue to another with this measuring device, quantifying the perception of sound experiences according to prescribed standards.

(URA) This reminds me of Jordan Lacey's work and his book *Sonic Rupture* (2016). His work draws on and expands acoustic ecology and acoustic communication through the lens of affect theory. He works with noise as a feature as opposed to something to suppress. We are stuck with noise and need to turn it into something productive.

(TS) And that's also what the musician Merzbow says. He makes such extreme noise music to encourage people to be aware of the noise of their everyday life. He uses noise to get people to appreciate or attend to other noises. It is quite an interesting philosophy; to generate noise so that people have to listen to it and then cannot ignore it in their everyday lives.

Soundwalking for health and well-being with Richard Bentley

I first met Richard Bentley through Twitter while we were both in the midst of our doctoral work. We both shared an interest in soundwalking and tranquillity and consequently led a *Seeking Tranquillity* event for *Sound Walk September 2020* together with Ximena Alarcon and Ron Herrema (Alarcon *et al.*, 2020). We have since walked together through the mapped tranquillity areas of Northumberland National Park and chatted on several occasions about the need for interdisciplinary collaboration in soundscape design, engaging communities in listening, and the role of artists in landscape and urban design more broadly.

Richard's approach to soundwalking is unique in his emphasis on mental health and well-being. I interviewed him on December 2021 to find out more about soundwalking for well-being and how artists can help landscape architects and urban designers in their listening for design journey.

Soundwalking is central to your research and practice – as an artist, can you tell us a little bit about your journey to soundwalking and how it has evolved in time?

I started by learning *kinh hành*, a Buddhist practice of mindful walking, from Thich Nhat Hanh (Nhat Hanh, 2011). Listening can be a part of that practice. It is a very meditative exercise that uses listening as a focus for meditation while walking. That was my first experience of walking and listening as an intentional exercise.

Later, I came across people like Hildegard Westercamp, Murray Schafer, Pauline Oliveros and others from the art world that were exploring the soundscape through walking and artistic expressions. That seemed to align in many ways with some of my experiences of *kinh hành,* the walking meditation, particularly Pauline Olivero's work on *Deep Listening* (The Center for Deep Listening, 2023). Many of those *Deep Listening* exercises were very familiar to me, albeit from a different angle.

I then moved to soundwalking as a practice to analyse aspects of the soundscape with urban planners and landscape architects, using soundwalking to engage the public or a particular group in evaluating the soundscape for their work in designing landscapes. My soundwalking journey has grown and diversified as I have got to know people and exercises from those various lines of work.

My own practice has maintained an element of the arts and well-being. In well-being, I include wider concepts such as meaning-making or spiritual development, a sense of developing some integration of yourself with what is commonly experienced as other than self. It is quite a different focus from other approaches to soundwalking from acoustic ecologists, planners, designers and other artists. Except for a few individuals, there is little work around soundwalking for well-being, which fascinates me as it brings together my interest in meditations, the arts and soundscapes.

You have developed tranquillity trails and well-being soundwalks from those interests and intersections. Are there any examples of soundwalks that you found particularly interesting or representative of your approach?

I did a recent project with NHS staff during the COVID lockdowns to enable staff a period of quiet, exploration of silence both externally and internally, and a connection with nature for well-being (*NHS Staff Sound and Well-being Workshops*). Silence is such a strange term, but by it, I mean positive silence that some people might equate to a sense of peace or tranquillity.

We started the session in the hospital but found that our conference room was not a suitable environment because of the associations with activities, meetings and work. We managed to move the sessions into a local church, close to a garden area and the Kennet River. We had two lots of five sessions. Broadly, the sessions started with meditation and visualisation for people to listen to what is happening inside them: that radio chatter that we have of our thoughts and the feelings in the body as well. We would quiet the mind and the body using mindful, slow movements and various other activities to bring the mind and body together.

We would then listen to the soundscape through various listening exercises and activities, including field recording and musical responses to the soundscape, to connect people gently with the environments they were listening to. We often finished by sharing experiences and sounds created during the session (Figure 4.4).

At the end of the project, it was interesting reading through the feedback indicating a need for this type of workshop. Some people felt guilty about having quiet time; others became very emotional as the quiet created space for difficult emotions to surface, which was interesting and challenging for the soundwalk and listening exercises. We used the Warwick-Edinburgh mental well-being scale (Warwick Medical School, 2023) to map the improvement in well-being, and, fortunately, in

Figure 4.4 NHS Well-being Soundwalk, Credit: Richard Bentley.

all the cases, there was an improvement in perceived well-being from the beginning to the end.

As well as doing these guided soundwalks and listening exercises, I also make audio tranquillity trails. One example is *Bourne Valley*, near Colchester, where I collaborated with Nature Nurture CIC (2023). That project aimed to connect local people with the natural green space on their doorstep, which very few used. We used a GPS-triggered audio tour that guided people around the path through a stretch of woodland.

We used characters to bring the history of the place to life and connect people with the history of the environment and its natural history. In addition, the trail also gave people an opportunity for reflection and space to sit and listen, either to the soundscapes and music that I was presenting them with or by taking the headphones off and listening to the natural soundscape (Figures 4.5–4.7; Soundtracks 4.1–4.3).

These tranquillity trails and soundwalks connect with the five ways to well-being (Aked *et al.*, 2008), including physical exercise (walking around these areas), mindfulness of the environment, learning something new as they go along, and connecting with and supporting each other. The feedback received from the *Bourne Valley* trail was that people felt connected to the space in a way they hadn't before and were more likely to visit those spaces afterwards, which I was really pleased to hear.

Great examples and very different settings and audiences, both centred on health, well-being and engagement. Can you tell us more about your approach to community engagement, particularly through soundwalks?

I try to get into the community rather than waiting for the community to come to me. If you set up a design consultation, or a soundwalk, the likelihood of people turning up is quite slim as it is perceived as quite a specialist activity. Soundwalks usually attract community members with a pre-existing interest in sound, urban planning or community development, so it is key to turn these events into something that people want to turn up to. Connecting local people with something personal to them that can really spark an interest; therefore, the key is to try and find out what it is about the soundscape, about sound, that fires people up to get them hooked. Once engaged, they are much more likely to offer their views on the soundscape and how it affects them.

Figure 4.5 Stop 4 on the Bourne Valley Tour: Giant Willow (Soundtrack 4.1), Credit: Richard Bentley.

Another important aspect is trust, at a personal level and in a wider sense. The belief that they are going to be listened to and that their views will be considered and acted upon.

Giving people space to share is also key. Individually, people may have difficulty articulating their likes, dislikes and annoyances. However, as soon as you get people

Figure 4.6 Stop 6 on the Bourne Valley Tour: Sit and take a moment to be mindful (Soundtrack 4.2), Credit: Richard Bentley.

talking to each other, there's a wealth of information because people feed off each other's questions and ideas.

Following the engagement with the community, what currently needs to be added is the linkup between the work we do as community artists and that of other bodies with an interest in soundscape (i.e., Community leaders, planners, designers and policymakers). As an artist, we focus on engaging people creatively with the soundscape, and it is difficult to link up with those who can take this initial work and use it constructively to inform policy or to make changes to a space. Sound expertise and skills in different disciplines need to come together because, if there is that collaboration, it is likely that we will achieve meaningful change regarding the soundscape.

This final reflection speaks to the aim of this book, the need for landscape architects and urban designers to draw from and collaborate with other disciplines with an interest and specialism in sound and with the community to change urban soundscapes. Action needs to be triggered at many levels.

Figure 4.7 Stop 7A on the Bourne Valley Tour: Fishing with monks at Blythe Pond (Soundtrack 4.3), Credit: Richard Bentley.

We need a joined-up approach. Community engagement, empowering people or giving people a voice is not enough.

We also need proper training for urban designers and planners on sound and listening. I have been surprised by how little sound is talked about within these circles. I spoke recently to Lisa Lavia from the Noise Abatement Society about the need for proper training as part of the qualifications needed to become a landscape architect or urban planner so that sound and listening become a natural part of the planning and design process.

You can instigate policy to trigger action, but there needs to be that awareness amongst designers and the community. Talking about sound and soundscape with my brother, Mark Bentley, a principal landscape architect at The Environment Partnershi, has been quite a revelation in some respects. The willingness is there amongst designers; it is just a question of training and opening conversations, with a nudge from policy as well.

I have spoken to many people from so many different fields working with sound during my Ph.D., and it has been fascinating. However, the work is very siloed. As well as training, we also need to enable time and space for collaboration because, without that collaboration, no one discipline will significantly impact the soundscape.

Is there any other advice you would offer landscape architects and urban designers interested in sound besides training and collaboration?

An important point to make that goes some way to address the question is that many artists feel uncomfortable with the language used by urban planners, landscape architects and acousticians because they come from a different world. It is important that the language used and the approach taken is accessible and inclusive to foster collaboration.

Artists also need to be taken seriously in terms of our contribution to the soundscape evaluation process. The data we produce naturally may be difficult to interpret. It may not be figures, decibel levels of sound pressure or graphs about the pleasantness of the soundscape. We don't work with those kinds of metrics. It is important to acknowledge what artists bring, and broaden our language when speaking about soundscape, to encompass creative approaches.

Finding a common language and a sense of mutual respect and equality within an interdisciplinary team is important to foster. It will be interesting to see if that collaborative soundscape process takes off and what kind of structure and format it takes.

An architect soundwalking with Antonella Radicchi

Antonella and I met at the *Internoise* conference in Madrid in June 2019, having previously connected on Twitter through a shared interest in tranquillity and quiet areas. Antonella was in high demand at the conference, a reflection of her extensive research on soundscapes and citizen science projects. Antonella's approach to soundwalking and sound research is unique in interweaving creative and technical approaches with citizen science technology.

I interviewed Antonella in November (2021) to learn more about her journey as an architect and urbanist into soundwalking and the background to the *Hush City* app that she has developed. The *Hush City* app is a free mobile app that invites people to 'identify and assess quiet areas in cities' and feeds into a web-based map of quiet areas, the *Hush City Map*. The app launched in 2017 through a pilot study in Berlin and has since been adopted by Berlin and Limerick City Councils to develop plans of quiet areas that can inform policies on health and well-being. In Berlin, the *Hush City* app was adopted within the context of the participatory process that led to the development of the *Berlin Plan of Quiet Areas* in 2018; in Limerick, it is still an ongoing process.

As an architect, when and how did your interest in sound and listening start?

I link it to my education and training in classical dancing, which took place parallel to my schooling. I grew up listening to music and performing with the body in a space, in context. I got this sense of rhythm and understood the power of sounds on our feelings and emotions from the very beginning of my life.

Then, while studying at the Faculty of Architecture in Italy, I encountered acoustics addressed from a technical perspective only. We had a course in technical physics that touched on lighting and sound, but mostly for indoor environments and from a technical perspective. I started to think of sound as an element of urban design and planning within the context of my Ph.D. I was very much into the work of Kevin Lynch and how he broke down the walls of academia and went out on the streets to involve people in assessing urban spaces. Wanting to deepen Lynch's approach, I studied his work at MIT. In the archives at MIT, I found an original study that he did with artist Gyorgy Kepes in New York in the 1950s. Together they studied all experiential qualities of the urban environment, including sound, and interviewed John Cage. The follow-up to this sensory study was *The Image of the City*, a contribution centred on visual studies and urban planning, where he demonstrated that we have these mental images of places grounded on five basic elements (Lynch, 1960). I then came across the work done by Southworth, a student of Lynch, and read his original master's thesis about the soundscape of the Boston peninsula in the MIT libraries. I had a look at these beautiful blue maps that Southworth drew to represent the soundscape of Boston which stemmed from his fieldwork, taking MIT professors around the peninsula of Boston in wheelchairs, blinded, too. It was fascinating, and this was something I wanted to explore.

While at MIT, I was part of a project studio titled *The Digital City*, which questioned how digital technology could be used to renew historical centres of cities. The environment at MIT was favourable to experiment, which led me to develop a project proposal to renew Florence's historical centre through technology and sound with Francisca Rojas, an MIT Ph.D. student (Radicchi and Rojas, 2009). The proposal never turned into a real project; however, we conceived an open-source community-led framework for using sensor and digital technology to redesign the soundscape of the historical centre of Florence. This was 2007 and therefore maybe too innovative for that time, as the project would employ smartphones and digital sensors to activate speakers and change the city's soundscape

81

by masking traffic noise with inputs from the community. Based on this project, I proposed a case study to the city of Florence, who was interested in principle but never implemented it.

Around that time, I started doing field recordings and soundwalks. I got in touch with the Italian branch of the Forum für Klanglandschaft (Forum Klanglandschaft Italia, 2023) and with one of its founders, Albert Mayr, an Italian composer who collaborated with Schafer in the Italian case study of the *Five Village Soundscapes* project (Schafer, Davis and Truax, 1977). Albert Mayr mentored me during my Ph.D. and introduced me to the theory and practice of soundwalking and a circle of artists and musicians active in the soundscape. As an architect with a creative background, this was a magic encounter as these artists and musicians were working with city sounds creatively. I experienced creative and inclusive ways of soundwalking. Some of these soundwalks were radical blinded soundwalks and, therefore, compelling, mind-blowing experiences. Albert Mayr encouraged me to lead soundwalks, which I was reluctant to do for many years. Once I started leading soundwalks, however, I found them extremely rewarding because of the social interaction with participants in the soundwalks. On soundwalks, I always love listening not only to the environment but also to people reporting on their experiences. When you talk about sound with people, they reveal very personal details because sound is linked to our mnemonic and emotional inner world. I must admit that I still prefer participating in a soundwalk rather than leading them because you have to be rational to lead. In contrast, when you follow, you can immerse yourself and enjoy the experience.

How has your soundwalking practice evolved since these initial soundwalks?

My experience with soundwalks has changed from two perspectives. The first is the move from participating to leading soundwalks, and the second relates to methodology. Initially, I mainly did creative, unstructured, silent soundwalks, just walking and listening. When I started doing the *Hush City* project, within the context of my post-doctoral research work, there was a need to provide data-driven evidence to impact policymaking and science. Hence, I elaborated on the method-purpose binomial and defined the '4-Variations Framework' for soundwalking according to civic, political, educational and research purposes (Radicchi, 2017). Since then, I have used this framework to operationalise my soundwalking practice employing 'silent soundwalks', 'commented soundwalks with simple evaluation points', 'solo soundwalks' and 'soundwalks with complex evaluation points' (ibid., p. 72).

Have you found any limitations in recruiting people for soundwalks, or in the makeup of participants?

I do not collect personal demographic data through the *Hush City* app (Radicchi, 2021). It was a decision made at the beginning of the project to privilege the privacy of the app users. In the soundwalks that I have organized, the recruitment process has always been easy. However, it depends on the context and the environmental conditions. For instance, if you run a soundwalk in winter in Berlin, you may barely find a couple of people because it is too cold to go outside and walk for one hour.

Regarding abilities, I once ran a soundwalk with the *Hush City* app in New York with a deaf participant, which I wrote about in a paper (Radicchi, 2019). I had an illuminating conversation with the participant, and in the written comments, they described looking at the environment and imagining how it could sound to them. It was not physiological listening, but *imaginative* listening if we can call it that. They were very enthusiastic about the topic and the app as well.

Talking about the app, how did you come up with the idea for the Hush City app? Did it emerge from the Florence case study that you have just described?

I was very much into digital technology from the early days. After the MIT project, I developed a digital sound map of Florence that invited people to share sounds, images and comments on sounds which they associate with emotions triggered by experiencing the city of Florence (Radicchi, 2015). One of the impacts of Florence's soundmap is that the data (images, sounds and text) were included in the *Open Data* System of the city of Florence (Comune di Firenze, 2013), becoming the first open dataset created by citizens included in a municipality system in Italy.

Then in 2014, a colleague working for the *Expo* of Milan challenged me to develop a sound map for the Expo. As Expos are usually very noisy, I thought it would be useful to have a map of the quiet spots instead. I developed a mock-up of an app called *Hush Expo* and dug more into the topic of quietness and relevant European environmental policies such as the END 2002 (European Parliament and Council, 2002). In the end, I did not develop the app for the Expo. However, I drew on this concept to develop the *Hush City* app, which I then developed and implemented at the TU Berlin as Principal Investigator of the '*Beyond the Noise: Open Source Soundscapes*' project (2016–2018) and the '*Hush City Mobile Lab*' project (2018–2020) (Figure 4.8).

Developing the Hush City app and map, would there be a place for city-wide, citizen-driven sound maps to complement noise maps to inform decision-making?

Absolutely. I made a proposal at a conference paper for integrating this kind of methodology into urban planning (Radicchi, 2018). The proposal mirrors the *Hush City Framework*, using the app and soundwalks to involve people in collecting

January – Lima, #561   February – Córdoba, #597   March – Stuttgart, #866   April – Geneva, #982

May – Amsterdam, #1012   June – Reading, #1058   July – Rüdesheim, #1112   August – New York, #1158

September – Berlin, #1330   October – Shanghai, #1376   November – Granada, #1593   December – Goa, #1655

Figure 4.8 Selection of quiet areas mapped through the Hush City App in 2018, Credit: Antonella Radicchi.

data that are then linked in real-time to the *Hush City* map. The aim would be for municipalities to integrate this data into their datasets or open data systems and keep them open for continuous review by citizens and policymakers. In other words, I proposed applying an open, circular process rather than the closed, linear one that the END's methodology indicates for creating noise maps, which policymakers must review every five years. When I discussed this framework in 2018 with the municipality of Berlin, the response that I got was that they do not have the necessary resources to curate such *living maps*. However, I remain optimistic, and a city advanced in participatory urban planning, such as Barcelona, could implement it in the future.

We have talked about the emotional impact of sound, about soundwalks and about tools for assessing soundscapes from human perception and measurements. What is holding us, as designers, from moving from this assessment stage into design?

It is a matter of education. We should change programs and integrate more modules dedicated to sound(scape) in architecture, design and planning programs. Everything can change if we change the knowledge that students can access. Changing training programs might need negotiation with the professional bodies for accreditation. However, the work should be done at this level because, in terms of publications, experiments and pilots, we have done a lot.

Besides adapting education, is there any other advice you would offer individual urban designers or landscape architects keen to start with sound?

To follow their passion, be wild with their imagination and not be afraid to make discoveries and develop something new, especially at the beginning of their training. It is a wonderful field yet to be fully accepted or developed; therefore, motivation and passion are key to following it through.

Listening and sounding exercises: soundscape narratives

Soundscape narratives was a short design studio with first-year Master of Landscape Architecture students at Newcastle University (UK) in 2020. The project was part of a studio module conducive to enabling students to learn the language of landscape both for deciphering and evaluating existing landscapes and for embedding narratives in designed landscapes.

This design studio unfolded in two parts: the first, concentrated on the designer as a user of the environment, listening to interact and navigate through it. The second, focused on the designer as the reader of the environment, listening to decipher and evaluate it, and as a starting point to envisage new futures. The studio was preceded by a lecture that introduced students to the role of listening in the multi-sensorial experience of the landscape, the tenets of acoustic ecology (including foreground sounds, background sounds and soundmarks) and soundwalking.

Soundscape narratives part 1

Students were tasked with carrying out a daily soundwalk for five consecutive days and recording it in a sound diary. Students could choose any route close to their home, lasting 30 minutes or more. At the end of the walk, students were required to:

1. Describe five sounds that caught their attention during the walk and their effect on their mood and behaviour. Students were given a set of questions to answer to help describe the sounds. Questions drew from ISO 12913-2 guidance and included: what type of sound did you think it was (biophonic, anthrophonic, geophonic)? How loud was the sound (high, medium, low)? What was its duration and periodicity (constant, intermittent, one-off, repetitive)? How was the sound altered by the environment (e.g., was there any echo)? Was the sound appropriate to the context, or did it surprise you? How did the sound affect you and your walk? Could you describe the sound using an affective adjective (i.e., calm, annoying, vibrant)?
2. Draw a map of the route that they had taken and locate the five sound sources on the map. The map could be of any scale or format (digital base or hand drawn) and served to supplement their description (Figure 4.9).
3. Repeat the same exercise for four consecutive days, walking the same route. Students could walk at different times of the day to notice temporal changes.

During the briefing of the exercise, a few students were sceptical about the task ahead, wondering whether there would be able to notice as many as five different sounds on their walks. At the end of it, most students were surprised by the amount of sounds heard, the variability of their immediate soundscapes in time and their response to it. The exercise coincided with the pandemic, and the start of a lockdown in the midst of it exacerbated temporal changes in the soundscape as human activity and anthrophonic sounds drastically changed from one day to the next. One of our students, working remotely from Wuhan at the time, noticed, in particular, the sounds of her own making during her soundwalks and changed her shoes daily to try and focus away from her footsteps and into middle and distant sounds.

Soundscape narratives part 2: collage or visualisation

The second part of the exercise aimed to read and evaluate a landscape exclusively through listening (to a field recording of an environment) and translating the heard environment and its affective evaluation into one or more visuals. Students were provided with two field recordings and were required to:

1. Listen to both recordings and choose one to explore in detail. Students were given little guidance on where the soundtracks were recorded other than they

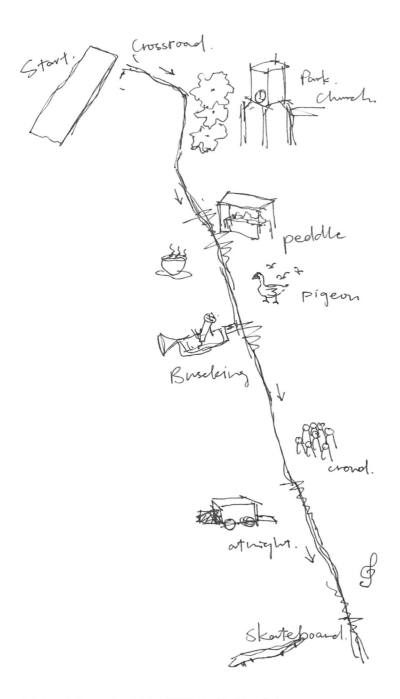

Figure 4.9 Sound diary route, October 2020, Credit: Estee Tsoi.

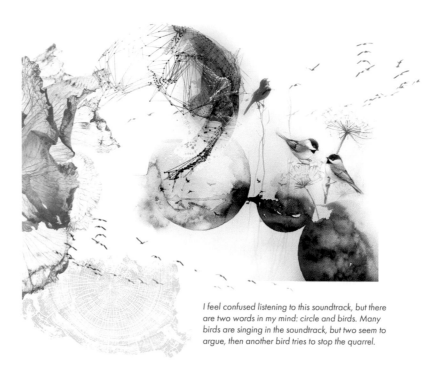

I feel confused listening to this soundtrack, but there are two words in my mind: circle and birds. Many birds are singing in the soundtrack, but two seem to argue, then another bird tries to stop the quarrel.

Figure 4.10 The first soundtrack on first listen, Credit: Mian Han.

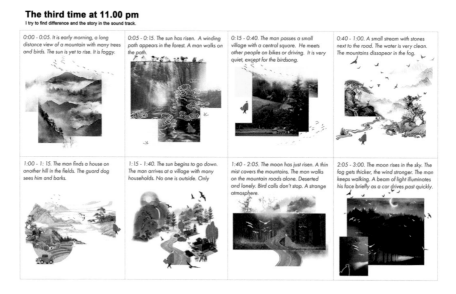

Figure 4.11 The first soundtrack on third listen, Credit: Mian Han.

were both recorded on the same day, at different times of the day, and at a distance of approximately 500 m. The recording's location (Hondarribia) and date (April 2019) were shared with the students after the exercise.

2. Produce a visual to portray the environment heard and experienced and the student's affective response. The visual could be a collage, diagram or drawing. The visual could be any size and be accompanied by a paragraph of text explaining the experience of the environment portrayed.

To aid with the exercise, while listening, students were encouraged to imagine the environment the field recording was portraying and try and answer the following questions: what are the spatial characteristics of the environment (hard or soft, open or enclosed)? Who is using the space, and what kind of activities might occur? What time of the day might it be, what season and what is the weather like? Which sounds contribute positively to your mood, and which contribute negatively? How would listening mediate what you would do if you were in the space?

Responses to this exercise were very varied in terms of the visuals produced. Most students could imagine the spatial characteristics of both environments quite well – whether open or enclosed, hard or soft – and the users and activities within them. One of our students, Mian Han, chose the first field recording (Soundtrack 4.4) and listened to it three times to produce three visual narratives. Through repeated listening, she revealed more details of the soundscape, producing imaginative visual narratives. Each one told a clear story and was highly evocative of different spatial, geographic, climate and aural realms, drawing the viewer into a layered, complex experience. Her third visual narrative no longer represented the soundtrack, but rather, through her imagination, the student expanded the recording into a fictional story spanning a full day. This fictional story starts at dusk and follows a man as he journeys alone from a trail in the forest to a road in a remote valley with cars passing by (Figures 4.10 and 4.11).

🎵 Soundtrack 4.4 Dawn chorus, Hondarribia, April 2019.

References

Aked, J., *et al.* (2008) *Five ways to wellbeing, new economics foundation.* Available at: https://neweconomics.org/2008/10/five-ways-to-wellbeing (Accessed: 13 March 2023).

Alarcon, X. *et al.* (2020) *Seeking tranquillity, walk, listen, create.* Available at: https://walk-listencreate.org/walkingevent/seeking-tranquillity/ (Accessed: 12 July 2023).

Comune di Firenze (2013) *Mappa sonora - Firenze Sound Map, Open Data i dati aperti del Comune di Firenze.* Available at: https://opendata.comune.fi.it/content/utiliz zatori-sviluppatori-api-daf?q=metarepo/datasetinfo&id=4c994148-0bf0-4de5-bda3-2157dda2c9a2 (Accessed: 20 April 2023).

European Parliament and Council (2002) 'Directive 2002/49/EC of the European Parliament and of the Council of the 25th June 2002, relating to the assessment and management of environmental noise', *Official Journal of the European Communities*, L189.

Forum Klanglandschaft Italia (2023) *Paesaggio Sonoro, Paesaggio Sonoro.* Available at: http://www.paesaggiosonoro.it/ (Accessed: 11 March 2023).

Lynch, K. (1960) *The image of the city.* Cambridge, MA; London: MIT Press.

Nature Nurture (2023) *Nature, nurture, nature nurture.* Available at: https://nature-nurture.co.uk/ (Accessed: 13 March 2023).

Nhat Hanh, T. (2011) *Walk like a Buddha, trycicle.* Available at: https://tricycle.org/magazine/walk-buddha/ (Accessed: 13 March 2023).

Radicchi, A. (2015) *Firenze sound map, Antonella Radicchi.* Available at: http://www.antonellaradicchi.it/portfolio/an-emotional-journey/ (Accessed: 11 March 2023).

Radicchi, A. (2017) 'A pocket guide to soundwalking', in Besecke, A. *et al.* (eds) *Stadtökonomie – Blickwinkel und Perspektiven.* Berlin: Sonderpublikation des Instituts für Stadt- und Regionalplanung der Technischen Universität Berlin, pp. 70–73.

Radicchi, A. (2018) 'Everyday quiet areas. What they mean and how they can be integrated in city planning processes', in *Inter-Noise and Noise-Con Congress and Conference Proceedings.* Chicago, IL, pp. 2984–3995.

Radicchi, A. (2019) 'A soundscape study in New York. Reflections on the application of stardardized methods to study everyday quiet areas', in *23rd International Congress on Acoustics.* Aaceh.

Radicchi, A. (2021) 'Citizen science mobile apps for soundscape research and public space studies. Lessons learnt from the Hush City project', in Skarlatidou, A. and Haklay, M. (eds) *Geographic citizen science design: No one left behind.* London: UCL Press, pp. 130–148. doi: 10.2307/j.ctv15d8174.14.

Radicchi, A. and Rojas, F. (2009) 'Soundscapes Oltrarno', in Frenchman, D. and Mitchell, W. (eds) *Technology, livability and the historic city. Future of Florence.* Cambridge, Massachusetts: MIT Press, pp. 80–85.

Schafer, R. M., Davis, B. and Truax, B. (1977) 'Five village soundscapes', *The Music of the Environment Series*, Issue 4,.

Smolicki, J. and Shaw, T. (2023) *About, walking festival of sound.* Available at: https://wfos.net/about.html (Accessed: 12 July 2023).

The Center for Deep Listening (2023) *About deep listening, the center for deep listening.* Available at: https://www.deeplistening.rpi.edu/deep-listening/ (Accessed: 13 March 2023).

Warwick Medical School (2023) *The Warwick-Edinburgh mental wellbeing scales - WEMWBS, The University of Warwick.* Available at: https://warwick.ac.uk/fac/sci/med/research/platform/wemwbs/ (Accessed: 13 March 2023).

PART II

Composition

Chapter Five

Reading the soundscape

> People can find meaning in their lives by communicating, talking, writing and telling stories. Landscapes and places are not able to do this. And yet they tell their stories to those of us who are able to decipher them.
>
> (Schäfer, 2014, p. 116)

Reading the soundscape

Landscapes can tell the stories of communities and places, of how those places came into being, how natural and cultural processes have shaped them and how they are inhabited. Landscapes hold past narratives and current narratives. Narratives that can be read and deciphered through fieldwork, by spending time in a place, and through a desktop review of maps, reports and policies. The act of reading the landscape includes unravelling the atmospheric qualities of a place, the communities who inhabit it and have shaped it, and past and present natural processes that have also moulded it. Through reading, we evaluate how these cultural and natural processes relate to a place's physical and atmospheric characteristics and experience. In the process, we uncover the character and identity of a place and seek opportunities for transformation (Timmermans, 2014).

Sounds are an integral part of the language of landscapes; thus, training our listening enables us to decipher the stories embedded within them. Deciphering stories enables us to bring attention to them through our interventions and to set the stage for communities and natural processes to start new chapters in those stories (ibid.).

DOI: 10.4324/9781003202981-8

The aim is to understand a site and its many layered stories through listening at a specific point in time, as landscapes and stories are constantly evolving and never finished.

Listening in its three interrelated modes – *affect* (1), *communication* (2) and *aesthetic evaluation* (3) – can form an integral part of the reading of the landscape:

1. Listening provides an affective engagement (of listeners and designers) with the environment and conditions their actions. As I have argued, this is the most basic and mundane mode of listening, and might integrate communication and affect.
2. Listening can help us understand a place, including its communities, culture, materiality and geometry. In doing so, it provides information about the stories and character of a place and what is happening around it.
3. Listening is an aesthetic pursuit and can contribute to how a space is valued. In turn, sound can be a creative avenue for fieldwork investigation and, later, transformation.

The purpose of reading the landscape through listening is to determine the qualities and character of a site and how the existing soundscape mediates the relation between human and non-human communities and their environment. At this stage, we identify opportunities for transformation and constraints that may limit or shape that transformation. We also determine the aural character and identity of a place. We can term this stage of the design process through listening as the *soundscape inventory and analysis*. The *soundscape analysis* can inform site-wide conceptual design responses and strategies to improve or conserve the existing soundscape.

The perception of the environment through listening depends on physical, environmental and individual and species variables, as discussed in previous chapters. Those variables can be grouped into three site inventory and analysis parameters: sound events, environment and listeners (Figure 5.1).

The *soundscape inventory and analysis* can be carried out through a combination of methods to capture and assess the variables that affect the perception of the environment through listening and determine aural character areas and identity. Methods for capturing and assessing these variables include soundwalks, field recordings (to extract sound measurements, if required), review of existing policies, noise and quiet area maps, citizen science apps and arts-led projects. These can be linked to and mapped alongside other site elements and qualities usually captured and assessed during these initial stages, such as historic maps or existing vegetation and fauna.

Therefore, the *soundscape inventory and analysis* are both objective (analysis of sound recordings, review of maps and ecological surveys, materiality and geometry)

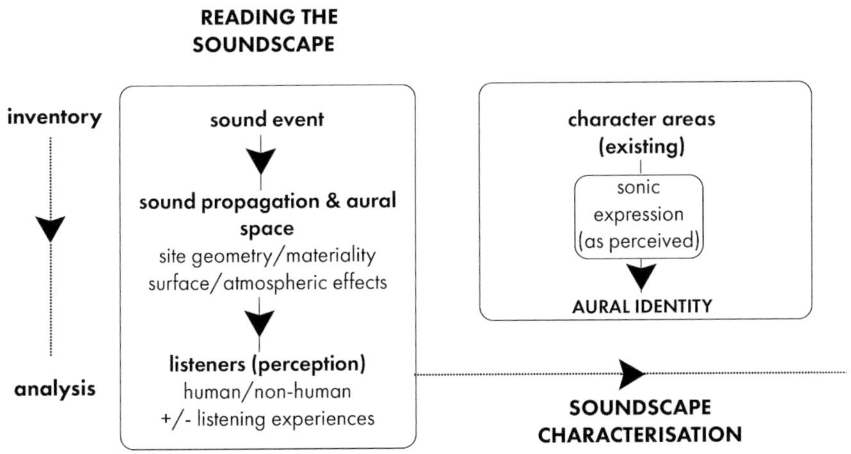

**READING THE
SOUNDSCAPE**

Figure 5.1 From soundscape inventory and analysis to characterization.

and experiential, as it captures aural qualities and experiences through soundwalks. Both are intertwined for the identification of opportunities and ideas for a site.

The scope of the *soundscape inventory and analysis* will vary according to the brief and scale of the project.

At a masterplanning or action plan scale, we can employ the soundwalking methodology recommended by ISO 12913 publications, adapting it to the scope of each project and expanding it to:

- Consider other living organisms, for example, by applying acoustic indices, as Chapter 9 details.
- Widen the community's input and participation through other methods, such as citizen science initiatives and artist-led engagements. Examples of both are included in the case studies found in Chapter 4.
- Incorporate additional detail as per the detail design scale.

At a detailed design scale, a more nuanced understanding of the soundscape and its context is required to engage communities and designers with a place through listening and develop an aural concept or strategies that can be integrated into the overall concept for the interventions on the site. In this volume, I concentrate on the detailed design scale and tools that can be incorporated into everyday practice to add to the existing methodology to assess the soundscape at the masterplan scale.

Soundscape inventory and analysis at masterplan scale

At a masterplanning scale, a soundscape assessment can be carried out through a combination of objective and experiential methods, including the review of noise and quiet area maps, soundwalks to collect information on the existing and future communities' perceptions of the soundscape and acoustic measurements, including psychoacoustic parameters and soundscape indices.

Review of noise and quiet area maps

Noise and quiet area maps drawn from sound pressure measurements are useful starting points for understanding noise levels from major airports, railways and roads. However, they provide limited information about other sounds and about listening as a mediator of the subject–environment relation. Nevertheless, they serve to identify areas where unwanted sound might be problematic, and the involvement of an acoustician might be required. They also serve to identify potential pockets of quietness and give an overall impression of a site that can be assessed in more detail through other methods.

Soundwalks in the ISO methodology

The purpose of the soundwalk, as described within the ISO 12913 publications, is to unveil the communities 'perception of the soundscape in its context' (BSI, 2018, p. 4). Through the soundwalk, information is collected on the parameters that influence the perception of the soundscape at specific points. Participants listen in silence for a couple of minutes before completing a questionnaire on the soundscape. Three alternative protocols for collecting data are available: two questionnaires (methods A and B) and an offsite interview (method C) (ibid.). All protocols aim to identify the uniqueness of a soundscape; the emotions that the soundscape elicits; how the soundscape mediates the dynamic relationship between people, place and activity; and lastly, the potential for design or improvement of the soundscape within the overall aim for the place. Method A, the most commonly employed, achieves those aims by recording sound sources and perceived affective quality and assessing the surrounding sound environment and its appropriateness (ibid.).

Many urban soundscape research projects have been carried out following the ISO methodology, and the reader is encouraged to review the breadth of research available. In my soundwalks with practicing landscape architects and students, I have used questionnaires adapted from the ISO methodology for assessing the soundscape and starting to think through listening as part of the design.

When working at a masterplan-scale level, at each assessed place along the sound-walk, a summary of positive and negative listening experiences can be developed and related to perceived opportunities and constraints, forming the starting point for site interventions and soundscape design. Arts-led methods, citizen science initiatives and acoustic indices can expand the soundscape assessment at this stage.

Soundscape inventory and analysis at detailed scale

Deciphering a place through listening can be integrated into the following stages of the site inventory and analysis process: (1) site inventory, (2) landscape characterization and (3) identification of constraints and opportunities.

Site inventory

The soundscape inventory can be linked and mapped alongside other site elements and qualities, typically:

- Historical maps, as sounds express or reflect the historical and contemporary culture of a place, including soundmarks.
- Existing vegetation and fauna, as these are, in turn, soundmakers and listeners and affect sound propagation.
- Movement patterns, as pedestrians and vehicles are sound events.
- Existing geometry and materiality, climate and microclimate, and topography of the site, as these affect sound propagation.
- Soils and hydrology, as these are sound events and affect sound propagation.

The purpose of this inventory is to identify the three variables that affect the perception of the environment through listening: *sound events*, the *environment* and its influence on sound propagation, the environment and its influence on sound propagation is all one category and the *listeners*, and how they are affected through listening. These three variables can be mapped within the above maps or in purposely created soundscape drawings.

Sound events

Sound events are the sources of sound. They are sounds experienced in their physical, social and environmental context (Truax, 1999).

Animate and inanimate objects and beings can be sources of sound. Anything can vibrate and therefore sound within a site and outside of it. Sound respects no site boundaries, and it is, therefore, difficult to control on a site, which is relevant when assessing a site and later when intervening upon it.

As part of the site inventory, sound events can be described and analysed according to their origin, acoustic properties and contribution to the character and identity of a place.

SOUND EVENTS – ORIGIN

When it comes to origin, sound events can be classified into *geophony* (geophysical sounds), *biophony* (biological sounds) and *anthrophony* (anthropogenic sounds) (Krause, 1987). This classification is useful to assess the overall composition of a soundscape and, therefore, the character of a place in a snapshot. Acoustic indices, such as the *Normalised Difference Soundscape Index* (NDSI), can be used to evaluate the proportion of biophonies and technophonies in a landscape. Acoustic or soundscape indices are employed within bio and ecoacoustics and are discussed in Chapter 9.

A more in-depth taxonomy for sound sources, particularly regarding sounds of human origin, is provided in the ISO 12913 part 2 (BSI, 2018). This taxonomy classifies outdoor acoustic environments first into 'urban, rural, wilderness, or underwater' and then into sounds of human origin (including anthropogenic sounds and biophonic sounds generated by humans) and those of non-human origin (ibid.) (Figure 5.2).

Classifying or grouping sounds into categories is a valuable tool when analysing data collated from soundwalks as part of a site analysis. The above classification provides limited information on non-human sounds, and depending on the nature of a project, a more in-depth description of these is required.

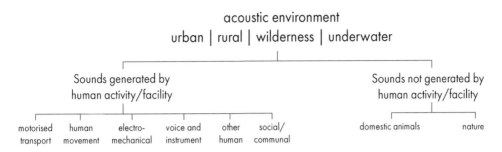

Figure 5.2 Taxonomy of sound sources, adapted from BSI (2018, Figure C.1).

SOUND EVENTS – ACOUSTIC PROPERTIES

Sound events can then be described and analysed according to their acoustic properties (acoustic indicators) and how these are perceived (psychoacoustic indicators). Acoustic indicators allow for the objective evaluation of sound, whereas psychoacoustic indicators are the acoustic parameters as perceived by people (BSI, 2018).

For a landscape architect or urban designer without acoustic or music training, acoustic and psychoacoustic indicators beyond sound pressure levels might not mean much and collaborating with acousticians might be beneficial at this stage, should a project require an in-depth analysis of these.

There are, however, other acoustic properties of sound events that any landscape architect or urban designer could identify and analyse, which provide information about the environment for its evaluation. These are the temporal and rhythmical acoustic properties and the type of sound in relation to its ambience (background, foreground and salient). With regards to temporality and rhythm, we can record whether a sound is permanent, temporal or one-off; whether a sound is cyclical (at certain times of the day) or seasonal (at certain times of the year); and whether a sound is monotonous or varied.

SOUND EVENTS – AURAL CHARACTER AND IDENTITY

The last aspect to consider regarding sound events, and the most important in thinking of listening to environmental sound as a relation, is how sounds contribute to the character of a place and its aural identity. Landscape character is defined as a 'distinct and recognisable pattern of elements, or characteristics, in the landscape that makes one landscape different from another' (Natural England, 2014, p. 8). These patterns of elements make each place distinctive, 'with its own individual character and identity' (ibid., p. 54). Landscape, as we have discussed, is a dynamic interaction between people and place, and landscape character is the result of natural, cultural and perceptual processes. These processes sound and are listened to, giving each place its unique soundscape. The emphasis here, once again, lies in understanding sound not as an object 'but [as] the medium of our perception' (Ingold, 2007, p. 11) and thus an interactive relation. Aural character and identity are discussed in detail later in the chapter.

In short, there are three aspects to record as part of the site inventory regarding a *sound event*:

- *Origin of sound event* (whether natural or cultural, biological or non-biological).
- *Acoustic properties* (including temporality and rhythm) and type of sound in relation to its ambience (background, foreground and salient).
- *Cultural, symbolic or functional relevance* of those sounds in relation to how they contribute to the character and navigation of space.

Environment and sound propagation

Sound waves are transformed as they travel through the environment. Therefore, the acoustic properties of the environment, determined by its geometry and materiality, as well as weather conditions, influence what we hear. Thus, listening in space can tell us invaluable information regarding the geometry and materiality of a place and help us determine aural space.

AURAL SPACE

Space and form determine the structure of the landscape and are thus the most important physical and visual characteristics of any landscape. We decipher space not only by looking but also by experiencing it with all our senses, including listening. Space is defined not only visually and physically but also aurally. Aural (also known as auditory) and visual space do not always correspond. Aural space is experiential and not defined by physical boundaries (Blesser and Salter, 2007). It is not defined by visual boundaries either: we can hear sounds out of sight, and sometimes the information we receive through listening and that received by looking do not correspond. Aural space is defined as much by 'virtual sonic boundaries', including background noise (ibid.), as it is by physical boundaries, atmospheric conditions, weather and listeners' abilities.

Several concepts related to aural space are useful to understand and decipher aural space, including *acoustic horizon*, *acoustic arena* and *auditory channel*.

The acoustic horizon is 'the farthest distance in every direction from [a source of sound] from which [the] sound may be heard' (Truax, 1999). The *acoustic horizon*, therefore, denotes the longest distance between the listener and the sonic event. The *acoustic horizon* is experiential and centred on the listener, thus varying between listeners.

An acoustic arena is an area 'where listeners can hear a sonic event because it has sufficient loudness to overcome the background noise' (Blesser and Salter, 2007, p. 27). The *acoustic arena* is centred on the sound event and delineates the area or space inside which listeners can hear the sound event.

Auditory channel refers to the connection established between a sound event and a listener (ibid.).

Acoustic horizons, *acoustic arenas* and *auditory channels* are all dynamic. For example, switching a TV off inside a room expands the *acoustic arena* of birds singing outside the window. Also, it expands the *acoustic horizon* of the listener inside the room (ibid.). Understanding *acoustic horizons* and *arenas* should form part of any site inventory, as depending on a site's physical, atmospheric and aural characteristics, including whether it is enclosed or not, sound waves can be contained within it or travel far beyond it. In turn, the sound resulting from our interventions can reach far beyond what the eye can see or reverberate within the site.

The theoretical diagram in Figure 5.3 serves to illustrate and understand these three concepts.

In Figure 5.3, listener 1 will hear sound X, as their *acoustic horizon* lies within the *acoustic arena* of X, creating an *auditory channel* (cX–1). Listener 2 will also hear sound X as their *acoustic horizon* partially lies within the *acoustic arena* of X, creating an *auditory channel* (cX–2). Listener 3 will not hear sound X, as their *acoustic horizon* does not overlap with X's *acoustic arena*. However, listeners 2 and 3 could communicate with one another if the *acoustic arenas* of their soundmaking equated to their *acoustic horizons*, thus creating another *auditory channel* (c2–3) (Hill, 2020).

In the environment, however, sound does not propagate as uniformly as shown in the diagram, as it is affected by atmospheric conditions, physical features and background sounds. Listeners' *acoustic horizons* also vary among individuals and are affected by a dynamic soundscape.

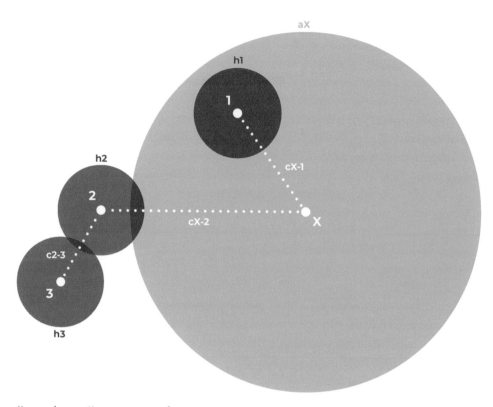

X = sound event; aX = acoustic arena of X
1, 2, 3 = listeners; h1, h2, h3 = acoustic horizons for 1, 2, 3
cX-1 = auditory channel that enables 1 to hear X; cX-2 = auditory channel that enables 2 to partially hear X
c2-3 = auditory channel that enables 2 and 3 to communicate

Figure 5.3 Theoretical diagram of acoustic horizons, acoustic arena and auditory channels, Credit: Dan Hill.

The listening and sounding exercises included in Chapter 6 were developed to help students understand and decipher aural space through listening. The reader might want to turn to these now.

SOUND PROPAGATION – MATERIALITY AND CLIMATE

Sound propagation is affected by *atmospheric* and *surface* effects (Truax, 1999).

Atmospheric effects include absorption, scattering or reflection of sound waves (ibid.) and are dependent on temperature, humidity and wind (Trikootam and Hornikx, 2019).

Absorption depends on temperature and humidity (ibid.). Due to water reflecting sound, there is higher absorption in low-humid, high-temperature places. This effect is more prominent for higher than lower frequencies (ibid).

Scattering depends on wind speed and direction. Wind speed increases with altitude, which creates a wind gradient and affects sound propagation through scattering. Sound levels increase when soundwaves travel downwind towards the receptor, as they are refracted towards the ground and then reflected from the ground. Sound levels decrease when travelling upwind away from the receptor (as they are refracted away from the ground) (Hannah, 2006).

Reflection depends on temperature gradients. In daytime, when the temperature is higher close to the ground and colder away from it, sound waves are refracted upwards. At night-time, the opposite happens, as the temperature is cooler closer to the ground, causing multiple ground reflections. (ibid.)

Surface effects include absorption, reflection and diffraction, which depend on the materiality of objects and surfaces (Truax, 1999). Reflection is the most frequent of these effects, as sound waves constantly interact with objects and surfaces (ibid.). Hard surfaces reflect sound waves, whereas soft surfaces, such as dense grass, absorb them (ibid). Therefore, sound waves rebound and echo in a space enclosed by hard surfaces, whereas sound waves are absorbed in a space enclosed by vegetation. Diffraction refers to a sound wave's ability to bend around an obstacle or pass through a slit, depending on its wavelength (ibid.). High-frequency sounds tend to be either absorbed or reflected. In contrast, low-frequency sounds 'have wavelengths that are much longer than most objects and barriers' and can therefore diffract around those larger objects and barriers (ibid.)

To summarise, regarding the environment during the soundscape assessment we can record:

- *Acoustic arenas* of key sound events and *acoustic horizons* of listeners at key each character area, if relevant.
- *Surface effects* caused by the materiality and geometry of a place. Examples of key *aural effects* that can be captured in the site inventory are provided at the end of this chapter.
- *Atmospheric effects*, which might relate to the specific timing of the assessment.

Listener's perception and affective response

Listening, as we have proposed, is always situated and embodied. This means that how we are affected by sound and respond to it varies in different contexts and situations and among listeners (humans and non-humans). As I have argued, listening *moves us to move* as part of the embodied interaction with the environment, triggering different emotions in different people (Fuchs and Koch, 2014). Take, for example, the walk I described in Chapter 2 along Leslie Street Spit on a hot summer's day. In this instance, the music from a nearby boat forced me to move on, as it was interfering with what I wanted to do in this space. Yet, I can only assume that the passengers on the boat were enjoying the music. Later in that same walk, while trying to listen to non-human sounds, a passer-by decided to stop and have a loud and long telephone conversation, forcing me once again to move on. However, the passer-by must have felt it was a perfect spot for a long conversation. These experiences invite two reflections:

- The affective response to the soundscape depends on the perceived level of control over it and the appropriateness of the sound events (Axelsson, 2015). Listening to sound provides a direct engagement with the landscape, which triggers an emotional response to it, as per the affective model introduced in Chapter 2. Throughout the walk, I engaged with many sounds, wanted and unwanted sounds, such as the music on the boat or the passer-by chatting on the phone. Those sounds triggered a response: irritation at first, then powerlessness, as these were sounds out of my control, and finally, physically moving away from the space. This affective response is more important than the acoustic properties of the environment for classifying it as positive or negative (ibid.). After all, the sounds that irritated me on this walk would be welcome elsewhere in the city and might not have troubled me if I had been engaged in a different activity in this space.
- How we are *moved to move* in listening depends on each listener. People (and animals, for that matter) do not hear and listen in universal ways (Hugill and Drever, 2023).

The examples above, and the two reflections that follow, demonstrate how judgments about sound vary according to context and individuals. Therefore, classifying a soundscape as good or bad is complex due to contextual and individual variations.

However, theoretical models of affection can help us predict how those soundscapes are perceived and plan our interventions accordingly. I return to these models in Chapter 7.

We can record communities' affective responses to the soundscape during the site inventory. Human communities' responses can be captured through questionnaires or arts methods. Capturing non-human communities' affective response is more complex and an area for future development.

Human affective response can be captured as an overall response at a particular place and moment (environment) and in more depth as a response to individual sounds heard. In both cases, affective responses can be captured through *descriptors* and *experiential aural effects*.

- *Descriptors* can be useful to capture the affective response at both an environment and sound event level. Examples of descriptors advanced by the ISO 12913 include: 'pleasant, chaotic, vibrant, uneventful, calm, annoying, eventful, monotonous' (BSI, 2018). It is also useful to capture the perceived degree of control over the soundscape and the appropriateness of the sound to the existing character, as these influence the affective response to the soundscape as reflected on earlier (Axelsson, 2015). Descriptors captured can be related to the character of the space. I return to descriptors and graphic representation in *The High Street Goodsyard* case study and Chapter 7 in relation to theoretical models of affection and *aural moods*.
- *Experiential aural effects* can also capture human affective responses and are introduced alongside *physical aural effects* at the end of the chapter.

Sound recordings for site inventory

Sound recordings can be used during the site inventory stage as objective and subjective observations of the site, as archives of the existing sonic environment, and to test or extract acoustic measurements and psychoacoustic parameters or acoustic indices. Regarding the latter, sound recordings are also an invaluable tool to assess and monitor the non-human world. By extracting acoustic indices, we can understand in a snapshot the biodiversity of a space and the balance between technological and biological sound sources (and, therefore, actors). Monitoring sound in time can also provide information regarding habitat evolution, phenology and animal behaviour.

Sound recordings can also form the basis of auralisations. Auralisations can have many different purposes: from auralisations that capture the character of a place, through auralisations that aid in idea and concept development, to auralisations that represent or express its final design and experience. Auralisations are theorised and discussed in full in Chapter 7.

Acoustic and psychoacoustic indicators

ISO 12913 recommends the measurement and reporting of a minimum set of acoustic and psychoacoustic indicators, and protocols for sound recording are detailed within (BSI, 2018). Acoustic and psychoacoustic indicators to report as a minimum include sound pressure level indicators and psychoacoustic loudness indicators (ibid.). Other recommended psychoacoustic indicators are sharpness, tonality, roughness and fluctuation strength. Psychoacoustic indicators are not developed further in this book, so the reader should turn to ISO guidance for further detail. Collaborations with acousticians might also be beneficial when pursuing quantitative soundscape assessments.

Landscape (and soundscape) characterization and *genius loci*

Landscapes can tell stories of communities and places to those who speak the language of landscape and can listen. As advanced in the introduction to this chapter, we read the landscape to unveil the natural and cultural processes of a place and to understand how these relate to the physical and atmospheric characteristics of the landscape. In the process, we uncover the character areas and identity of a place, its *genius loci* or 'spirit of place'.

Establishing a site's character areas helps us intervene in it. Through the soundscape assessment, we seek to identify the aural qualities of an area that contribute to its distinctiveness and how listening contributes to the aesthetic and perceptual appraisal of the landscape. Aural qualities are the aural expression of natural and cultural elements and events of a place. These aural qualities can be identified in the site inventory and assessed in conjunction with the broader elements that contribute to the character.

To determine how the perception of sound events contributes to the character of a place, classifying them into *background, foreground and unique sounds* is a useful exercise. In any given place, there will be unique sounds, either in how they interact or are perceived. For example, a seascape might have a constant background sound of waves breaking at the shore, punctuated by foreground sounds of seabirds, dogs barking and people enjoying themselves on the beach. It might also have a particular fog horn (Soundtrack 5.1) or some other cultural feature of the local community.

🎵 Soundtrack 5.1 Fog Horn at Seahouses, Northumberland, April 2021.

Another evaluation that can be useful to determine how sound events contribute to the character of a place is thinking about how appropriate those sounds are to the overall character of the place and the events and interactions that occur there.

The overall identity of a place or *genius loci* has an aural expression, which I term *aural identity*. It is the overall aural expression of a place that makes it unique, an aural expression of the stories embedded in the site's materials, communities and processes. Within the field of ecoacoustics, each wild habitat has its own *acoustic signature* that expresses the life within it (Krause, 2013). Signature, in sound, refers to the unique characteristics of a sound. *Acoustic signature*, in turn, can also denote the 'unique character … of the space in which' a sound is heard (Thompson, 2012, p. 119). Therefore, *acoustic signature* or *aural identity*, as I will term it from this point onwards, refers not only to the characteristic sounds themselves but also to the characteristics of a place that determine how those sounds interact, propagate and are perceived.

A place's character areas and *aural identity* can be captured or expressed in many ways: through field recordings, annotations and descriptions or as part of the overall creative expressions of the character areas and identity of the site. In the *Old Pottery* case study in Chapter 6, we mapped aural qualities as part of character areas and created sound compositions to express the aural identity of the site.

Aural narratives

Reading the landscape enables us to identify opportunities for change and get ideas to inform the design interventions that follow. These ideas might spring from a place's identity or *genius loci*, the existing narratives uncovered during the reading stage, or other sources of inspiration, as I will discuss in Chapter 7.

Some places may not have *genius loci* or existing narratives to draw from. These 'non-places' demand a more creative and inventive approach from the landscape architect or urban designer, who needs to develop an *ingenious loci* (Baines, 2021).

Non-places might still have aesthetic properties or stories buried within them, which can be the starting point for new ideas or narratives, as discussed in Chapter 7.

Constraints and opportunities

Once the site inventory is complete, all information is assessed in line with the brief for the transformation of the site to determine the *aural opportunities and constraints* of a place. These can be summarised in a diagram or map.

Aural opportunities might include retaining or bringing attention to positive listening experiences or the chance to introduce new listening experiences that can contribute to the design principles and strategies for the site. Aural design principles and strategies are discussed in Chapter 7.

Aural constraints might derive from a place's geometry and materiality, which causes *aural effects* that impede communication. Alternatively, they might be negative listening experiences that originate outside the site and might prevent the enjoyment or legibility of a place.

Two different examples of site inventories and assessments, *The High Street Goodsyard* and *Old Pottery*, are included as case studies in the next chapter. These examples also include different approaches to representing sound in drawings. The reader might also want to turn to the chapter entitled *Mapping the Acoustic City: Noise Mapping and Sound Mapping* in Gascia Ouzounian's volume *Stereophonica* (2020) for a historical overview of noise and sound mapping.

Aural effects

Sonic effect is a term coined by researchers at the *Centre de reserche sur l'espace sonore et l'environment urbain (CRESSON)* to refer to the discernible sound effects that result from the interaction of 'the physical sound environment, the sound milieu of a socio-cultural community, and the *internal soundscape* of every individual' (Augoyard and Torgue, 2005, p. 9). Some *sonic effects*, such as reverberation, are linked to the morphology and materiality of space. Others depend on the listener or community, including semantic effects and those that relate to memory (ibid.). CRESSON's *sonic effects* are described in detail in the volume *Sonic Experience: A Guide to Everyday Sounds*, edited by Jean-Francois Augoyard and Henry Torgue (2005), where the reader will find a full description of all sonic effects introduced in the following pages. In this book, I employ the term *aural effect* instead of sonic to shift the emphasis from the sound itself to its perception through listening.

I return now to Hondarribia, Spain, the village that opened this book, to experience, through a walk, key *aural effects* found in the urban fabric. Location numbers in the text refer to those shown in Figure 5.4. Chapter 6's *Old Pottery* case study also includes *aural effects* captured in the overall soundscape assessment.

Hondarribia walk

My walk in Hondarribia takes place midweek in August, mid-afternoon, 2021. The walk starts close to the Old Town, alongside the pathway that follows the former moat of the city walls. August is a busy month for the town. Late afternoons, weekdays and weekends are full of people; tourists, summer residents and full-time residents. I start walking southward. The path runs parallel and adjacent to one of the main road arteries of the town. Soon, the path sinks lower than the road, and I come across a water fountain. It is an unusual place for a fountain, and I briefly stop to appreciate how the flowing water partially *masks* the sound of the traffic (location 1 Soundtrack 5.2). Masking of one sound by another is due to similar frequency distribution (Augoyard and Torgue, 2005) and is a strategy frequently used for soundscape design (Figure 5.4).

🎵Soundtrack 5.2 Masking of traffic with water, Hondarribia.

I continue the walk, a straight line that follows the traffic flow. The continuous traffic flow causes a *drone* effect (location 2) as there is 'no noticeable variation in intensity' or pitch of the traffic sound (ibid., p. 40). The stone wall that bounds the road on the east reverberates and exacerbates the drone. Tired of this drone, I turn towards the walls, towards the recently restored *erreginaren baluartea* (queen's stronghold), which has a lower and an upper section connected by a sloping tunnel. The city walls date back to the XV and XVI century and were built of heavy pieces of sandstone quarried from the nearby Jaizkibel mountain. On entering the walls through a narrow tunnel, I experience a *cut-out* effect, as the traffic noise intensity suddenly falls as I pass through the threshold arch (location 3). A *cut-out* effect can also happen when moving 'from reverberant to dull spaces' (ibid., p. 29).

The tunnel leads me to an inner patio, enclosed by stone walls of different heights on all four sides. Surprisingly, the *drone* of the traffic is back, as sound waves rebound on the high walls to the west and south and within the courtyard. Footsteps and voices *filter* down from the tunnel at the southeast corner of the patio, which ultimately connects to the upper platform (location 4). *Filtration*, in this case, is caused by the slight angle and difference in height between the direction of the tunnel and

Figure 5.4 Location of aural effects identified through a walk in Hondarribia's Old Town. Map data ©2023 Google Earth

where I am standing, which prevents me from receiving the sound waves directly from the source. *Filtration* is caused by 'features of the environment separating the source and listener' (ibid., p.49). The voices' soundwaves are reflected off the ground and walls within the tunnel and outside, losing energy and causing 'the original timbre and intensity' to modify (ibid., p. 49). High frequencies do not propagate as far as low frequencies, contributing to the *filtration* effect (ibid.) (Figure 5.5).

Figure 5.5 Location of aural effects 2 (drone), 3 (cut-out), 4 (reverberation) and 5 (echo) alongside walk in Hondarribia.

I follow these footsteps and voices into the narrow tunnel. In here, my footsteps and those of others seem to multiply due to *reverberation* as I walk upwards (location 5 Soundtrack 5.3). The reflection of the footsteps causes reverberation sounds on the walls and ground surfaces of the tunnel, which are then 'added to the direct signal', resulting in an environment perceived as louder than the original signals (ibid., p. 111).

♫ Soundtrack 5.3 Reverberation, Erreginaren baluartea, Hondarribia.

Exiting the tunnel, I turn towards the steps leading to the upper section of the stronghold, which is covered in grass. The area sits higher than both the old town and the road. Here, despite the many visitors around me, I feel momentarily suspended in both time and space. In this suspension, the walls call me to remember their past as a fortification. As the main line of defence for the town, the walls were sometimes filled with the thundering of artillery sounds. Later in September, during the town's festivities, those thundering sounds become a reality in the Arma Plaza when a military parade opens fire to commemorate the 1638 victory over the French army following a long siege (Hondarribia Turismo, 2023). Here, I am reminded of this thunderous display through an aural effect termed *phonomnesis* (location 6), which refers to the ability of a particular context and situation to trigger a sound memory (ibid.) (Figure 5.6).

I come out of the *erreginaren baluartea* onto the inner perimeter of the wall and walk once again parallel to the wall, but this time I am nine metres higher than the outer perimeter of the wall. There is a distant sound of traffic that seems to come from all directions; it is difficult to locate the source of the traffic sound as the path is bound by the three-metre upstand of the perimeter wall, and I can hear out but not see. The higher altitude, the fact that the walls are surrounded by roads alongside their full perimeter, and the fact that I cannot see what lies below the wall cause this

Figure 5.6 Location of aural effects 6 (phonomnesis), 7 (ubiquity), 8 (reverberation) and 9 (filtration) alongside walk in Hondarribia.

ubiquity effect (location 7). *Ubiquity* refers to the 'difficulty … of locating a sound source … the sound seems to come from everywhere and from nowhere at the same time' (ibid., p. 130). In the city, this typically happens when the listener is in a highly reverberant space, where direct and indirect signals mix, creating a complex and ambiguous sonic environment (ibid.).

It is hot, and the hard landscape emanates heat in all directions. Looking for shade, halfway through the street, I come down a set of stone steps into one of the narrow streets of the old town, Etxenagusia Margolaria Kalea. I stop by an old well at the end of the steps, hoping to cool down in the shade and through listening to and perceiving the humidity of the trickling water. I am one of two pedestrians on the street. Yet, hearing the *reverberation* of the others' footsteps, as soundwaves bounce from one surface to the next, tricks me into thinking that I am accompanied by more (location 8). Whereas *echo* is described as 'a single reflection that is delayed long enough to be perceived as a separate acoustic event', *reverberation* results from multiple reflections that 'causes them to fuse together into a complex spatial impression' (Truax, 1999).

I continue walking until I reach the intersection threshold with the principal street of the old town, Nagusi kalea. Here, voices *filter* and *echo*, portraying the street as busier than it is (location 9). I cross Nagusi kalea and follow another narrow street until I come to a small plaza, Apezpiku Plaza, that opens into a lower open space in another grassed turret. A band is playing here, and I can hear it clearly from the plaza. I continue walking northwards, and the music is *cut-out* by the buildings, reappearing again as I turn the corner and reach the boundary of the edge of the church (location 10) (Figure 5.7).

I follow the perimeter of the church and come to rest in another small square, this time between the northern elevation of the church and a 10th-century

Figure 5.7 Location of aural effects 10 (cut-out), 11 (cocktail party) and 12 (reverberation).

castle, now a hotel. I sit down on one of the wooden benches for a while. Voices filter. From the Arma Plaza, the cafe of the hotel, and the church, with many visitors at this time of the year. There are trees in this square, too – their shade welcome in the heat. I concentrate on the faint rustling of the leaves and the slightest of breezes, which cools this space. I record in this space, and when I play it back in the evening, I am surprised that the recorder does not portray what I thought I heard (location 11). The rustling was much louder live than in the recording, a result of another sonic effect: the *cocktail party* effect. This effect refers to our ability to be selective listeners, focusing on a sound and disregarding others (Augoyard and Torgue, 2005).

I walk a short distance to the Arma Plaza and sit here again for a while. The plaza is busy, with people sitting and chatting in the outdoor cafes and kids playing. A recycling van comes to collect empty bottles from one of the cafes. I close my eyes and listen. The plaza becomes even louder and busier, with sounds multiplying through reverberation. Whereas the previous square had some vegetation in walls and trees, this plaza has a triangular shape and all hard surfaces and walls of similar heights, making soundwaves *reverberate* as they hit the surfaces.

As the clock strikes four, the church's bells start to call and *reverberate* in the plaza, adding to the vibrancy of the space (location 12 Soundtrack 5.4). The bells always call twice on the hour to ensure that residents who missed the first call can catch up with the time or events that the bell announces. On the second call, I pay attention to the resonance of the bell, set in a rhythmical movement and think about the sonic footprint or acoustic arena of the bell calls that extends all the way to the beach 1.8 km away. The church might not always be visible, yet it is always heard (Soundtrack 5.5).

♪ Soundtrack 5.4 Reverberation, Arma plaza, Hondarribia.

♪ Soundtrack 5.5 Acoustic arena of church bells.

I repeat this same walk mid-April, mid-day 2023 – a quieter day, with noticeably less traffic and people. *Aural effects*, however, remain. The recordings and photographs included in these pages relate to this last walk. Soundtrack 5.5 was recorded on Christmas Day 2021, 750 m away from the church, and showcases the extent of the acoustic arena of the bell.

This walk has taken us through the main *aural effects* found in the urban fabric. These effects can be identified and assessed during fieldwork to understand how they contribute to the overall perception and navigation of the landscape and each place's character. Through the assessment, we can decide whether they should be retained, reinforced or amended. Sound can be altered at source, in its propagation or at the listener (receptor), and it is important to note the degree of control we might have over existing *aural effects*. For example, we might be powerless to control sound filtering into our site. Accordingly, we might need to think of strategies to control or direct sound within the site or adapt the types of uses and locations the site can accommodate. The existing *aural effects* can therefore influence the development of the design and brief.

Aural effects will also be created through our proposals, consciously or unconsciously. Thus, understanding key effects is also a useful starting point for designing with our ears. The facilitation of *aural effects* can form part of our landscape strategy, for example, to reinforce soundmarks through *echo* and *reverberation* or create opportunities for *phonomnesis*, linking communities with their history and stories.

The case studies narrated in Chapter 6 provide alternative approaches to reading the landscape through listening. *Bristol Soundwalks* is a participatory project founded by Sarah Jones-Morris and aimed at mapping and protecting quiet places in Bristol through regular soundwalks. *The High Street Goodsyard* could be described as a non-place where, together with Oobe landscape architects, I uncovered a historical narrative of the site and its context to drive a design focused on listening. The *Old Pottery, Corbridge*, is our (Dan Hill and Usue Ruiz Arana) sonic laboratory, which has helped us develop an understanding of aural identity and ways to express it. This chapter concludes with listening and sounding exercises developed with landscape architecture students and practitioners to read the landscape and space through listening.

References

Augoyard, J.-F. and Torgue, H. (2005) *Sonic experience: A guide to everyday sounds*. 1st englis. Montreal, Ithaca: McGill-Queen's University Press.

Axelsson, Ö. (2015) 'How to measure soundscape quality', *Euronoise 2015*, pp. 1477–1481. Available at: https://www.conforg.fr/euronoise2015/proceedings/data/articles/000067.pdf.

Baines, B. (2021) *GROSS.MAX, The Berlage keynotes*. Available at: https://www.youtube.com/watch?v=VB4wjMN0rkU (Accessed: 12 June 2023).

Blesser, B. and Salter, L. (2007) *Spaces speak, are you listening? experiencing aural architecture*. Cambridge, MA: MIT Press.

BSI (The British Standards Institution) (2018) 'ISO / TS 12913–2 : 2018 BSI Standards Publication Acoustics — Soundscape', BSI Standards Publication.

Fuchs, T. and Koch, S. C. (2014) 'Embodied affectivity: On moving and being moved', *Frontiers in Psychology*, 5(June), pp. 1–12. doi: 10.3389/fpsyg.2014.00508.

Hannah, L. (2006) 'Wind and temperature effects on sound propagation', *New Zealand Acoustics*, 20(2), pp. 22–29.

Hill, D. (2020) *Ecoacoustic identity: A soundwalk methodology for establishing the recognisability of the soundscape (unpublished)*.

Hondarribia turismo (2023) *Hondarribia and its festivities*, Hondarribia. Available at: https://hondarribiaturismo.com/en/hondarribia-and-its-festivities/ (Accessed: 12 June 2023).

Hugill, A. and Drever, J. L. (2023) *Aural diversity, aural diversity*. Available at: https://auraldiversity.org/index.html (Accessed: 30 May 2023).

Ingold, T. (2007) 'Against soundscape', in Carlyle, A. (ed.) *Autumn leaves*. Paris: Double Entendre, pp. 10–13.

Krause, B. (1987) 'Bioacoustics, habitat ambience in ecological balance', *Whole Earth Review*, 57 (Winter), pp. 14–18.

Krause, B. (2013) 'The voice of the natural world'. Available at: https://www.ted.com/talks/bernie_krause_the_voice_of_the_natural_world?language=en&subtitle=en.

Natural England (2014) *An approach to landscape character assessment*, Natural England. Available at: http://www.programmeofficers.co.uk/Cuadrilla/CoreDocuments/CD40/CD40.20.PDF.

Ouzounian, G. (2020) *Stereophonica: Sound and space in science, technology, and the arts*. Cambridge, MA: The MIT Press.

Schäfer, R. (2014) 'The narrative of landscape', *Topos*, 88, p. 3.

Thompson, E. (2012) 'Sound, modernity and history', in Sterne, J. (ed.) *The sound studies reader*. Oxon and New York: Routledge, pp. 117–129.

Timmermans, M. (2014) 'Reading a landscape', *Topos*, 88, pp. 20–27.

Trikootam, S. C. and Hornikx, M. (2019) 'The wind effect on sound propagation over urban areas: Experimental approach with an uncontrolled sound source', *Building and Environment*, 149(November 2018), pp. 561–570. doi: 10.1016/j.buildenv.2018.11.037.

Truax, B. (ed.) (1999) *Handbook for acoustic ecology*. 2nd ed. Cambridge Street Publishing. Available at: http://www.sfu.ca/sonic-studio-webdav/handbook/index.html.

Chapter Six

Reading the soundscape in practice

Bristol Soundwalks with Sarah Jones-Morris

Bristol Soundwalks was founded in 2017 by an acoustician and a landscape architect to raise awareness of noise and its impact on health and well-being through qualitative methods and to influence urban policy-making in Bristol (2020). Through free public monthly soundwalks over the past five years, and with the help of Dr. Antonella Radicchi and her citizen-science research programme *Hush City* app, the team collated over 200 soundwalks collected by citizens of Bristol and beyond, that have contributed to a collective map of quiet spaces in the city.

I first encountered *Bristol Soundwalks* in a conversation with Antonella Radicchi in 2019. At a Landscape Institute event, I then met up with Sarah Jones-Morris, landscape architect and urban designer, founding member of *Bristol Soundwalks* and a UK Ambassador for *Hush City*. We have since collaborated in various Landscape Institute events and kept in touch through a mutual interest in urban soundscapes.

I caught up with Sarah in mid-February 2022 to find out about the origins of *Bristol Soundwalks* and the takeaways from it that might help other city makers.

How does the idea of Bristol Soundwalks come about?

Around 2017, I set up my own Landscape Architecture Practice, Landsmith Associates, and participated in an air quality citizen science project, *The Bristol Approach* (2023), with Knowle West Media Centre led by Sustainable Neighbourhoods Programme Manager Zoe Banks-Gross. A significant barrier to people with air quality is that it can be intangible. However, noise can have an instantaneous

DOI: 10.4324/9781003202981-9

effect; if somewhere is noisy, you move away. Thinking about air quality led me to think about noise. I came across the work of Antonella Radicchi through Twitter and got in touch with local acoustician Paul Driscoll, from Formant, who was very interested in soundscapes too. Around that time, the World Health Organization changed guidance about measuring noise beyond decibels, and DEFRA bought out a planning guidance note on noise action plans, specifically creating and allocating (Department for Environment Food and Rural Affairs, 2019). *Bristol Soundwalks* started through a timely coming together of all those events and people interested in soundscapes.

Different people have different approaches to soundwalking. What happens at a Bristol Soundwalk?

Our soundwalks have evolved over the years in response to the experience of leading them. During the first year, we did the soundwalks monthly and as one-offs for conferences and festivals. I contacted Antonella Radicchi, and we started following her guide and using the *Hush City* app to assess spaces (Radicchi, 2019). In time, we adapted the approach, and a key soundwalk for it was the one we did in Bath. The Bath soundwalk was attended by acousticians and musicians and became more meditative while keeping with the *Hush City* principles. Paul was familiar with the initial acoustic ecology soundwalks of the 1970s, and our soundwalks became a way of immersing ourselves in the environment.

What happens at Bristol Soundwalks now?

We usually have a rough idea of where we will walk. When we first start, we have a minute to focus our listening; we close our eyes and listen. And then, we start the soundwalk via *Hush City* app without saying anything until we have completed the survey. Then, we discuss the space (the built form, character, etc., what we think contributes to the soundscape) and move in silence, or as quiet as possible, to the next spot. In the end, we discuss the walk itself and changing sounds (Figure 6.1).

This structured approach works well as we don't walk for more than 45 minutes. Otherwise, people start switching off. However, during the COVID-19 pandemic, we could do a minimal amount of soundwalks, and we decided to concentrate on creating a quiet areas and routes map for central Bristol based on the data collected. Also, we started to partner with *Tranquil City* (2023) to widen the scope and partnerships.

I have also found about 40 minutes to be the right length for a soundwalk to keep people's attention. Do you ask all participants to download the Hush City app in advance? And do you log in responses individually or collectively at each space?

Figure 6.1 Participants on a soundwalk led by Paul Driscoll and Sarah Jones-Morris, as part of *Festival of Therapeutic City* in Bath, 2019, Credit: Sarah Jones-Morris.

Individually. We plan a route to take in three or four spaces to assess. When we get to an area, everybody goes to a different point in that space because, in Bristol, there are places relatively small but with varying soundscapes (Figure 6.2).

For example, a space near a boatyard right on the harbour is a transect of five pedestrian walkways. Within 10 metres, there is quite a variation in decibels and soundscape quality. Through this approach, people understand how varied and complex the soundscape of a place can be and how difficult it is to capture this richness in traditional computer noise models. This method also helps envision future design and planning for more tranquil spaces. Variations of the soundscape at different times of the day and seasons also need to be considered.

Have you had conversations with the City Council throughout the process to determine how your findings might influence city planning?

Figure 6.2 Participants on a Bristol Soundwalk discussing a city centre space. Part of *Bristol Open Doors* 2018 and led by Paul Driscoll and Sarah Jones-Morris, Credit: Sarah Jones-Morris.

When we started, we had several meetings with the Council. One of the issues we face is that *Hush City* app uses Google mapping, which the Local Authority cannot use due to costly licensing agreements. It's a manageable issue, as the Council knows and can reference our work. We also recently contributed to a leaflet titled *Bristol City of…Sounds* that brought awareness of Bristol's rich soundscape (2021).

There are several barriers to considering noise a central issue for planning. For example, local authority procurement has a solid division between art and health projects. Our work tends to be framed as an arts project, which disregards noise's health and well-being effects. That said, we have had interest from the University of Bristol's medical departments and also from SHINE (Bristol Health Partners, 2023), who have come to a few of our walks and see a genuine link between soundscape and healthy neighbourhoods. However, unless health gets more embedded within built environment aspects and planning, I don't see a change in the importance of noise.

In 2022, we started collaborating with *Tranquil City* as they are involved in a *Quiet Route* mapping for Bristol City Council to explore how a city soundscape policy would look like (Waters, 2022). However, it's based on the DEFRA road and railway noise level maps (Extrium, 2023). Therefore, a quantitative approach to mapping based on dB measurements that misses the richness that is required.

Another barrier is knowledge and training. Wales introduced soundscape legislation and has recently consulted on further soundscape policy; but sadly, it has not come with the knowledge or activity associated with it (Welsh Government, 2018; Welsh Government with the Noise Abatement Society, 2022). So, it has become more of an aspiration rather than legislation that can be implemented – we will see how this may change in the future.

Training is a big issue.

Victor and Jameson, acousticians who are now also part of Bristol Soundwalks, talk about getting the *Institute of Acousticians* more involved in soundscapes because their training still focuses on quantitative approaches to noise. Jameson, for example, has been part of an art installation creating a sonic trail around Bristol (Musyoki, 2021).

What is next for Bristol Soundwalks?

I would love to do a quiet map of Bristol, a simple output accessible to everyone that highlights the city's more tranquil spots. However, it is a complex task. First, we need to set the parameters that define a quiet space: is it about the decibels, or should we consider other factors too? Second, sounds are dynamic and constantly changing; a map of quiet spots would only present a moment in time.

Out of the 250 spaces we have mapped, we only have around 11 'quiet spots' in Bristol, and we have uploaded three of those key spaces to our website (Jones-Morris, 2020).

In 2022, the team was approached by Bristol City Council and the WECIL group (2023) to focus on co-creating a quiet area plan for neurodivergent people. It will also be working with *Tranquil City* on this project.

A quiet map is valuable for urban planning. Sometimes the most straightforward outputs are the most effective in reaching a broad audience.

Exactly, just some dots on a plan to identify the quietest areas. We could then reference the data's origin and the parameters used to define quiet areas.

What about participants? What kind of feedback have you received?

It varies. We get comments like *This is amazing, I've never really thought about it*, as the soundwalks challenge perceptions from people from a built environment background. Others either love it or wonder, *what are we doing this walk for* and don't fully get it.

Over the years, participants have also varied depending on how we have promoted the events. We were invited by Bristol Open Doors (Bristol Open Doors, 2023), to do a couple of soundwalks for them. Bristol Open Doors has a mailing list of over 30,000 people, and their events are very popular and attract a broad audience. In one of those soundwalks, we had 25 attendees, more than we have ever had by advertising through Twitter! Thankfully, nearly everybody had downloaded the app, and some people found it fascinating … others didn't.

An interesting challenge that has come up through the walks and is worth mentioning is the complexity of retrofitting positive soundscapes into existing urban areas. As some suggest, removing the noise is idealistic and will not happen in the short term.

Unless you bring in another pandemic.

All cars and all external ventilation units gone! Until that happens, it is essential to understand why some spaces are quieter than others. One space that stands out is Berkeley Square in Bristol, a little green space off a busy street. It is quiet, and that's because of the altitude, geometry and materiality of the space. It is a Georgian square with tall buildings that act as a buffer and has staggered access. Whatever noise filters from the main road is lowered because it is on a hill and dissipates because it hasn't got straight through tunnel-like access.

Architectural aural effects. We pay little attention to them when designing.

It is almost like you need a checklist of aspects to consider when designing with sound: thinking through materials, layout and all things that can be reviewed.

Thinking about your practice, how do you think the soundwalks have influenced your work?

I do raise the issue of noise and positive soundscapes with clients. One influence I have had is in the *Building with Nature* standards (2023), which now includes a section on noise as part of their accreditation evaluation. Noise is also a biodiversity indicator. The standards talk about *Environmental Net Gain (ENG)* and seeking quiet spaces. We must also know that only some people like quiet spaces; some areas need positive sounds.

Vibrancy and animation.

Many of our soundwalks have been noisy yet relaxing. Some people seek active and vibrant places and find them more relaxing than quiet spaces. There might be a cultural component and perception of feeling safe when more people are around it.

There are other aspects related to how we perceive and cope with noise. In a soundwalk that we did around Bristol Temple Meads Station, one participant commented on how he used to live near a busy street and used to pretend the noise came from the sea. He was unaware that the body is still affected by the noise, reacting to it, even though he was trying to trick himself into thinking otherwise.

We might consider the psychological effects of noise first, as physiological effects might manifest after a while. Picking up on your comment about Building with Nature accreditation and Environmental Net Gain, the benefits of natural soundscapes are frequently mentioned in urban design.

I gave a talk on ENG, noise pollution and positive soundscapes at a conference a couple of weeks ago for Building with Nature (2023). The Urban Mind project (Mechelli, 2023) developed an app to investigate the effect of nature on well-being. Birdsong was identified as a positive contributor to well-being. From an ENG perspective, if you want birdsong to benefit mental health, you must have suitable habitats and wildlife connections. ENG is positive for nature, people and the economy because places with birdsong and green space have a higher economic value. In contrast, noisy areas near busy roads have a lower economic value.

Everything is interrelated; we need to make those links explicit.

It is disappointing that the *Environment Act*, which focuses on Biodiversity Net Gain, doesn't mention noise pollution (UK Parliament, 2021). Also, we need to address links between neurodivergent people (as defined by BSI, 2022) and the impact noise pollution has on their health and well-being, for example, by being able to access city centres knowing there are quieter areas.

Speaking of noise pollution, many people became aware of the sounds of plant rooms and extractors during the lockdown. Without traffic noise, suddenly we heard these machines sounding.

We extensively work with the University of Bristol's external estate department. An issue that came out of a stakeholder engagement was the projection of noise from the plant room of a lab into the nearby public space. Nobody sits in that space due to this low-frequency noise. The lady in charge of grounds maintenance said she felt physically sick after working there for over half an hour. It is back to quantitative versus qualitative noise assessment. Those vents might not register as problematic if you're doing a decibel reading. Luckily, the university has taken some of it on board for future planning, the need to consider the location of plant rooms and their impact on public space. Especially now, with a growing student population and an increased demand for outdoor space and seating following the COVID-19 pandemic, noise must be noticed; there is scope for change.

The high street Goodsyard, Glasgow

Background and project brief

In the spring of 2017, Oobe Landscape Architects were invited to submit design proposals for the public realm associated with a new residential development in Glasgow. The proposed 7.5-acre site for the new neighbourhood was located close to the city centre, east of the Merchant City, in an area undergoing regeneration (Figure 6.3).

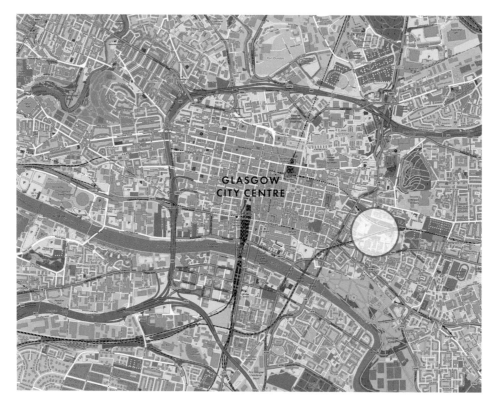

Figure 6.3 Site location, Base map data: © Open Street Map contributors (openstreetmap.org).

The project architects, Stallan-Brand, had progressed the architectural design to outline design stage, and the client sought to employ a landscape architect through an invited design competition. I was part of the team at Oobe responsible for developing the proposals for the public realm for the design competition.

Soundscape inventory and analysis

Desktop review

Before visiting the site, we reviewed the area's relevant planning policies, ecological records and historical maps. We discovered through the review of the historical maps that the Molendinar Burn flows culverted underneath the existing car park, dissecting the site in a north-south direction. The Molendinar was once central to the development of medieval Glasgow, as it provided water for the mills and craft industry in the area and shaped the development of the local landscape and built environment around it. Yet, no visible traces of the burn and its stories remained on site.

In advance of visiting the site, we also reviewed the latest noise maps for the area (Scottish Government, 2023), which identified the majority of the area as overall quiet (<55 dB Lden, <50 dB Lnight), with a louder boundary alongside Bell Street on the southern boundary (60–65 dB Lden, 50–55 dB Lnight) (Figures 6.4 and 6.5).

Site visits – inventory and analysis

I then visited the site over two days in May (2017) and carried out several soundwalk at different times of the day in and around the site to produce a basic soundscape assessment to inform the design. Typical of many projects in practice, there was little time to carry out the site assessment for the competition, which limited the possibility of involving the community in the soundscape assessment. Nevertheless, I was accompanied by a Glasgow resident during these walks who provided a 'non-expert' perception of the site.

On the first day, we carried out soundwalks without any recording equipment to experience the soundscape with the naked ear, without distractions. We also defined the character areas for the site and our *listening stations* for follow-up visits. We recorded and assessed our impressions of the soundscape on the second day. We spent time at each listening station and completed a custom-made table to assess the soundscape. We also evaluated the courtyard of a neighbouring residential

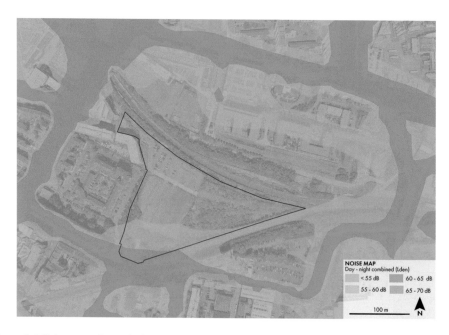

Figure 6.4 Noise map, day and night combined, data derived from Noise Scotland (Scottish Government, 2023), Map data: ©2023 Google earth.

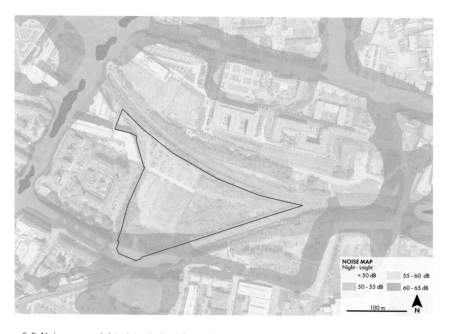

Figure 6.5 Noise map, night, data derived from Noise Scotland (Scottish Government, 2023), Map data: ©2023 Google earth.

development (listening station 5), as the proposed building layout was due to create a similar enclosed space at the centre of our site.

Over those two days, I also visited several other streetscapes and parks in Glasgow and recorded these as aural precedents for the site and as the basis to carry out auralisations.

The soundscape assessment is summarised on the following three drawings and the custom table used to assess the soundscape during daytime. The custom table was completed for all character areas, for day and night-time assessment (Figures 6.6 –6.10).

Soundscape inventory and analysis summary

SOUND EVENTS

Sound events within the site included occasional vehicles coming in and out of the car park, seagulls flying through the site, insects – mainly bees – buzzing in the

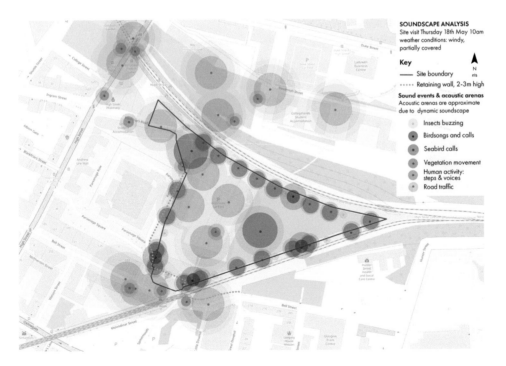

Figure 6.6 Acoustic arenas of foreground and background sounds within the site and vicinity, daytime. Thursday 18th May, 10 am, Base map data: © Open Street Map contributors (openstreetmap.org).

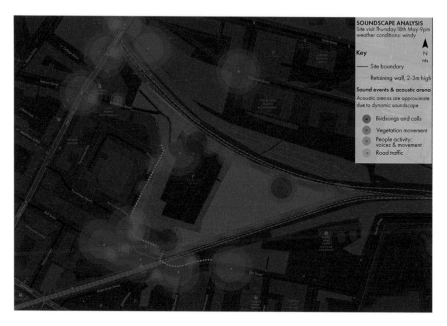

Figure 6.7 Acoustic arenas of foreground and background sounds within the site and vicinity, early night. Thursday 18th May, 9 pm, Base map data: © Open Street Map contributors (openstreetmap. org).

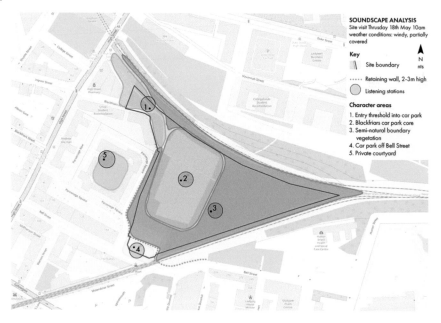

Figure 6.8 Landscape character areas and listening stations, Base map data: © Open Street Map contributors (openstreetmap.org).

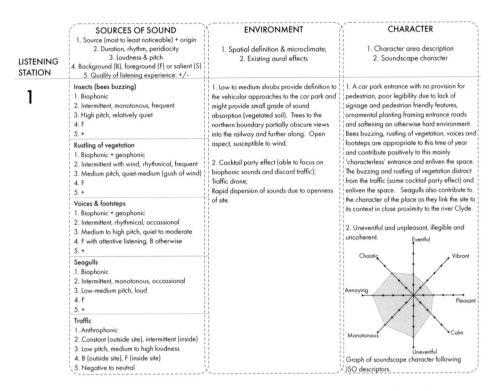

LISTENING STATION	SOURCES OF SOUND 1. Source (most to least noticeable) + origin 2. Duration, rhythm, peridiocity 3. Loudness & pitch 4. Background (B), foreground (F) or salient (S) 5. Quality of listening experience: +/-	ENVIRONMENT 1. Spatial definition & microclimate; 2. Existing aural effects	CHARACTER 1. Character area description 2. Soundscape character
1	**Insects (bees buzzing)** 1. Biophonic 2. Intermittent, monotonous, frequent 3. High pitch, relatively quiet 4. F 5. + **Rustling of vegetation** 1. Biophonic + geophonic 2. Intermittent with wind, rhythmical, frequent 3. Medium pitch, quiet-medium (gush of wind) 4. F 5. + **Voices & footsteps** 1. Biophonic + geophonic 2. Intermittent, rhythmical, occassional 3. Medium to high pitch, quiet to moderate 4. F with attentive listening, B otherwise 5. + **Seagulls** 1. Biophonic 2. Intermittent, monotonous, occassional 3. Low-medium pitch, loud 4. F 5. + **Traffic** 1. Anthrophonic 2. Constant (outside site), intermittent (inside) 3. Low pitch, medium to high loudness 4. B (outside site), F (inside site) 5. Negative to neutral	1. Low to medium shrubs provide definition to the vehicular approaches to the car park and might provide small grade of sound absorption (vegetated soil). Trees to the northern boundary partially obscure views into the railway and further along. Open aspect, susceptible to wind. 2. Cocktail party effect (able to focus on biophonic sounds and discard traffic); Traffic drone; Rapid dispersion of sounds due to openness of site.	1. A car park entrance with no provision for pedestrian, poor legibility due to lack of signage and pedestrian friendly features, ornamental planting framing entrance roads and softening an otherwise hard environment. Bees buzzing, rustling of vegetation, voices and footsteps are appropriate to this time of year and contribute positively to this mainly 'characterless' entrance and enliven the space. The buzzing and rustling of vegetation distract from the traffic (some cocktail party effect) and enliven the space. Seagulls also contribute to the character of the place as they link the site to its context in close proximity to the river Clyde. 2. Uneventful and unpleasant, illegible and uncoherent. Graph of soundscape character following ISO descriptors.

Figure 6.9 Excerpt from soundscape assessment table showing assessment of listening station 1 during daytime.

flowering shrubs, birds singing in the tree canopies, occasional footsteps and voices, and the rustling and swaying of vegetation in the wind. Sound events filtering into the site were very similar and included seagulls, traffic from vehicles circulating in the vicinity roads and occasional distant voices and footsteps.

The area was very open and exposed, and there was scope to reduce the filtration of sounds through architectural proposals to bring attention to existing natural sounds and increase the variety of listening experiences within the site.

ENVIRONMENT

The site was an open space used as a car park. It consisted mainly of tarmac surrounded by a vegetated boundary with semi-natural scrubland and trees to the north, east, west and southern boundaries, and scrub and grassland (in flower at the time of visit) alongside the northwestern approach. The site was bound by a railway

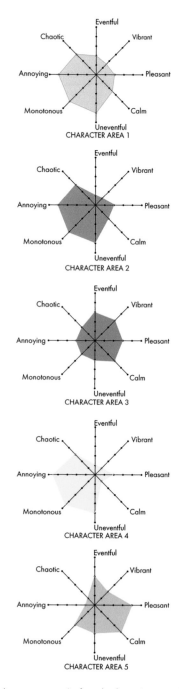

Figure 6.10 Soundscape character assessment of each character area following ISO descriptors.

line to the north and east, which was unused during the visits. To the west and southern boundaries, the site as bound by an industrial retaining brick wall, 2–3 m high, with the site situated at the higher level of the wall. To the other side of the wall a residential development to the west, a private car park and Bell Street to the south. The area was mainly flat, and due to its open aspect, the acoustic horizon of the listener was large, bound by distant traffic noise and built structures. Neighbouring sounds filtered into the space, mainly along the northern and southern boundaries, and sounds emanating from the site dispersed quickly. No aural effects linked to the morphology and materiality of the space were observed within the site.

CHARACTER AREAS AND AFFECTIVE RESPONSE

There were four distinct areas within the site, and another that we studied outside the site, as indicated in Figure 6.6: (1) entry threshold onto the car park from the northwest with scrub and grassland planting, (2) car park core, (3) semi-natural boundary (alongside railway corridors and remnants of industrial retaining walls), (4) a lower level car park off Bell Street and (5) private residential courtyard. Besides the existing brick walls, there was little on the site that referenced the rich history of the site or neighbouring communities. The site also suffered from poor legibility and coherence.

Perceptual aural effects experienced include a certain *cocktail party effect*, particularly in listening stations 1 and 3, where the salient sounds of birds, buzzing of bees and swaying vegetation animated the space and distracted from the traffic sound. There was also a certain *ubiquity* as distant traffic hum in the background is permanent, yet it cannot be seen, and therefore, it is difficult to pinpoint which direction is coming from.

The site lacked a distinctive identity and did not reflect the rich history of the site associated with the Molendinar burn and with the communities that lived and live within it. The site could be described as a *non-place*, and the overall soundscape assessment reinforced this description and characterisation, as the site was, in the most, uneventful and unpleasant. The site, however, was full of potential, with a rich history and narrative hidden from view and with opportunities to introduce sound and listening to support the design principles for the site.

The site's aural narrative, principles and strategies are narrated in the second part of this case study in Chapter 8.

Old Pottery, Corbridge

Introduction

In 2021, we (Usue Ruiz Arana and research assistant Dan Hill) were commissioned by the current owners of the Old Pottery, Corbridge, to develop a landscape design for the site informed by listening. Since then, the Old Pottery has become our sonic laboratory where we are testing the different roles that listening and sound-making could play in landscape design, from using listening as a vehicle to unearthing the identity of a place and inform landscape design, to establishing a kinship with non-human others and designing from that established kinship.

The Old Pottery, also known as Walker's Pottery, lies between the northern out-skirts of Corbridge, Northumberland, and the A69, surrounded by agricultural land (Figure 6.11).

The site is a former family-owned fireclay pottery that produced many goods, including firebricks, pipes and tiles, from 1840s to 1930s. Several buildings still stand

Figure 6.11 Location map, Base map data: Google Earth ©2023 CNES/Airbus ©2023 Maxar Technologies.

and are Grade II listed, including two imposing bottle kilns, a downdraft kiln and chimney, horizontal kilns and drying rooms. Together with other buried and earthwork remains, the resulting complex is designated as a Schedule Monument, as a 'reasonably well-preserved rural pottery' (Historic England, 2016). The complex also houses a cottage, home to Mike Goodall, Cathy Edy and their son, who took ownership of the Pottery in 2016. At the time, many of the buildings had been overrun by dense scrub and trees, causing damage to some of the structures and making the site impenetrable in places. Mike and Cathy carried out urgent repairs and are devising potential futures for the site with the help of a team of designers … and listeners (Figure 6.12).

By the time of our involvement, Doonan and EDable architects had produced preliminary proposals for the site. Those proposals aimed to ensure a sustainable and economically viable restoration and development of the Pottery to future-proof the site in the long term. The proposals were founded on the following key themes:

• Family: ensuring a suitable environment and privacy
• Community: allowing public access to key areas and a programme of artistic interventions
• Skills and education: from opportunities to engage the public with the history of the site to crafts-based training courses and qualifications
• Security: clear separation of public, semi-private and private areas
• Heritage: preserving and utilising existing assets
• Character: building on the distinct existing character areas: wild, magical, picturesque, romance, decay, wild.

Figure 6.12 Existing site photographs, July 2021: looking southwards (left), small kiln (right).

Several scenarios had been considered for the site, from an *artist retreat* with artists in residence, studios and community space to rent; through an *inhabited market garden* with growing areas and produce selling markets; to an *accommodation max* that would maximise short- and long-term rentals and would allow the site to be hired out for events such as weddings. As per the following site plan, all scenarios would clearly distinguish between private, semi-private and public uses and management. The southern part of the site is already accessible to the public (Figure 6.13).

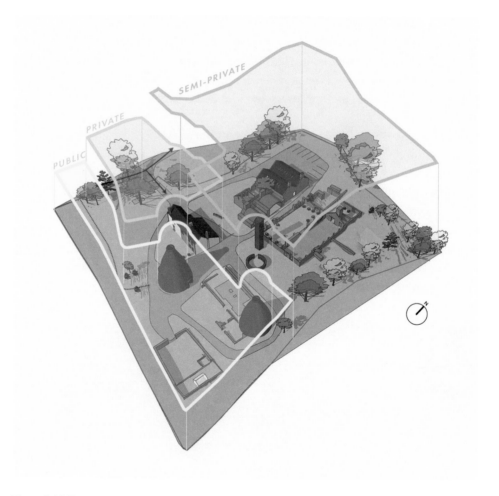

Figure 6.13 Proposed management for the site, Base axonometric credit: EDable Architecture.

Listening to the site: soundscape inventory and analysis

I (Usue) first visited the Pottery on the 18th of July 2021 on a warm (19C) and clear afternoon (12 pm) with my soundwalking partner, Alan. We had a walking interview with Mike and Cathy to find out what it is like to live on the site, their future plans and how they perceive the soundscape of the site. Before my arrival, Mike had warned me of the proximity of the A69 and the constant traffic sound that permeates the site; *I don't know if you will be able to do much. We are very close to the traffic.* Indeed, as I got out of the car at the site entrance, my first impression on arrival was that the traffic sound dominated the soundscape. Surprisingly, it seemed to come from the West instead of the North, as I had imagined from looking at the map, an impression Cathy shared. Cathy remarked how she didn't find the traffic sound annoying, due to its constancy, *just like the flow of the sea*, but that the tires of lorries, breaking that flow, were particularly noticeable.

After that initial walkabout, I walked the site once more on my own, stopping to make binaural recordings and take notes and sound pressure measurements (L_{ceq}) with a precalibrated app on my phone (Decibel X), while Alan played the violin in the kilns to test their reverberance. My note-taking was informed by questionnaire (method B), ISO 12913-2 (BSI, 2018). The binaural recordings enabled Dan to go on a virtual soundwalk of the site afterwards and make his own annotations.

Initial impressions from the soundwalk, notes taken from the interview with Mike and Cathy, and sound pressure level measurements have informed the following diagrams that constitute the sonic inventory and analysis of the site. The first set of drawings captures the soundscape's perceived loudness, pleasantness, eventfulness and appropriateness.

- Perceived loudness: *Traffic noise seems to come from the West. We hear, in particular, the low rumbling of lorries* noted residents, which was experienced by participants. This is due to the topography of the site and the slight bend of the motorway, and the presence of an off-road into Corbridge. A new residential development will be built West of Milkwell Lane, partially alleviating traffic noise. There is a correlation between measured sound pressure and perceived loudness in most places. However, reading the dB measures was a surprise, as the site seems louder than what the measurements tell (Figures 6.14 and 6.15).

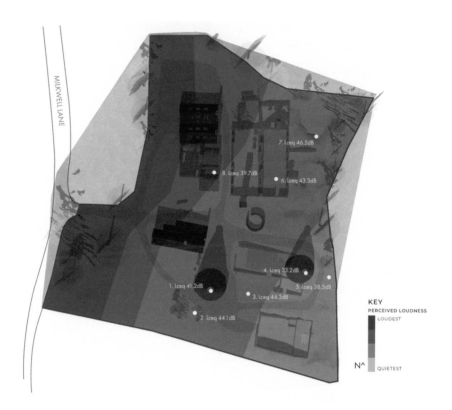

Figures 6.14 Perceived loudness. Base drawing credit: EDable Architecture

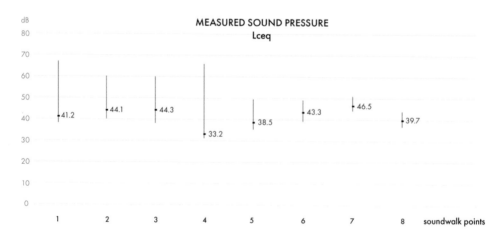

Figure 6.15 Measured sound pressure.

- Perceived appropriateness. Along the northern and western boundary, the traffic hum contrasts with the rural and wild character of the site. To the south, however, calls of birds, buzzing and stridulation of insects, rushing of vegetation and the distant church bells ringing and human sounds correspond to the pastoral setting. To the centre of the site, the traffic hum and absence of sounds contrast somehow with a site perceived as once full of life (Figure 6.16).
- Perceived pleasantness. Pleasantness is multisensorial and related to both perceived appropriateness, eventfullness and loudness. There are many pleasant moments on the site, such as the discovery of the stillness of the kilns and their reverberation, the rhythmical stridulation of the crickets or the church bells heard in the distance (Figure 6.17).

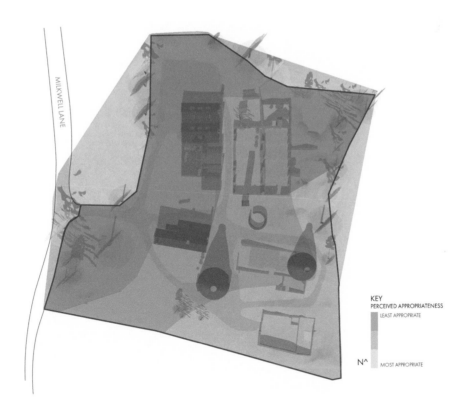

Figure 6.16 Perceived appropriateness, Base drawing credit: EDable Architecture.

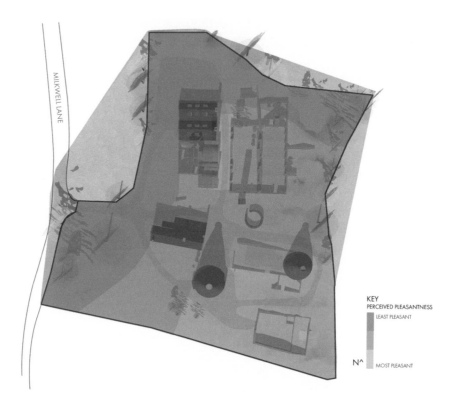

Figure 6.17 Perceived pleasantness, Base drawing credit: EDable Architecture.

- Perceived eventfulness. The southern part of the site is perceived as the most eventful, with natural sounds dominating the soundscape. In contrast, the core of the pottery – the ruinous buildings – appears as the least eventful, as one imagines a site that was once very active (Figure 6.18).

Next, the drawing on Figure 6.19 summarizes our (Dan, Alan & Usue's) experiential notes on the soundwalk and responses captured in the questionnaire (BSI, 2018, method B). The diagram captures key sound events and aural effects. The numbers refer to the spots where we stopped to listen: our listening stations.

Following the initial visit and experiential annotations, environmental and experiential aural effects were summarised in site sections, as these are key to how the

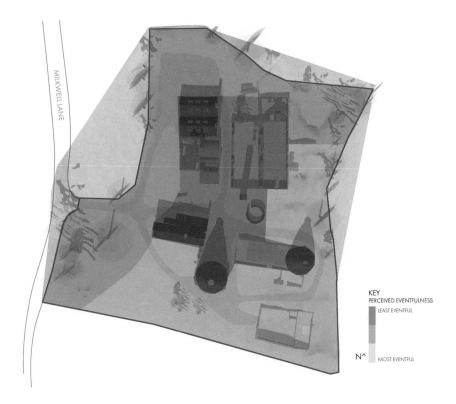

Figure 6.18 Perceived eventfulness, Base drawing credit: EDable Architecture.

soundscape is currently experienced and how the soundscape might be re-imagined. The sections are accompanied by some of the field recordings of the visit (soundtracks) (Figures 6.20–6.24).

We concluded the site survey and analysis stage by identifying opportunities and constraints for the soundscape, in line with the landscape character areas identified, and with the development of a sound composition that encapsulates the aural identity of the site. Opportunities and constraints are summarised in the following diagram, and the aural identity is described in the next section. These opportunities and constraints guide the aural strategies proposed for the site in Chapter 8 (Figure 6.25).

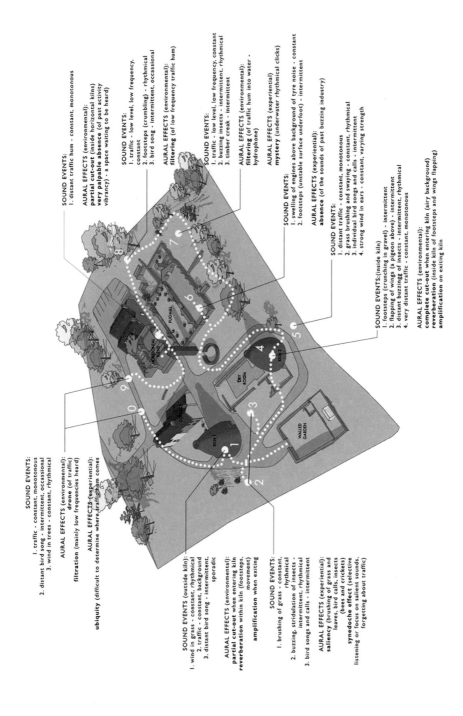

Figure 6.19 Soundscape assessment: key sound events and aural effects on listening stations along the soundwalk, Base axonometric credit: EDable Architecture.

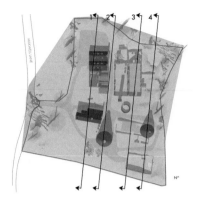

Figure 6.20 Location of site sections, Base drawing credit: EDable Architecture.

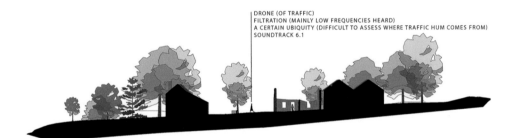

DRONE (OF TRAFFIC)
FILTRATION (MAINLY LOW FREQUENCIES HEARD)
A CERTAIN UBIQUITY (DIFFICULT TO ASSESS WHERE TRAFFIC HUM COMES FROM)
SOUNDTRACK 6.1

♬ Figure 6.21 Site section 01 (Soundtrack 6.1), Base section credit: EDable Architecture.

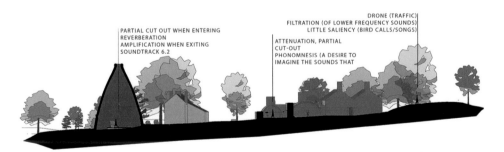

PARTIAL CUT OUT WHEN ENTERING
REVERBERATION
AMPLIFICATION WHEN EXITING
SOUNDTRACK 6.2

DRONE (TRAFFIC)
FILTRATION (OF LOWER FREQUENCY SOUNDS)
LITTLE SALIENCY (BIRD CALLS/SONGS)

ATTENUATION, PARTIAL
CUT-OUT
PHONOMNESIS (A DESIRE TO
IMAGINE THE SOUNDS THAT

♬ Figure 6.22 Site section 02 (Soundtrack 6.2), Base section credit: EDable Architecture.

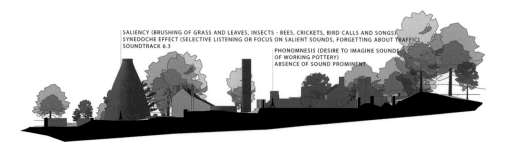

🎵Figure 6.23 Site section 03 (Soundtrack 6.3), Base section credit: EDable Architecture.

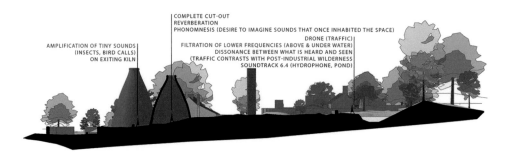

🎵Figure 6.24 Site section 04 (Soundtrack 6.4), Base section credit: EDable Architecture.

The approach taken for the survey and analysis draws from the ISO methodology to the extent that:

- human perception was prioritised, and loudness, pleasantness, eventfulness and appropriateness were considered,
- the soundwalk methodology was followed (with experiential data collected using questionnaire methods: B – soundwalk participants and C – interview with residents),
- binaural recordings were taken following the described protocol.

The main purpose of this exercise, however, was to develop a simple methodology that could be used by any landscape architect or urban designer as a part of normal fieldwork, site inventory, and analysis without having to invest in

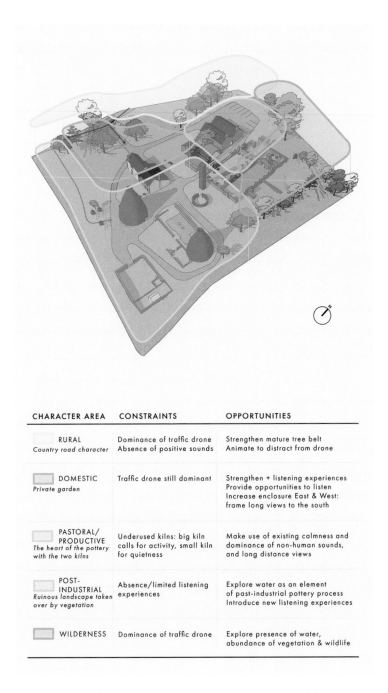

CHARACTER AREA	CONSTRAINTS	OPPORTUNITIES
RURAL *Country road character*	Dominance of traffic drone Absence of positive sounds	Strengthen mature tree belt Animate to distract from drone
DOMESTIC *Private garden*	Traffic drone still dominant	Strengthen + listening experiences Provide opportunities to listen Increase enclosure East & West: frame long views to the south
PASTORAL/ PRODUCTIVE *The heart of the pottery with the two kilns*	Underused kilns: big kiln calls for activity, small kiln for quietness	Make use of existing calmness and dominance of non-human sounds, and long distance views
POST- INDUSTRIAL *Ruinous landscape taken over by vegetation*	Absence/limited listening experiences	Explore water as an element of past-industrial pottery process Introduce new listening experiences
WILDERNESS	Dominance of traffic drone	Explore presence of water, abundance of vegetation & wildlife

Figure 6.25 Landscape character areas with aural opportunities and constraints, Base axonometric credit: EDable Architecture.

expensive equipment or expert data analysis; a methodology informed simply by listening. We prioritised affective listening. Affective listening, for this project and as discussed in this book, refers to the intertwined physical, emotive, and intersubjective response that listening to sound elicits. We listened to uncover the aural identity of the Pottery, relate to the inhabitant's experiences of the site and soundscape, establish a kinship with others and design from that established kinship. We also set out to work creatively with sound, and the purpose of our binaural recordings was not to extract data but to develop creative auralisations for the site.

Aural identity: composition I, murmuration I

This first piece was composed from field recordings of the site (1st visit) and is accompanied by a graphic score (refer to Figure 6.26 and Soundtrack 6.5). In conjunction, graphic score and composition transport the reader to the Old Pottery and our perception of it. We drew inspiration from the *Scoring the City* project conceived by Gascia Ouzounian and John Bingham-Hall, which turned to music and scores to 'challenge the static nature of the architectural blueprint' (Ouzounian and Bingham-Hall, 2022). The Old Pottery's landscape has changed and is constantly evolving, a dynamism that the media of music and scores can encapsulate.

The drive behind this composition, and the next (detailed in Chapter 8), was to move away from the familiar comforts of top-down mapping, planning and drawing, which, although useful tools for any spatial designer, can also distance from the experiential aspects of a place. Instead, we proposed working from an internal position, looking and listening outwardly to narrate The Pottery's story from the experience of it. Traditional maps and plans carry the weight of certainty, a strong objectivity that resists dispute. However, this work's interest lied in the intersubjective matter of perception. Pauline Oliveros links sonic perception to memory through every individual's complex web of previously experienced events and associated sounds (Oliveros, 2015). Thus, in Oliveros' view, individuals may have a different neural response to any sonic event based on past experiences. In undertaking these works, we attempted to reveal a practice that was less about obtaining objective truth but rather aimed to reveal intersubjective experiences.

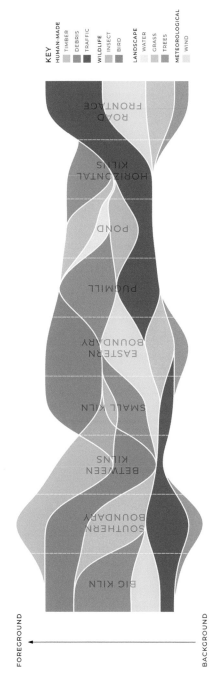

KEY

HUMAN-MADE
TIMBER
DEBRIS
TRAFFIC

WILDLIFE
INSECT
BIRD

LANDSCAPE
WATER
GRASS
TREES

METEOROLOGICAL
WIND

FOREGROUND

BACKGROUND

Figure 6.26 Murmuration I graphic score (Soundtrack 6.5), Credit: Dan Hill.

147

Dan is still to visit The Pottery in person, yet after listening to it attentively for many hours over months feels he knows it more intimately than his own bedroom. Though he has seen photographs, plans and maps of the site, The Pottery exists to him foremost as a series of sonic moments: bursts of birdsong, crumbling debris underfoot and reverberant chambers exaggerating the sound of batting wings. Each moment is isolated in its recording, but perception has irreversibly merged them into a unified whole.

The recordings were taken at spatial nodes along Usue's curated soundwalk of the site. Dan created the score included in Figure 6.26 as a means of aurally navigating the site. As he listened, he noted what he heard and tried to quantify its presence through each space and, in time, a map for the ears. The coloured waves represent the ebb and flow of each sound character moving in and out of the soundwalk. Their weights are guided by the sound's volume, their vertical position and their experienced proximity in the recording. He then translated his findings back into sound using the score as a guide, now accounting for his perceived experience of each location. This enabled him to articulate the different parts of the route with musical character, imbuing each space with its own timbre and texture.

By learning about the site almost exclusively through listening, Dan could represent his experience more authentically through sound than through visual media. Trialling this process has become a critical part of our approach in working with this site through listening.

Listening and sounding exercises

Sounding bodies, sounding space

Sounding bodies, soundings space was a two-week design studio with first-year Master of Landscape Architecture students at Newcastle University (UK) in 2022. The studio was set up to encourage students to decipher space by listening as a first step towards considering space as not only visual and physical but also aural. The studio started with a lecture that introduced students to *aural space* and its importance to the work of landscape architects, the *deep listening* practice developed by composer and accordionist Pauline Oliveros (The Centre for Deep Listening, 1999), as well as key concepts to help understand and decipher aural space, such as those introduced in Chapter 4: *acoustic horizon, acoustic arena* and *auditory channel*.

The studio unfolded in two parts.

Part 1

In the first part, students put into practice scores or instructions to cultivate their listening and aural awareness of space. The scores drew from Oliveros' *deep listening scores* developed over a lifetime (The Centre for Deep Listening, 1999). Olivero's scores consisted of 'listening and sounding exercises' that sought to connect listeners with the acoustic environment and all its inhabitants (ibid). Our scores were designed to focus on listening to space and listening to our own bodies (and those of others) while moving, and therefore sounding, through space.

   Below are two examples of our scores and students' creative responses:

SCORE 01

Go on a 30-minute walk around your neighbourhood. Be silent for the full duration of the walk and concentrate your listening on your footsteps. Note down on a map the walk you have done and the parts of the route where you could hear your footsteps. A step further: sketch those spaces where your footsteps were the loudest and the quietest and reflect on the relation between aural space and visual/physical space (Figure 6.27).

SCORE 05

Sit on a bench in a park, any park. Listen for 5 minutes. Focus on the smallest sound you can hear – who makes that sound? Can you describe the sound through an onomatopoeia? Now focus on the loudest sound you can hear and repeat the same exercise. Then listen to all other sounds in between and try and make a scale of sounds (and onomatopoeias) – from smallest to loudest. Include your own sound-making as part of the process. The onomatopoeias could be in any language of your choosing (Figure 6.28).

Part 2

In the second week of the studio, students worked in groups to develop their own set of scores or instructions for sounding space and/or body. Students were encouraged to be creative using various media, including written words, collages

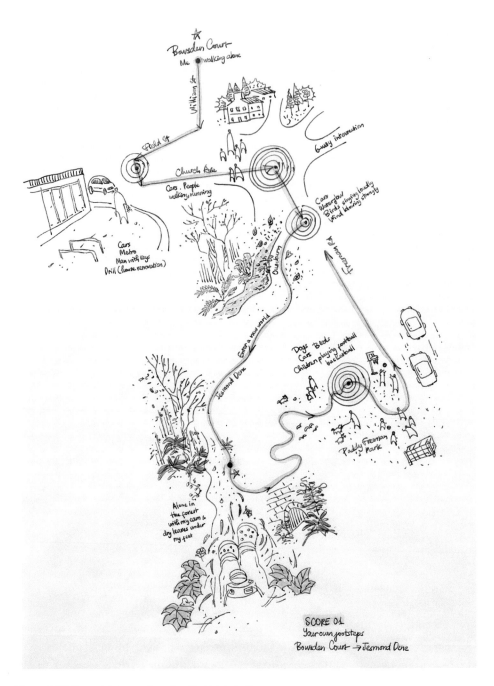

Figure 6.27 Score 01 in practice, Credit: Hai Anh Nguyen.

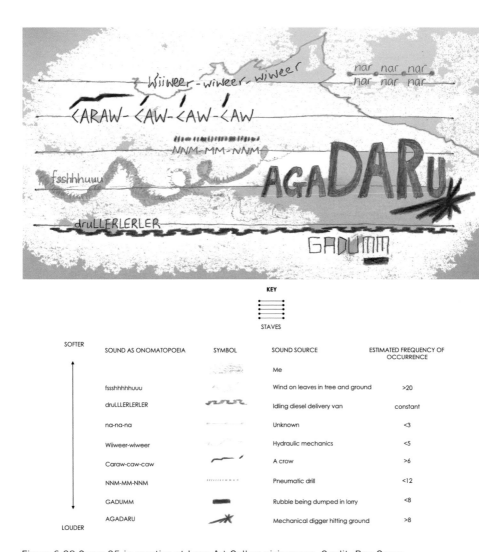

Figure 6.28 Score 05 in practice at Lang Art Gallery civic space, Credit: Ben Crowe.

and drawings. Each group created and tested three scores, and we collated all scores into a booklet titled *Sounding bodies, sounding space*. We circulated the booklet within our school and beyond to encourage others to listen by putting our scores to the test.

Soundwalks for students and practitioners

Over the years, I have led many soundwalks with landscape architecture, urban planning students and landscape architects in practice. The format and purpose of these soundwalks have varied, according to participants, and as a reflection of my listening, sounding and experimenting journey. Some soundwalks have been pure listening exercises: walking in silence in small groups along a pre-planned route, taking in all sounds as they come and becoming aware of our own sound-making and interacting with the sound-making of others. Others have sought to spark people's imagination through sound (e.g., the soundwalk I led for the *Walking Festival of Sound* introduced in Chapter 4). Others have sought to provide practitioners and students with tools to analyse the soundscape, consider it an integral part of the landscape, and start thinking about how to intervene in it. An example of this last is the soundwalk that I led with stage 2 Master of Landscape Architecture students in September 2022, where we followed the ISO 12913 method A questionnaire (BSI, 2018), with additional open-ended questions that prompted students to think of potential interventions in the spaces traversed. The format of the walk and representation and purpose of data collected is detailed next, as it might provide a framework for the reader to develop their own soundwalks.

Format of the walk

The walk was designed to last approximately 40 minutes (3 km), plus an additional 5 minutes in each of the three listening stations where we stopped to analyse the soundscape. I planned the route to take in a wide variety of listening experiences and aural spaces and bring attention to non-human soundmakers. In advance of the soundwalk, students were given instructions to help calibrate their listening and soundwalking, as well as a link to an online questionnaire to be filled, on their mobile phones, at each of the listening stations.

We walked on a Tuesday afternoon in late September, with 20 participants led by me. An overcast day, warm and dry, and slightly windy. We started the walk from our studio towards Lovers Lane, a quiet and relatively narrow lane on Campus flanked by towering mature trees and five to six storey buildings. We stopped at the end of the lane, our first listening station. We then walked along Claremont Road and crossed the A167 over a pedestrian bridge. We reached the Town Moor, a 400-ha open grassland where cows graze from spring to autumn. We climbed the tallest hill of the moor, amongst the cows, and stopped to take on the long-distance views over the cityscape and surrounding roads while listening at our second listening station. We then went down to Exhibition Park, a Victorian park with various facilities and a small boating lake. Our last listening station was here by the lake, home to varied waterfowl (coots, mallards, moorhen, swans) and popular with gulls.

We walked as a group in silence for the duration, coming together at the end to share insights and thoughts. Following the walk, and once participants had submitted their questionnaire responses, I collated and analysed the quantitative and qualitative data to give feedback to the students.

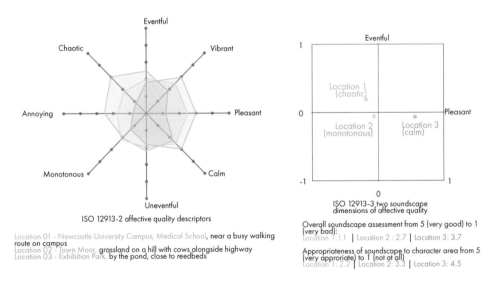

Location 01 - Newcastle University Campus, Medical School, near a busy walking route on campus
Location 02 - Town Moor, grassland on a hill with cows alongside highway
Location 03 - Exhibition Park, by the pond, close to reedbeds

Overall soundscape assessment from 5 (very good) to 1 (very bad):
Location 1: 1.1 | Location 2: 2.7 | Location 3: 3.7

Appropriateness of soundscape to character area from 5 (very appropriate) to 1 (not at all)
Location 1: 2.2 | Location 2: 3.3 | Location 3: 4.5

Figure 6.29 Soundscape assessment summary at each listening station.

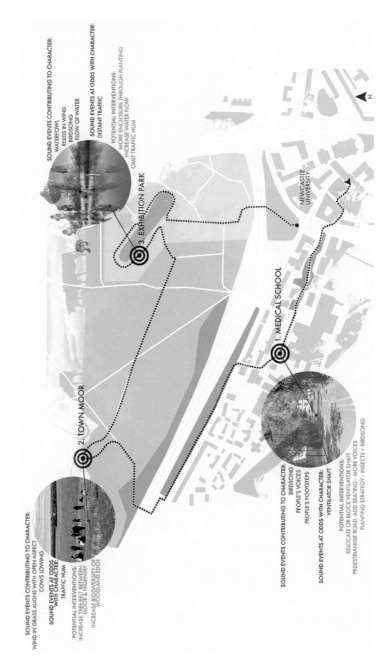

SOUND EVENTS CONTRIBUTING TO CHARACTER:
WATERFOWL
REEDS IN WIND
BIRDSONG
FLOW OF WATER

SOUND EVENTS AT ODDS WITH CHARACTER:
DISTANT TRAFFIC

POTENTIAL INTERVENTIONS:
MORE ENCLOSURE THROUGH PLANTING
INCREASE WATER FLOW
OMIT TRAFFIC HUM

3. EXHIBITION PARK

NEWCASTLE
UNIVERSITY

1. MEDICAL SCHOOL

2. TOWN MOOR

SOUND EVENTS CONTRIBUTING TO CHARACTER:
WIND IN GRASS ALIGNS WITH OPEN ASPECT
COWS LOWING

SOUND EVENTS AT ODDS WITH CHARACTER:
TRAFFIC HUM

POTENTIAL INTERVENTIONS:
INCREASE TREE BELT BETWEEN
MOOR & HIGHWAY

INCREASE BIODIVERSITY OF
WOODLAND EDGE

SOUND EVENTS CONTRIBUTING TO CHARACTER:
BIRDSONG
PEOPLE'S VOICES
PEOPLE'S FOOTSTEPS

SOUND EVENTS AT ODDS WITH CHARACTER:
VENTILATOR SHAFT

POTENTIAL INTERVENTIONS:
RELOCATE OR BLOCK VENTILATOR SHAFT
PEDESTRIANISE ROAD, ADD SEATING - MORE VOICES
PLANTING STRATEGY - INSECTS + BIRDSONG

Figure 6.30 Map of soundwalk with characteristic sound events and proposed interventions.

154

The questionnaire consisted of five parts:

- Parts 1–4 followed ISO 12913, questionnaire method A, with questions on sound source identification, perceived affective quality (perceptual attributes), and assessment and appropriateness of the surrounding sound environment. Quantitative data collated were analysed according to ISO 12913 recommendations: as ordinal scales, with median and range values. The perceived affective quality responses were translated into a two-dimensional model of pleasantness and eventfulness, following the formulas provided on ISO 12913 part 3 (2019), with pleasantness plotted on the *x*-axis and eventfulness on the *y*-axis (Figure 6.29). The dimensions of pleasantness and eventfulness, and as discussed in Chapter 7, encompass most other soundscape descriptors researched to date (Aletta, Kang and Axelsson., 2016).
- Part 5 consisted of open-ended, qualitative questions that prompted students to consider potential landscape interventions at each listening station. Answers were thematically analysed and linked, following an inductive approach (Figure 6.30). Of note in these responses was how listening station 3, by the lake, which was experienced at the end of the walk, was calm and wild, contrasting to noisier spaces traversed to get there. Many participants commented on how the experience would have been different should the walk have been done in the opposite direction. This studio helped students think how they could integrate listening into the early stages of a project to enhance the soundscape, and through it, the landscape.

References

Aletta, F., Kang, J. and Axelsson, Ö. (2016) 'Soundscape descriptors and a conceptual framework for developing predictive soundscape models', *Landscape and Urban Planning*, 149, pp. 65–74. doi: 10.1016/j.landurbplan.2016.02.001.

Bristol Health Partners (2023) *Supporting healthy and inclusive neighbourhood environments HIT*, Bristol Health Partners. Available at: https://www.bristolhealthpartners. org.uk/health-integration-teams/healthy-neighbourhood-environments-shine/ (Accessed: 5 July 2023).

Bristol Open Doors (2023) *Explore the city*, Bristol Open Doors. Available at: https:// bristolopendoors.org.uk/ (Accessed: 5 July 2023).

BSI (The British Standards Institution) (2018) 'ISO/TS 12913 - 2 : 2018 BSI Standards Publication Acoustics — Soundscape', BSI Standards Publication.

BSI (The British Standards Institution) (2022) *PAS 6463: Design for the mind - Neurodiversity and the built environment - Guide.*

Building with Nature (2023) *Building with nature.* Available at: https://www. buildingwithnature.org.uk/about (Accessed: 5 July 2023).

Department for Environment Food and Rural Affiars (2019) *Noise action plan: Agglomerations environmental noise (England) regulations 2006, as amended.* Available at: https://assets.publishing.service.gov.uk/government/uploads/system/uploads/ attachment_data/file/813663/noise-action-plan-2019-agglomerations.pdf.

Extrium (2023) *England noise and air quality viewer*, Extrium. Available at: http:// www.extrium.co.uk/noiseviewer.html (Accessed: 5 July 2023).

Faram, J. (ed.) (2021) *Bristol / city of sounds, Bristol/city of...* Available at: https://www. bristolcityof.co.uk/sounds_folded_screen.pdf (Accessed: 5 July 2023).

Historic England (2016) *Walker's Pottery*, Corbridge, Historic England listing. Available at: https://historicengland.org.uk/listing/the-list/list-entry/1006441? section=official-listing (Accessed: 18 March 2021).

Jones-Morris, S. (2020) *Bristol soundwalks, Bristol soundwalks.* Available at: https:// bristolsoundwalks.wixsite.com/brisoundwalks (Accessed: 5 July 2023).

Mechelli, A. (2023) *Urban mind, urban mind.* Available at: https://www.urbanmind. info/about#aboutop (Accessed: 5 July 2023).

Musyoki, J. (2021) *Hidden sounds of spike Island, walk, listen, create.* Available at: https:// walklistencreate.org/walkingpiece/hidden-sounds-of-spike-island/ (Accessed: 12 December 2023).

Oliveros, P. (2015) *The difference between hearing and listening, TEDx talks.* Available at: https://www.youtube.com/watch?v=_QHfOuRrJB8 (Accessed: 27 March 2023).

Ouzounian, G. and Bingham-Hall, J. (2022) *Scoring the city, scoring the city.* Available at: http://scoring.city/about/ (Accessed: 21 March 2022).

Radicchi, A. (2019) *Hush city map, hush city mobile lab.* Available at: https://map. opensourcesoundscapes.org/view-area (Accessed: 22 September 2019).

Scottish Government (2023) *Scotlan's noise, Scotland's environment.* Available at: https://noise.environment.gov.scot/noisemap/ (Accessed: 23 May 2017).

The Bristol Approach (2023) *Home*, The Bristol Approach. Available at: https:// www.bristolapproach.org/ (Accessed: 5 July 2023).

Tranquil City (2023) *About us*, Tranquil City. Available at: tranquilcity.co.uk (Accessed: 5 July 2023).

UK Parliament (2021) *Environment act.* Available at: https://www.legislation.gov.uk/ ukpga/2021/30/contents/enacted.

Waters, G. (2022) *Tranquil city launches in Bristol with go Jauntly!*, Tranquil City. Available at: https://tranquilcity.co.uk/2022/05/26/tranquil-city-launches-in-bristol-with-go-jauntly/ (Accessed: 5 July 2023).

WECIL (2023) *WECIL supporting independent living*, WECIL. Available at: https://wecil.org.uk/ (Accessed: 5 July 2023).

Welsh Governemnt (2018) *Noise and soundscape action plan*.

Welsh Government with the Noise Abatement Society (2022) *Technical advice note (TAN) 11: Air quality, noise and soundscape. Supporting document 1: soundscape design*.

Chapter Seven

Composing the soundscape

Everything we seek we have already found.

(Wainwright, 2023)

From aural narratives to detailed design

We read the landscape to intervene in it – to write it or transform it. Reading the landscape enables us to identify opportunities for change and conceptualise ideas to inform the design interventions that follow. Conceptual ideas might spring from the identity or *genius loci* of a place, from existing narratives uncovered during the reading stage, or from other sources of inspiration. Conceptual ideas are turned into a set of themes or principles to drive the design. Many potential solutions might address the project brief and respond to the site's opportunities and constraints. These solutions are 'arrived at by a combination of trial and error and the designer's own unique voice' (Waterman, 2022, p. 96).

Many landscape architects stress the importance of developing a clear, simple concept or idea for a site, which is carried through the entire design process (see, e.g., Cormier, 2015). The best concepts or ideas emerge from the site and its stories. They should be strategic and adaptable to reveal the qualities that already exist on the site and set the stage for other chapters in the story to open out. A concept that emerges from the experience of the site grounds a design in its physical and cultural context.

Concepts might also be *layered* and include several ideas that work in conjunction to intervene on the site (Dee, 2001, p. 37). A landscape comprises many layers.

DOI: 10.4324/9781003202981-10

Thus, concepts that emerge from the landscape are also likely to be multi-layered, with a series of design principles or strategies that uncover the existing stories in the landscape and respond to the assessment and brief to drive the design forward.

As suggested in the previous chapter, some sites might not have existing stories to hook onto to drive the design. These *non-places* require an *ingenious loci* that emerges from the designer's creativity (Baines, 2021).

Whether starting from a *place* or a *non-place*, a *genius loci* or an *ingenious loci*, the designer adds their *own voice* through the design process, turning initial ideas into a scheme that addresses the brief and responds to the constraints and opportunities identified in the assessment (Waterman, 2022). A design can then add new contemporary layers to the site, marrying these with the existing ones to ensure that the contemporary scheme can accommodate existing and future communities and their stories.

Once the outline design has been agreed upon with the client and, where possible, with the end users, proposals are developed into a final design and materials details. A set of technical drawings and specifications is produced, as well as visualisations or other forms of representation, such as models, which help us to represent and sell the proposed scheme. Visualisations are used for various purposes, including planning applications, client presentations, community engagements and marketing.

In reading the landscape through listening, we also seek opportunities to intervene in the landscape; thus, we play a part in its composition. However, listening requires time. We cannot grasp landscapes in an instant. Thus, listening encourages us to value what is already there and might lead to subtler interventions than those devised through looking. Listening, therefore, can help us uncover qualities and processes in the landscape otherwise missed and design from or with what is already there instead of starting anew. Through listening, we decipher stories embedded in the landscape to bring attention to them through our proposals and to set the stage for communities and natural processes to start new chapters in those never-ending stories (Timmermans, 2014). Sound can be an integral part of the layered design concept for a site: of the stories, principles and strategies that drive the design.

Sound can also be a creative element in the concept and detailed design process, expressing or emphasising the overall concept and thus engaging existing and future listeners with a site's stories. Sound plays an important role in how a site functions, aiding with legibility and navigation, supporting context-based activities and adding complexity, where needed, to enrich the multisensorial experience and quality of place. Finally, auralisations, as a counterpart to visualisations, can also be used for a variety of purposes, together with visualisations or on their own: from aiding the designer in the creative processes through helping designers and communities envisage how proposals will sound, to supporting planning applications, client presentations and marketing. In this last, we can use the affective engagement that listening elicits to engage listeners with a potential project or site.

In the next few pages, I will uncover how sound can be integrated within the design principles and strategies of the site, helping to uncover stories embedded in the landscape and to root a scheme in its physical and cultural context.

Aural principles and strategies

The layered concept, comprising design ideas, principles and strategies, forms the basis for developing outline and detailed design proposals for a site (Figure 7.1). These are often drafted in the form of conceptual and spatial diagrams that indicate the character areas or distinctive spaces proposed for the site, with the array of activities and communities each will host. At this stage, a soundscape strategy can be developed with a set of principles and strategies to strengthen the layered concept for the site. It should work with each character area and use proposed and increase positive listening experiences and reduce negative ones identified through reading the landscape. In this way, the soundscape strategy is integrated into the overall design principles and strategies for the site. Thus, it is concerned not only with the experience of the soundscape but also with the experience of the landscape.

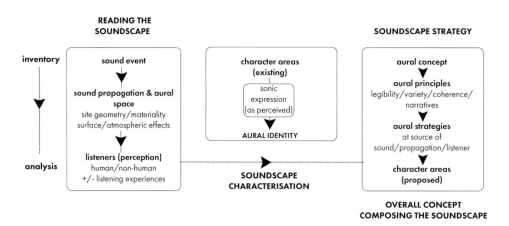

Figure 7.1 From reading to composing the soundscape.

Design principles

The four core principles for successful landscape and urban design schemes are legibility, variety, coherence and narrative. This section describes how those principles have been arrived at and explains aural principles and strategies conducive to their implementation.

The four core principles emerge from the following sources: Kaplan and Kaplan's (1989) environmental behaviour research, as highlighted by Dee (2001); acoustic design principles proposed by Truax (1984); placemaking or placekeeping literature and practice; and my own project experience as a landscape architect and educator.

Dee, in *Form and Fabric in Landscape Architecture* (2001), draws attention to the qualities Rachel and Stephen Kaplan identified to understand and explore the environment: *legibility, coherence, complexity* and *mystery* (1989). The qualities of *legibility* and *coherence* are linked to understanding the environment (ibid.). *Legibility* is linked to wayfinding and the ability to 'understand and remember' the environment to navigate it (ibid., p. 55). *Coherence* is related to order in the environment and how the different elements of the environment can be read and understood as a whole (ibid.). The qualities of *complexity* and *mystery* are linked to exploration. Complexity is linked to 'how much is going on' in a place, which is linked to visual, physical and aural elements (ibid., p. 53). Lastly, *mystery* refers to an enticing environment that invites the user to discover something that might not be immediately perceptible and requires further exploration (ibid.). Understanding and exploring the environment are abilities that determine people's preference for particular environments over others. Thus, designing environments that can be understood and explored is key if people are to use and adopt those places (Dee, 2001).

Truax, similarly, identifies *complexity* and *coherence* as two key principles for successful environmental sound design (1984, p. 100). Truax employs the term *variety* in place of complexity to describe a sonic principle required to keep our listening active and thus receive information to understand and engage with the environment. Monotonous soundscapes, Truax argues, numb our listening, as perceiving difference in the environment is required to acquire information. *Variety*, however, should be manageable for the listener, as 'too much information, or information that is unordered' is equally ineffective (ibid.). This is where *coherence* comes into play. Both *variety* and *coherence* are required for successful sound environments. (ibid.). Truax's principles concur with later theoretical models developed to evaluate and predict affective responses to a soundscape, which I will explain later in the chapter.

Lastly, placemaking is a collaborative process connecting people with places around them (Project for Public Spaces, 2022). Placekeeping, as a counterpart to placemaking, encourages working with what is already there – keeping and enhancing places instead of making them anew (Hickey, 2023). Placekeeping invites us to consider the impact of our interventions and our place in the myriad of relations that make up the planet (ibid). Placekeeping, therefore, is a term more suited to the design and management of places through listening, as listening is a temporal activity which mediates the relations between subjects and the environment and invites them to value what is already there. Placekeeping facilitates high-quality interventions that emerge from a place's 'physical, cultural, and social identities' (Project for Public Spaces, p. 2).

Successful places integrate four qualities:

1. They are accessible, connected and easy to navigate.
2. They are comfortable and welcoming.
3. They facilitate an array of activities and uses.
4. They encourage social interaction and become places in their neighbourhoods that people return to (ibid.)

We can link these four placekeeping principles to the Kaplans' principles introduced above. Thus, places that are accessible and connected are legible. Places that are comfortable and welcoming are coherent. Places that offer an array of activities and uses are varied. Finally, places that encourage social interaction, whilst not mysterious, are open in a way that invites continuous exploration; we could say that these places have a narrative or story that links the local community to the place. Accordingly, these are the four principles explored and carried forward in this section, termed as follows: *legibility, coherence, variety* and *narrative* (Figure 7.2).

Aural strategies: modification of listening experiences to implement design principles

There are three points of intervention where listening experiences can be modified: at the source of a sound event, at the propagation of sound and at the perceiving end (the listener).

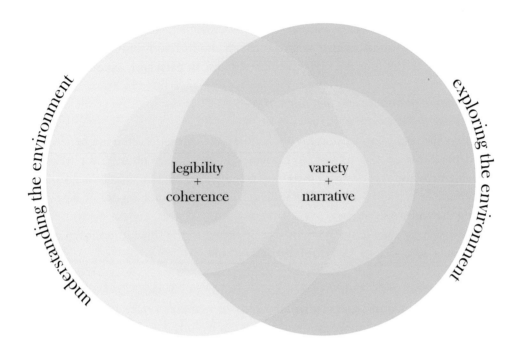

ENVIRONMENTAL PREFERENCE + PLACEKEEPING

Figure 7.2 Core principles for successful design.

At source

We are bound by the boundaries of our sites. Thus, in most cases, the modification of sound sources is limited to the sound sources within that site, including those that are seasonal, cyclical and temporal. Certain sound sources, such as people, birds and other animals, might only be temporarily in our site, and their presence and activity might evolve unexpectedly. For example, new community uses might emerge that were not originally envisaged, hence the importance of flexibility in strategies.

At propagation – aural effects

As mentioned in Chapter 5, sound waves are altered by the environment that they travel through; by atmospheric, geometrical and surface effects. Therefore, the proposed design's geometry, materiality and microclimate will affect how existing sounds and new sounds, which originate in our site or travel through it, propagate, contributing to the four principles identified above, in particular to coherence.

At listener end (human and non-human)

As I have discussed throughout this book, the soundscape affects the listener. Listening depends on individual listening capacities, as well as on culture and physiology (hearing capacity). Listening is, therefore, individual as well as socially determined. Perceptual aural strategies that affect individual and social listening can be employed during the landscape design.

These three points of intervention can be linked to the three interrelated modes of listening advanced at the beginning of the book:

- Interventions at the source of sound can be linked to *aesthetic listening* when considering the acoustic and aesthetic qualities of sound as a material object.
- Interventions in the propagation of sound can be linked to *listening as communication*. Sound is an expression of the activities taking place within a space and the physical and atmospheric characteristics of the space. The propagation of sound, therefore, affects the effectiveness of the communication that takes place through listening.
- Interventions at the listener end can be linked to *affective listening*, which in turn can encompass *aesthetic* and *communicational listening*. Listening influences how we are affected by the environment and how we respond to it. Thus, intervention at the listener's end can affect the embodied and contextual response to sound.

As we become skilful listeners and composers, we will become aware of the aural expression of our design and management interventions, how these might affect the communities within them and how we might actively emphasise listening and sound-making through the design process. The listening experience can be choreographed or composed by applying the aural strategies introduced next. For example, the listening experience can be choreographed by bringing attention to the existing aural qualities of a place, or it can be composed through amendments to the form of the public realm. However, there will always be limitations, as there are with design overall, as landscapes are alive and unpredictable, and aural space extends beyond physical place. Thus, aural strategies, similar to wider site strategies, should always

	strategies at source	strategies at propagation	strategies at listener	
legibility	omit, reduce, hide distract reveal, reinforce, amplify	aural effects landscape elements	soundmarks sensorial distraction	
variety	curation of listening experiences: active passive natural/other sounds	form materiality	sensorial play	
coherence	aural moods	adjacencies of aural moods	appropriateness degree of control	
narrative	aural narratives	aural effects	perceptual aural effects	

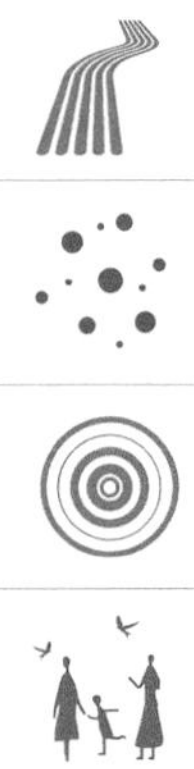

Figure 7.3 Core principles and corresponding aural strategies at the source of sound, propagation and listener.

be open, flexible and capable of adapting in time to respond to evolving landscapes (Figure 7.3).

Legibility: strategies

Legibility is linked to accessibility and connection; that is, the ability of any user to access a place, use it, find their way around it and exit from it. In Chapter 1, I introduced the concept of *acoustic communities*, where human and non-human beings can communicate and thrive, which relates to human-scale and non-human-scale design. A human-scale space is related to 'human ear and human voice' and is one where background sound does not mask the human voice (Schafer, 1970, p. 23). Accordingly, a non-human scale space would relate to each species' mode of vocalisation, and it would be one where background sound does not mask their vocalisation and communication. Thus, both concepts would require a *hi-fi* environment where individual sounds can be heard amongst ambient background noise (Schafer, 1977, p. 43).

The following aural strategies can be implemented to increase the legibility of a proposed design.

Strategies at the source of a sound event

OMIT, REDUCE AND HIDE

The soundscape assessment would have identified a series of negative listening experiences that might be detrimental to legibility. Those negative listening experiences could be linked to specific sound events within the site that we can omit, reduce or hide. We can also predict future negative listening experiences that can be omitted or reduced at this stage.

For example, on the soundwalk with Master of Landscape Architecture students described in Chapter 6, we stood at a well-used pedestrian-priority street at the point just before it bifurcated in two. The Medical School flanked us on one side, and a series of front gardens with mature trees on the other (Figure 7.2). At a distance, the spot appeared quite pleasant, buzzing with people and enclosed by mature trees full of birds. Yet, when we stood at the spot, which was one of our listening stations, our listening was dominated by the mechanical sound of a powerful extractor fan from the ground level of the Medical School. This salient sound prevented us from engaging with the wider soundscape, which might have helped us orient ourselves and decide which of the two routes to take. If this extractor had been identified as a negative sound source at the design stage of the building, it could have been relocated so that it did not face into the public realm (Figure 7.4).

Figure 7.4 Soundwalk, September 2022, listening station by Medical School (left) and at Lovers Lane (right).

DISTRACT

If we cannot omit or reduce the source of a sound, we can look at introducing positive sounds to distract from the negative ones through a masking effect (soundtrack 7.1). For example, in the walk along Hondarribia narrated in Chapter 5, the water fountain adjacent to the road distracted me from the constant traffic hum. Adding fountains is a common strategy to distract from traffic noise, particularly when constant (Coensel, Vanwetswinkel and Botteldooren, 2011).

🎧 Soundtrack 7.1. Footsteps on gravel distracting from traffic drone, Glasgow.

REVEAL, REINFORCE AND AMPLIFY

This is a simple case of revealing what is already there, choreographing a listening experience across a site that encourages users to listen to particular sounds at a particular place. This approach aligns with the origin of the word 'design' as to 'mark out' (OED online, 2023). All a site might need might already be present and listening might encourage us to keep and reveal it. For example, earlier on the walk described above, with the landscape architecture students, we stopped at a point where the street is bound on one side by mature vegetation within hospital grounds and by amenity street trees on the other. Towering trees flank the street on either side, enclosing and sheltering passers-by. This street, Lovers Lane, is partially shaded yet feels comfortable and full of birdsong, offering a respite from the busyness of other areas of campus and a multitude of roads. We sat to listen on a low wall halfway up the street. The provision of seating here, or a series of seats along the street, would be a great addition to an otherwise successful street, enabling people to slow down and enjoy the many positive listening experiences already here – people's laughter as they pass by in deep conversation, a variety of bird calls, the brushing of leaves and the soft crunching of footsteps in bound gravel.

We can design our public realm to bring attention to the sounds already there, for example, by inviting users to slow down through a change in the direction of a path, a change of surface materials or a change in level which needs to be navigated. Thus, amplification can be facilitated by bringing the listener closer to the sound event, for example, by redirecting a path or by allowing activities currently not permitted, such as sitting on the grass, to bring people closer to the rustling of the grass and insects that live within it. As described next, we can also accentuate or amplify positive listening experiences through *aural effects*.

Strategies at propagation of sound

AURAL EFFECTS

In Chapter 5, we discussed *aural effects* and how these influence the perception of the soundscape. Some *aural effects* are linked to how sound propagates in space, and so they are dependent on forms, elements and materiality of the space, while other effects are linked to the listener. At the design stage, we can remove or amend *aural effects* that reduce the legibility of the place and introduce *aural effects* that might contribute positively to the experience of place and navigation through it.

Aural effects which hinder legibility include some of the ones noticed during the walk in Hondarribia, mainly *ubiquity* (where sounds seem to come from everywhere) and *reverberation,* where they contribute negatively to the navigation of space. With regards to form and materiality of space, *ubiquity* is linked to *reverberation*, as the more reverberant a space, the more difficult it is to locate the source of sound (Augoyard and Torgue, 2005). To avoid *reverberation*, we can look at softening the hard surfaces of an existing or proposed space. For example, in the case of the walk in Hondarribia, introducing vegetation along the narrow street with parallel walls (location 8) would help to reduce *reverberation*. *Ubiquity* can also be linked to the listener's position, as was the case in Hondarribia, where I was moving through an environment where traffic sounds seemed to come from everywhere because of multiple roads in the periphery of the space (location 7).

Practical aural strategies are of two types. The first is tailored towards reducing negative listening experiences, while the second seeks to accentuate or amplify positive listening experiences through spatial and surface alternations and landscape elements. These strategies draw from the soundscape actions identified by landscape architect Gunnar Cerwén to reduce unwanted sounds (2020).

AURAL STRATEGIES TO REDUCE NEGATIVE LISTENING EXPERIENCES

These include using *earth berms* or *noise walls* close to the sound event (e.g., traffic) to reduce the propagation of sound waves. When it comes to *earth berms*, the soil absorbs sound, and if they are planted, absorption increases and, therefore, propagation decreases (Natural England, 2023). Shallow, planted *berms* can be more effective than *noise walls* as they limit sound reflection at the source and perform better in downwind conditions (Van Renterghem and Botteldooren, 2012). An example of *earth berms* integrated successfully into landscape design as sculptural landforms can be found at *Buitenschot Park* by H+N+S Landscape Architects. Located southwest of Amsterdam's Schiphol Airport, the landforms have been designed to reduce low–frequency ground-level noise caused by airplanes taking off through absorption and dispersion. These geometrical and angular *earth berms* came into being when nearby residents affected by noise observed that noise from the airport was lower when the agricultural fields between the airport and their homes were ploughed (H+N+S Landscape Architects, 2023) (Figure 7.5).

Tree belts close to the source of sound can also help with *mitigation*. This results from tree trunk scattering of sound waves, particularly high frequencies, and their absorption by the planted soil on the ground. Studies have demonstrated that both a 15-m and a 30-m deep belt can provide a similar level of traffic noise level reduction to a screen wall of 2–3 metres high (Van Renterghem, De Coensel and

Figure 7.5 Aerial image of Buitenschot Park by H+N+S Landscape Architects, Credit: Paul de Kort.

Botteldooren, 2013). Emerging studies have also looked at shallower belts, with a high density of tree trunks, trunks of large diameter and a degree of randomness in trunk location, with promising results (Van Renterghem, 2014).

AURAL STRATEGIES TO ACCENTUATE AND AMPLIFY POSITIVE LISTENING EXPERIENCES

There might be instances where positive listening experiences are hardly audible due to the presence of other sounds or the openness of a space, which results in sound waves dissipating or absorbing quickly. In these cases, we might seek to accentuate or amplify those listening experiences through the following strategy.

Enclosure: Enclosing a space partially or fully through soft landscaping (densely planted *trees* or *earth berms*) or hard landscaping (walls) could limit other sounds from entering the space, as discussed earlier for berms, trees and walls, or provide some *echo* or *reverberation* within the space, in the case of hard walls. A change of surfacing from soft to hard might also help minimise ground absorption of sound. Depending on the degree and nature of the enclosure, we might seek to create a *cut-out effect*, with a sudden change in the listener experience, as described in the walk through Hondarribia in Chapter 5 and the *Old Pottery* case study, when entering the kilns.

Strategies at the listener

Interventions at the listener end can also aid with legibility. Legibility depends on both the spatial characteristics of a place and on how the user interprets those characteristics to aid navigation and use of the space. Strategies at the listener end include the following.

SOUNDMARKS

Soundmarks, as introduced in Chapter 1, are the aural counterpart of landmarks. Landmarks are the salient features of a place that help the user orientate and navigate a place. These need to be enduring to enable that orientation and navigation to occur. Soundmarks, therefore, are the salient aural features of a place that equally help the user orientate and navigate the said place. These are not one-off salient features but are present daily or seasonally, whether constantly or at regular intervals. For example, the bells in Hondarribia are a *soundmark* of the town that help users place themselves in relation to a key building and key events within it. Other permanent soundmarks in the town include, for example, the many fountains that aid with orientation.

Soundmarks can also operate at larger scales. For example, in 1996, Japan designated 100 community *soundmarks*, which ranged from bells, such as the bell of Hakodate Russian Orthodox Church, to wildlife sounds, such as the calls of black-tailed gulls in Kabushima (Japan Ministry of the Environment, 1996).

Soundmarks can be actively introduced or existing *soundmarks* incorporated into the design to aid with legibility. Soundmarks can be geophonic, biophonic or anthrophonic.

PERCEPTUAL AURAL EFFECTS

Perceptual aural effects can also aid with legibility and wayfinding. Notably:

Distracting with the other senses or sensorial distraction. All senses work together in understanding and engagement with the environment. Each sense provides information differently, which can be useful in the design process. For example, research has demonstrated that the sight of vegetation can distract from traffic noise and contribute to a more positive evaluation of the environment (Van Renterghem and Botteldooren, 2016; Aletta, Oberman and Kang, 2018). This can help with the legibility and use of that environment. These and other sensorial distractions might be useful when sound sources cannot be amended.

Variety: strategies

Variety is required to keep our listening active and receive information. Thus, it aids understanding of the environment and engagement with it (Truax, 1984). Perceiving difference in the environment allows us to acquire new information about it (ibid.) and invites us to explore that environment. The following aural strategies can contribute to adding variety in the public realm.

Strategies at the source of sound event

CURATION OF NEW LISTENING EXPERIENCES

Aural variety in a place might be actively sought or a byproduct of the wider variety sought through the design proposals. In both instances, to prevent soundscapes from becoming monotonous, sounds within them should balance a degree of *regularity* and *variation* (Truax, 1984, p. 101). *Regularity* and *variation* are characteristic of human activity sounds and thus would be considered as 'having a human character' (ibid.).

AURAL VARIETY (ACTIVELY SOUGHT OR DIRECT)

Facilitating natural sounds. Even though judgments about sound are ultimately individual and vary according to context, we have an affinity for natural sounds. Natural sounds are associated with tranquillity (Jackson *et al.*, 2008) and physiological, cognitive and emotional restorative effects (Levenhagen *et al.*, 2021). They also contribute to evaluating an environment as pleasant. Consequently, facilitating natural sounds through our proposals can increase human health and well-being.

Not all natural sounds are conducive to tranquillity. This is related to the appropriateness of the sound to place and activity. For example, birdsong deemed tranquil throughout the day might be classified as annoying early in the morning outside one's bedroom. Some birdsong, such as the calls of seagulls, might not be tranquil at all. The impact of human activity on those natural sound sources should also be considered as we strive to design for human and non-human communities.

Natural sounds can be introduced in design by establishing new habitats that will increase the biophony of the place; the planting of new trees and vegetation, as well as the introduction of flowing water. This last can be achieved through sustainable urban drainage systems, streams or fountains, thus linking green and blue infrastructure to positive soundscapes for human and non-human communities.

Curating other sounds. Natural sounds (geophonic and biophonic) are not the only sounds to be actively sought. Aural variety can come from geophonic sound sources (e.g., wind, flowing water, rain tapping on hard and soft surfaces), biophonic sound sources (human and non-human communication, circulation, movement, play, performance) and anthrophonic sound sources (such as music), or any combination of these (e.g. footsteps in gravel) that can contribute positively to the public realm.

AURAL VARIETY (BYPRODUCT)

Positive listening experiences are intrinsically linked to the users and activities of the space, as well as its form and materiality. Users and activities sound. Form and materiality affect sound propagation and might add sounds to the space. Positive listening experiences are an indirect effect of successful design.

A streetscape redesigned to restrict traffic and facilitate informal play and social interaction, for example, will animate the street and provide an aural transformation from the constant hum of traffic (monotonous, *lo-fi*) to a hubbub of human activity (varied, *hi-fi*). The redesigned streetscape might also include tree planting, which might host birds that call and sing. Trees will also sound; rustling sounds in the wind to be enjoyed outdoors in the street. The street's soundscape might also filter indoors to residents facing the street, keeping residents engaged with their surroundings. All those sounds will vary while having a certain regularity, as they are not one-off sounds but everyday sounds with different temporal and rhythmical patterns.

Even though we may not seek aural variety intentionally, as skilful listeners, we can predict the aural variety that we are facilitating indirectly through our designs.

Strategies at propagation

FORM

At the design stage, we can add variety by introducing *aural effects* or removing effects that might have a detrimental effect on how aural variety is perceived. The effects mentioned for legibility are also applicable here. For example, *reverberation* can add variety by amplifying key sounds in the space. Reducing sound propagation through *earth berms, tree belts or walls* can also help reveal the variety of sounds already thereby removing background noise that could be masking their perception. The forms that we create in the landscape and how those forms are enclosed in all dimensions (ground, vertical and ceiling planes) will give rise to one or several *aural effects* that might contribute to variety and legibility. Some forms, such as the triangular form of *Arma Plaza* in Hondarribia, enclosed by hard surfacing, cause multiple reverberations that might make aural variety excessive and render a space illegible. Other forms and layouts, and the activities they facilitate, might lead to desirable effects for variety, such as *cut-out*.

As well as the *aural effects* mentioned thus far, the material palette selected during the detailed design stage influences variety through propagation.

MATERIALITY: AURAL PALETTE

How materials sound should be a consideration when curating a materials palette for a scheme. Materials, whether hard or soft, will alter the absorption, reflection and diffraction of sound waves traveling through space as well as being the source of sound themselves. With regards to the first, we have already discussed the absorption of vegetation soils and tree trunks, particularly at higher frequencies, and the reflection and reverberation caused by hard surfaces. Forms in the environment also define microclimates within them and alter the propagation of sound in the process.

There are, however, other *aural effects* derived from the proposed materiality of a place. For example, footsteps vary depending on the surfacing being walked upon: from the crunching of gravel surfaces to the sharpness of smooth granite paving. Materials sound under certain weather conditions, such as rain tapping on a variety of hard and soft surfacing or wind filtering through spaces and making loose materials sound. The *Old Pottery* case study is an example of how the aural informed the selection of materiality for the scheme.

Strategies at the listener

PLAYING WITH THE OTHER SENSES OR SENSORIAL PLAY

When discussing variety, we discussed *distracting with the other senses*, using the different ways of perceiving the environment through the different senses to distract from unwanted sounds. The richness of the senses can also be employed to add variety through the design of spaces that provide diverse sensorial stimuli to create a varied environment.

Listening can provide engagement with the environment, either as a complement to other sensorial stimuli or in the absence of other sensorial stimuli, thus adding variety to an otherwise monotonous space. For example, on one of my many walks along Leslie Street Spit in Toronto, I followed long stretches of monotonous road. This road was wide and straight, with dense vegetation that blocked the view on one side and bare areas under construction on the other. Walking along this monotonous road, the aural took over from the visual in my engagement with the landscape. I failed to spot any variation through sight, but listening enlivened the road. Birdsong above, calls of waterfowl in the distance and waves breaking at the shore, which I could hear but not see. Listening attentively invites the listener to explore areas otherwise perceived as monotonous, abandoned or untidy.

A frequent comment of my soundwalk participants is how, in many places, the aural does not correspond with the visual, and this often catches participants by surprise. Through listening and in time, some spaces become more interesting than initially thought just by looking at them. In other cases, places are less pleasant than initially thought, for example, if next to a motorway hidden from view. The interplay of the senses, particularly sight and sound, leads to evaluating spaces differently and can be used strategically in the design process.

Coherence: strategies

Coherence is related to how the different elements of the environment come together and are read as a whole (Kaplan and Kaplan, 1989). Aurally, coherence is linked to variety and how listening experiences relate to the existing and proposed identity of a place and character within it.

Strategies at the source of sound event

AURAL MOODS

Outline design proposals for a site are often drafted as conceptual diagrams and spatial diagrams that indicate the character or functional areas proposed for a site, with the array of activities each will host. Character areas have key characteristics that make them distinctive to those experiencing and perceiving the place. In turn, character areas have distinctive soundscapes that express the physical characteristics of the environment, the communities living within them and their interactions and activities. An aural character can be actively designed or composed through *aural moods* or indirectly result from those characteristics and interactions.

We should consider activities, interactions and uses as sound sources in composing *aural moods*. Sound sources are altered by the acoustic properties (physical characteristics) of the spaces proposed, affecting the behaviour and activities of the people experiencing those spaces. Thus, we need to be able to imagine and predict how our projected character areas will sound and be experienced similarly to how we can visualise them. In talking about *aural moods*, we talk about collective or intersubjective listening experiences and behaviours. Developing *aural moods* appropriate to each intended character area will strengthen and enhance the perception of the space. For example, a vibrant soundscape will enliven an urban square, whereas a calm soundscape would be more appropriate for a pocket park.

We can look at theoretical models of soundscape affective perception to develop *aural moods*. These models follow prevailing theories of affect that focus on two orthogonal dimensions: *valence* (pleasure) and *arousal* (Russell, 1980) and are primarily focused on calm and vibrant moods.

An incipient theoretical model was developed by Hedfors and Berg, who argued for thinking through sonic atmospheres in Landscape Architecture (2003).

Their model was based on *clarity* in a figure/ground model, where the figure refers to prominent sounds and the ground to background sounds. *Clarity*, the ability to listen to prominent sounds against the background sounds, applies to quiet and vibrant spaces, as clarity is required to make a space interesting and provide a strong identity. *Clarity* also enables the listener to feel that they have a degree of control over what they are listening to (ibid.).

The *Positive Soundscape Project* (PSP) developed a model for soundscape perception based on two dimensions: *calmness* and *vibrancy* (Davies *et al.*, 2013). *Calmness* is strongly linked to pleasantness, while *vibrancy* depends on two registers: *cacophony-hubbub* and *constant-temporal*. *Cacophony-hubbub* is linked to the number of sound sources and how they mix harmoniously (*hubbub*) or not (*cacophony*). *Constant-temporal* relates to the degree of monotony and rhythm (ibid.), which can, in turn, be related to Truax's dimensions of *variety* and *coherence* *(1984)*. The categories of *calmness, hubbub* and *temporal* are related to positive listening experiences, and cacophony and constant relate mainly to negative ones (Davies et al., 2013).

Two later models by Axelsson et al. (2010) and Cain *et al.* (2013) encompass the majority of other soundscape descriptors researched to date (Aletta, Kang, and Axelsson, 2016). Axelsson's orthogonal model of perceived affective quality consists of two descriptors in one dimension, *pleasantness* and *eventfulness,* at a 45-degree angle from another two descriptors*, calmness and excitement* (2010). Cain *et al.'s* model uses the descriptor *vibrancy* instead of *excitement*. Both models correlate with the findings of the PSP. Axelsson added a further descriptor, appropriateness, which adds to affective quality, although on its own, it is not a measure of soundscape quality (2015). Aptly, ISO 12913 part 3 provides a formula to turn the eight descriptors captured through method A questionnaire of part 2 into a two-dimensional model of affect: *eventfulness* and *pleasantness* (BSI, 2018). The soundwalk case study in Chapter 6 provides an example of soundscape descriptors plotted into a two-dimensional model.

There are limitations to the ISO12913 data analysis and representation, as highlighted by Mitchell *et al.* (2022)., including the difficulty in capturing variation in time and amongst the many users of the assessed spaces. As a response, Mitchell et al. have developed an open-source representation tool that the reader is invited to explore (ibid.).

According to these affective models, a vibrant soundscape would include a fair number of sound events (varied), perceived to harmonise with one another (coherent and pleasant), appropriate to the setting (legible) and with a degree of variation over time. A calm soundscape could be described very similarly, but with fewer or quieter events that still provide a degree of engagement and are audible against the ambient noise.

Although the main *aural moods* developed through these models are calm at one end of the continuum and vibrant at the other, many moods can be created from the two main dimensions described: *pleasantness and eventfulness* and through considering *appropriateness*. These in-between ranges can be achieved by varying the number and type of sound events (human and non-human, appropriate to the setting, rhythmical and variation over time), the *aural effects* that affect their propagation in space and time, or the listeners' experience, as *aural moods* are spatial, temporal and embodied. *Aural moods* should always link to the wider proposals to avoid considering sound in isolation from its context and embodied perception.

Strategies at propagation

ADJACENCIES OF AURAL MOODS

Aural space, as discussed in Chapter 5, differs from physical and visual space, and in many cases, it does not correspond with it. We might be able to define spaces and character areas on a plan and physically on a site. However, their aural expression might extend beyond the site boundary, permeating adjacent areas. All elements and activities should come together for a site to be coherent, including their sonic expression. For example, if I am seated, reading, at a quiet spot in a park and suddenly a food van parks nearby and starts playing loud music, I am likely to move and search for an alternative spot. Accordingly, we need to think that some activities can share an acoustic space, and it might be beneficial to do so, for example, to create vibrancy, as detailed above. Others, however, might need isolation. Equally, we need to consider how the aural expression of the activities belonging to one space might impact the activities of nearby others and whether we might want to apply strategies to contain them or whether filtering one to another provides a degree of connection and coherence.

Strategies at the listener

APPROPRIATENESS AND DEGREE OF CONTROL

The *appropriateness* of sound events to a place adds to the affective quality of the soundscape, as introduced above. The affective response to a soundscape also depends on the *perceived level of control* over it (Axelsson, 2015.). These are two strategies that the designer can employ at this stage.

Concerning *appropriateness,* as designers, we should consider how the proposed aural environment might influence the behaviour of its users within the space. For example, back in *Arma Plaza*, my last stop on my walk through Hondarribia in Chapter 5, the sound expression of the outdoor cafes, due to reverberation, could be too overpowering to spend time sitting on the benches of the square. In this case, the designer might look at providing further separation within the square by enclosing the seats, for example.

With regard to *the perceived degree of control*, as designers, we can provide *clarity* within a space. If the listener can distinguish sounds clearly within a space, they feel they have control over what they are listening to. This clarity correlates with a *hi-fi* soundscape and the previously introduced human and non-human scale spaces. *Clarity* might be achieved in the design by avoiding constant hums, for example, by keeping car circulation and car parking to the perimeter of a masterplan and encouraging pedestrian priority streetscapes.

Narratives: strategies

As I have emphasised, listening can *move us to move*, instigating bodily reactions, thoughts, emotions and actions (Fuchs and Koch, 2014). Listening, therefore, is a conduit for the unfolding of stories and narratives: old stories embedded in the landscape and new chapters of those stories embedded in the environment and co-created by the communities inhabiting them. Listening and sounding can be an integral part of the layered design concept for a site; of the stories, principles and strategies that drive it. To that end, collaborating with or drawing from sound artists can greatly benefit a scheme. The breadth of sound artists' work is vast; this section introduces just a few examples. The reader is encouraged to explore sound artists further to enrich their work.

Strategies at the source of sound event

Aural narratives can drive the design of a site. *Aural narratives* link to the existing or proposed character, ecology or communities within a site. Here, I explain what aural narratives might mean through several examples.

AURAL NARRATIVES DERIVED FROM A SITE'S HERITAGE

An example of an *aural narrative* to provide the design is provided in the case study High Street Goodsyard in the following chapter. In this case, sound was used to reveal a buried history of *a non-place,* that of the culverted Molinburn. The aural concept sought to expose the burn through sound in the landscape, to expose the site's rich history. The aural concept was accompanied by other design principles that, in conjunction, drove the design of the site.

SOUNDWALKING NARRATIVES

For an example of a *soundwalking narrative*, I turn once more to Leslie Street Spit, Toronto. One Saturday in September 2015, I arrive at the Spit early afternoon. It feels much calmer than last time. I can see no one from the entrance. It is warm yet rather windy. Two salient sounds catch my attention by the entrance and accompany me throughout the walk: the waves breaking at the shore and the stridulation of crickets. I cannot see the source of either, yet I can vividly hear them. The stridulating crickets, in particular, become the metronome for my walk. It is as though my walking legs and my body follow the rhythm set by them. It is extremely calming.

Unbeknownst to me at the time of this walk, the calming effect of listening to crickets was discovered and employed during the Tang Dynasty in China by the royal family, who would keep and carry crickets on walks. The practice was later extended to the general public and re-enacted digitally by artist Lisa Hall for her Walking with Crickets soundwalk series (2016). Participants of the soundwalk explored urban spaces with and through cricket stridulations, altering how they perceived the spaces traversed. Mediated soundwalks, such as these by Lisa Hall, can take many forms, with participants usually listening to a pre-recorded soundtrack, mostly on headphones, whilst walking through a specific environment, thus transforming their usual engagement and experience. Much earlier examples of non-digital mediated (sound)walks are *The Songlines,* created by and for the Indigenous communities of Australia, which produced a soundmap of the country, connected through narrated routes which helped people to find resources and 'orient themselves physically and spiritually' (McCartney, 2014, p. 4).

Soundwalking narratives can be embedded into a scheme by curating or choreographing a walk to bring attention to key sound events (both existing or proposed) to be listened to with the naked ear or through the introduction of mediated narratives, listened to digitally.

Strategies at propagation

Aural effects that are both environmental (propagation) and perceptual (listener) can be employed to invite exploration of a place, thus adding mystery. Within Cerwén's *sound-scape actions,* introduced earlier, the three described below are relevant to narratives, and the reader is encouraged to review Cerwén's work to find more (2019, 2020).

Tranquillity by contrast, is linked to the *cut-out* effect introduced earlier and is an aural spatial contrast which can induce tranquillity through the sudden transition from a loud environment to a quiet one (Cerwén, 2020). I experienced this tranquillity effect in the *Old Pottery* case study, described in Chapter six, on entering the kilns. In this case, there was a sudden transition from a loud to a quiet environment, with the effect that small sounds seemed to amplify, adding to the clarity of the soundscape. This principle was also employed by sound artists Will Schrimshaw and Jamie Allen for their *Acoustic Subtraction* installations at Kielder Forest, Northumberland and other locations. Here, they played white noise for 20 minutes and stopped abruptly, cleansing people's listening and encouraging them to listen more (Schrimshaw, 2010).

Shrouded sounds refer to sources of sound that can be heard but not seen. They can add mystery to a place, inviting further exploration (Cerwén, 2020), which was the case, for example, with the breaking of waves and stridulation of crickets during my walk at Leslie Street Spit, narrated earlier.

Hide and reveal is an example of an aural walking narrative, where sounds are hidden and revealed as the user moves along a path, which could again invite further exploration of the spaces alongside the path (ibid.). This strategy applies to both sound events and propagation.

Strategies at the listener

Perceptual *aural effects* can also invite further explorations of a place, as listening can evoke thoughts and memories and alter the engagement and perception of a place.

Two perceptual *aural effects* are useful here:

Anamnesis is the instinctive recall of a memory through listening and can bring back a past atmosphere to the current experience of place (Augoyard and Torgue, 2005). Augoyard and Torgue emphasise the role of the listener in triggering this effect rather than that of the sound. Anamnesis might be linked to everyday spatial experiences, where temporal changes can bring back memories (ibid). Therefore, an urban design that encourages everyday uses and has a varied layout with changing experiences could be conducive to *anamnesis*. *Anamnesis* can also be linked to particular spaces and cultures (ibid.). For example, sounds specific to a culture, such as the yearly thunderous shooting display in Hondarribia, or the song played by the parading bands on that day, can trigger memories of events in previous years. Regarding spatial *anamnesis*, this can be triggered by a space that reminds us of another. In a large-scale masterplan, for example, spatial *anamnesis* could be achieved by a series of thresholds into a site that might have similar configurations, elements and materialities and can help with legibility and wayfinding and linking memories to places through listening.

Remanence refers to the perceptual listening effect of perceiving a sound that can no longer be heard, just as the sound event disappears, which is an aural illusion (ibid.). For example, after hearing the last bell calls in Hondarribia, they resonate in the ear for a while, perhaps due to their previous domination of aural space. On a walk in rural Northumberland, I experienced a similar effect in a different setting while following a path that ran close to a small flowing burn for quite some time. When the path split away from the burn and led me to a forest, the sound of the flowing burn seemed to remain in my ears for some time, even though recordings of the soundwalk tell a different story. In design, this perceptual effect can be linked to *soundmarks*, which can remain in the ears even after the sound event can no longer be heard, thus prolonging their physical effect.

These pages have taken us through core design principles and accompanying aural strategies, which can be incorporated into any design, regardless of scale or location. The reader is invited to test and adapt these strategies in their future designs. Next, we move on to discussing auralisations and their use throughout the life of a project.

Auralisations

As we observed in the last section, narrative, imagination and creativity are key drivers of the design process. Thinking through sound and listening can be integral to this creative and iterative design process. Auralisations, as aural counterparts of projection drawings and visualisations, can help at different stages of the iterative design process. Auralisations can be imagined as soundscape compositions which range from those that capture the existing soundscape to those that help us think creatively and spatially and communicate proposals in an immersive and affective format. One of the most difficult things to do in the representation of landscape architecture and urban design is to capture the passage of time, as environments are constantly evolving and changing, and a drawing only ever captures a single moment in time. Auralisations can help us to overcome this shortcoming, thus expanding the scope of visualisations.

Landscape architect James Corner distinguishes between projection drawings *from the ground*, such as survey and analysis drawings, and those projected *onto the ground*, such as masterplans which propose a new unrealised landscape (Corner, 1992). Between these two stages, between the existing and the proposed, the real and the ideal, landscape architecture practice Gross Max finds the space for creating visuals that are not just representational but also transformational (Hooftman, 2022). These images demonstrate intention, yet they are highly speculative and let people experience for themselves, using their imagination (ibid.).

Barry Truax proposes another practice sequence for sound compositions: *sonification, phonography* and *virtual soundscapes* (Truax, 2012). *Sonification* can be understood as the aural counterpart of data visualisation (ibid.). *Phonography* is the documentation or mapping of the world through field recordings (ibid.). Finally, *virtual soundscapes* are virtually composed soundscapes that can emerge from a specific context or an imagined one and trigger 'the inner world of memory, metaphor or symbolism' (ibid., pp. 194–195). In between *phonography* and *virtual soundscapes*, Truax situates a range of practices with varying degrees of abstraction, but where both context and sounds are identifiable (ibid.).

Auralisations for landscape and urban design can be envisaged following a three-stage sequence that maps to both the drawing and the sound composition sequences introduced above: *phonographs*, as projection from the ground and documentation; *aural speculations*, as spatial speculations that emerge from the context and are situated between the real and imaginary, and *auralisations*, as aural projections onto the ground (Figure 7.6).

Phonographs

Field recordings can be used as part of the site inventory to document the existing soundscape. These can be done with a handheld recorder or mobile phone and can be the starting point for more abstracted auralisations later in the design process. It is useful to record for at least five minutes at each key space to capture a wide range

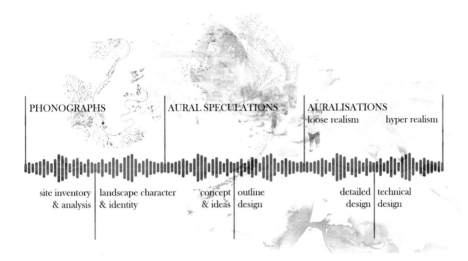

Figure 7.6 Three-stage sequence of auralisations mapped to design stages.

of activities and uses and have sufficient material for future work. Sections of the recordings might be rendered unusable due to many factors, for example, someone stopping to talk on the phone right beside you, a gush of wind, a car that parks next to you with the motor running, an aeroplane passing by, etc. These all represent the site but might not be the desired focus for auralisations.

Depending on the nature of the project, it is also often useful to record at different times of the day, on different days and in different seasons. The soundscape can change considerably from one week to the next and according to the weather conditions.

A wide range of audio and music-making software is available for the simple manipulation of field recordings and the production of other forms of auralisation. These include Audacity (free), Reaper and Adobe Audition (part of Adobe creative suite).

Gateshead-based acousticians, Apex Acoustics, featured in a case study in the next chapter, have started to use their field recordings in innovative and creative ways during the early stages of a project. Apex Acoustics use field recordings as the aural counterpart of precedent images to help clients choose how they would like different spaces in their buildings to sound. A similar approach can be employed for outdoor spaces, using field recordings alongside precedent images to demonstrate how different spaces might be experienced.

Examples of field recordings used as part of the site inventory and analysis are provided in the next chapter.

Aural speculations

Aural speculations are situated between the real and the imagined, between the existing and proposed. These *aural speculations* can help us develop and express a narrative for the site, as for the *Old Pottery* case study. They do not represent a proposed scheme but express intention and spatial speculation. As is the case for the overall narrative of the site, aural concepts or narratives and their expression through *aural speculations* can emerge from any contextual aspect that triggers the designer's creativity and imagination.

Aural speculations can vary in degree of abstraction and can start from field recordings of the site, manipulated through software such as Audacity, Reaper, and Adobe Audition. We do not need to become sound artists or musicians to compose *aural speculations*, as these can be straightforward technical manipulations. Designers might also seek to collaborate with sound artists and musicians for more elaborated sonic outputs.

Auralisations: from loose reality to simulation or hyperreality

Once the design process starts, *auralisations* can help the designer think about how their schemes might sound and be experienced in a way that parallels how different types of visualisations are employed. Visualisations range from illustrative to technical (Landscape Institute, 2019). Illustrative visualisations showcase a development's essence and communicate proposals to stakeholders and clients (Ruiz Arana, 2021). Technical visualisations are produced as part of Townscape and Visual Impact Assessments or Landscape and Visual Appraisals and are accurate, objective and unbiased. They enable local authorities to assess the effects of development on the existing character of an area (ibid.).

Illustrative visualisations, in turn, are varied and range from *loose realism* to *hyperrealism* (Kullmann, 2014). *Loose realism* images are developed early in the design process to showcase the essence of the development and test ideas before committing to them and, as such, are invaluable tools for designers. *Hyperrealism* images tend to be produced towards the end of the design process once the design has been fully detailed, and they are attempts to represent the proposals as accurately as possible (ibid.). *Loose real* images have the advantage of being open to interpretation by 'requiring a point of view by the author and the viewer', as well as being within most designers' drawing and technical skills (ibid., p. 30). *Hyperreal* images have certain disadvantages: they restrict interpretation, as they appear so real, they require advanced technical skills from designers, and they are time-consuming. (ibid). *Hyperreal* images can also unintentionally mislead viewers, presenting a future that will never be fully depicted. There are usually inaccuracies in these visualisations. For example, they may be temporal inaccuracies, such as mature trees shown alongside pristine, recently installed hard surfacing. These visualisations also portray usage inaccuracies, with many activities taking place simultaneously, which could never happen in real life (ibid.).

Through this short overview of visualisations, I have demonstrated the value of *loose realism* images for the everyday practice of landscape architecture and urban design to make a case for their aural counterpart, *loose realism* auralisations.

Loose realism auralisations

Loose realism auralisations are quick to produce, everyday auralisations that help designers think and communicate draft ideas and plans. Similarly to the sonic speculations introduced earlier, these auralisations can vary in their degree of abstraction and can start from field recordings of the site. This is the case for the auralisation included in case studies *High Street Goodsyard and Rewilding the Gardiner Expressway*. In both cases, the sound compositions or auralisations started from field recordings in the site or nearby comparable spaces.

Hyperrealism and technical auralisations

Hyperreal or *technical* auralisations seek to represent proposals aurally as accurately as possible. Simulation software for indoor environments is readily available, although it requires technical skills from acousticians. For outdoor environments, technical auralisations are an emergent field of research and development (Hornikx, 2016; Kang, 2019). These auralisations will likely remain highly technical and time-consuming and will only likely be produced once the design has been agreed. Due to technicality and costs, these auralisations are also likely to remain out of reach for most landscape architects and urban designers, and collaboration with acousticians would help develop them.

Between *loose realism* and *hyper-realism* auralisations, we find tools such as the *City Ditty* soundscape design digital tool developed by *Sounds in the City* partnership. *City Ditty* seeks to enable built environment professionals to design with sound. *City Ditty* allows users to design a soundscape by adding *sound objects* to a 3D city model and allows for temporal variation (Yanaky, Tyler, and Guastavino, 2023). Some existing 3D modelling software also allows sound simulation, such as *Revit Enscape TM*, by adding sound sources to the model.

Whilst awaiting further development of modelling software for auralisations, *phonographs*, *aural imaginaries* and *loose realism*, auralisations have the potential to enhance everyday practice. All these forms of auralisations can:

- Help designers think creatively and spatially through sound-making and listening
- Help communicate proposals in an immersive, open-ended and affective format, with the potential to evoke the inner sound world of listeners and engage them early in the design process
- Foster collaborations with sound artists to develop a sonic narrative and enrich the design
- Spark an interest in sound amongst stakeholders, clients, and wider design teams
- Be produced through different techniques and for different purposes, adapted to the skills of different designers: from simple field recording arrangements to abstracted compositions
- Complement later auralisations aimed at stimulating designed landscapes

References

Aletta, F., Kang, J. and Axelsson, Ö. (2016) 'Soundscape descriptors and a conceptual framework for developing predictive soundscape models', *Landscape and Urban Planning*, 149, pp. 65–74. doi: 10.1016/j.landurbplan.2016.02.001.

Aletta, F., Oberman, T. and Kang, J. (2018) 'Associations between positive health-related effects and soundscapes perceptual constructs: A systematic review', *International Journal of Environmental Research and Public Health*, 15(11), pp. 1–15. doi: 10.3390/ijerph15112392.

Augoyard, J.-F. and Torgue, H. (2005) *Sonic experience: A guide to everyday sounds*. 1st englis. Montreal, Ithaca: McGill-Queen's University Press.

Axelsson, Ö. (2015) 'How to measure soundscape quality', *Proceedings of Euronoise 2015, C. Glorieux, Ed.*, Maastricht, pp. 1477–1481. Available at: https://www.conforg.fr/euronoise2015/proceedings/data/articles/000067.pdf

Axelsson, Ö., Nilsson, M. E. and Berglund, B. (2010) 'A principal components model of soundscape perceptiona)', *The Journal of the Acoustical Society of America*, 128(5), pp. 2836–2846. doi: 10.1121/1.3493436.

Baines, B. (2021) *GROSS.MAX, The Berlage keynotes*. Available at: https://www.youtube.com/watch?v=VB4wjMN0rkU (Accessed: 12 June 2023).

BSI (The British Standards Institution) (2018) 'ISO / TS 12913 - 2 : 2018 BSI Standards Publication Acoustics — Soundscape', BSI Standards Publication.

Cain, R., Jennings, P. and Poxon, J. (2013) 'The development and application of the emotional dimensions of a soundscape', *Applied Acoustics*, 74(2), pp. 232–239. doi: 10.1016/j.apacoust.2011.11.006.

Cerwén, G. (2019) 'Listening to Japanese gardens: An autoethnographic study on the soundscape action design tool', *International Journal of Environmental Research and Public Health*, 16(23), pp. 1–30. doi: 10.3390/ijerph16234648.

Cerwén, G. (2020) 'Listening to Japanese gardens II: Expanding the soundscape action design tool', *Journal of Urban Design*, 25(5), pp. 607–628. doi: 10.1080/13574809.2020.1782183.

Coensel, B. De, Vanwetswinkel, S. and Botteldooren, D. (2011) 'Effects of natural sounds on the perception of road traffic noise', *The Journal of the Acoustical Society of America*, 129(4), pp. EL148–EL153. doi: 10.1121/1.3567073.

Cormier, C. (2015) 'Claude Cormier happy design: Current projects'. Available at: https://vimeo.com/111575234.

Corner, J. (1992) 'Representation and landscape: Drawing and making in the landscape medium', *Word and Image*, 8(3), pp. 243–275. doi: 10.1080/02666286.1992.10435840.

Davies, W. J., *et al.* (2013) 'Perception of soundscapes: An interdisciplinary approach', *Applied Acoustics*, 74(2), pp. 224–231. doi: 10.1016/j.apacoust.2012.05.010.

Dee, C. (2001) *Form and fabric in landscape architecture: A visual introduction*. online. London: Spon Press.

Fuchs, T. and Koch, S. C. (2014) 'Embodied affectivity: On moving and being moved', *Frontiers in Psychology*, 5(June), pp. 1–12. doi: 10.3389/fpsyg.2014.00508.

H+N+S Landscape Architects (2023) *Land art park Buitenschot, H+N+S*. Available at: https://www.hnsland.nl/en/projects/land-art-park-buitenschot/ (Accessed: 14 June 2023).

Hall, L. (2016) *Walking with crickets*, Lisa Hall. Available at: http://www.lisa--hall.co.uk/walking-with-crickets.html (Accessed: 2 November 2018).

Hedfors, P. and Berg, P. G. (2003) 'The sounds of two landscape settings: Auditory concepts for physical planning and design', *Landscape Research*, 28(3), pp. 245–263. doi: 10.1080/01426390306524.

Hickey, M. (2023) *Through an indigenous lens: A shift from placemaking to placekeeping, evergreen*. Available at: https://www.evergreen.ca/blog/entry/through-an-indigenous-lens-a-shift-from-placemaking-to-placekeeping/ (Accessed: 23 June 2023).

Hooftman, E. (2022) 'Every picture tells a story', in Amoroso, N. and Holland, M. (eds) *Representing landscapes: One hundred years of visual communication*. New York: Routledge, pp. 199–208. doi: 10.4324/9781003183402-24.

Hornikx, M. (2016) 'Ten questions concerning computational urban acoustics', *Building and Environment*, 106, pp. 409–421. doi: 10.1016/j.buildenv.2016.06.028.

Jackson, S., *et al.* (2008) 'Tranquillity mapping: Developing a robust methodology for planning support', *Report to the Campaign to Protect Rural England*, Available at: Tranquillity Mapping: Developing a Robust Methodology for Planning Support (cpre.org.uk)

Japan Ministry of the Environment (1996) *100 soundscapes of Japan*. Available at: https://www.env.go.jp/search/search_result.html?cx=003400915082829768606%3Awiib6pxwlwc&ie=UTF-8&q=100+soundscape&sa=+.

Kang, J. (2019) 'Urban sound planning - A soundscape approach', *Proceedings of Acoustics 2019*. Capa Schanck, Victoria, Australia: Available at: p11.pdf (acoustics.asn.au)

Kaplan, R. and Kaplan, S. (1989) *The experience of nature: A psychological perspective*. Cambridge: Cambridge University Press.

Kullmann, K. (2014) 'Hyper-realism and loose-reality: The limitations of digital realism and alternative principles in landscape design visualization', *Journal of Landscape Architecture*, 9(3), pp. 20–31. doi: 10.1080/18626033.2014.968412.

Landscape Institute (2019) 'Visual representation of development proposals', *Landscape Institute Technical Guidance Note*, 06/19, pp. 1–58.

Levenhagen, M. J., *et al.* (2021) 'Ecosystem services enhanced through soundscape management link people and wildlife', *People and Nature*, 3(1), pp. 176–189. doi: 10.1002/pan3.10156.

McCartney, A. (2014) 'Soundwalking: Creating moving environmental sound narratives', in Gopinath, S. and Stanyek, J. (eds) *The Oxford handbook of mobile music studies, Volume 2*, New York: Oxford University Press, pp. 1–27. doi: 10.1093/oxfordhb/9780199913657.013.008.

Mitchell, A., Aletta, F. and Kang, J. (2022) 'How to analyse and represent quantitative soundscape data', *JASA Express Letters*, 2(3), p. 037201. doi: 10.1121/10.0009794.

Natural England (2023) *Green infrastructure planning and design guide: Designing nature-rich, healthy, climate-resilient, and thriving places.* Available at: https://designatedsites.naturalengland.org.uk/GreenInfrastructure/downloads/Design Guide - Green Infrastructure Framework.pdf.

OED online (2023) *design, v., Oxford University Press.* Available at: https://www.oed.com/view/Entry/50841?rskey=16BETF&result=2&isAdvanced=false#eid (Accessed: 23 June 2023).

Project for Public Spaces (2022) *PLACEMAKING what If we built our cities around places ?, A Placemaking Primer.* Available at: http://www.pps.org/wp-content/uploads/2016/10/Oct-2016-placemaking-booklet.pdf.

Ruiz Arana, U. (2021) 'Creative auralisations for public realm design: A case study', poster presented at *Urban sound symposium*, Ghent University (online).

Russell, J. A. (1980) 'A circumplex model of affect', *Journal of Personality and Social Psychology*, 39(6), pp. 1161–1178. doi: 10.1037/h0077714.

Schafer, R. M. (1970) *The book of noise.* Vancouver: Priv. print by Price Print.

Schafer, R. M. (1977) *The soundscape: Our Sonic environment and the tuning of the world.* Rochester, VT: Destiny Books.

Schrimshaw, W. (2010) *Acoustic substraction, will schrimshaw.* Available at: https://willschrimshaw.net/acoustic_subtraction.html (Accessed: 2 November 2018).

Timmermans, M. (2014) 'Reading a landscape', *Topos*, 88, pp. 20–27.

Truax, B. (1984) *Acoustic communication, Springer handbook of Ocean engineering.* Norwood, NJ: Ablex Publishing Corporation. doi: 10.1007/978-3-319-16649-0_15.

Truax, B. (2012) 'Sound, listening and place: The aesthetic dilemma', *Organised Sound*, 17(3), pp. 193–201. doi: 10.1017/S1355771811000380.

Van Renterghem, T. (2014) 'Guidelines for optimizing road traffic noise shielding by non-deep tree belts', *Ecological Engineering,* 69(August), pp. 276–286 Available at: http://journal.um-surabaya.ac.id/index.php/JKM/article/view/2203.

Van Renterghem, T. and Botteldooren, D. (2012) 'On the choice between walls and berms for road traffic noise shielding including wind effects', *Landscape and Urban Planning,* 105 (3), pp. 199–210.

Van Renterghem, T. and Botteldooren, D. (2016) 'View on outdoor vegetation reduces noise annoyance for dwellers near busy roads', *Landscape and Urban Planning*, 148 (April), pp. 203–215. doi: 10.1016/j.landurbplan.2015.12.018.

Van Renterghem, T., De Coensel, B. and Botteldooren, D. (2013) 'Loudness evaluation of road traffic noise abatement by tree belts', *Proceedings of the 42nd international congress and exposition on noise control engineering (Internoise 2013)*, Innsbruck, Austria

Wainwright, E. (2023) *Sounding senses: Inhabiting riverside* (unpublished).

Waterman, T. (2022) *The fundamentals of landscape architecture*. 2nd ed. London: Bloomsbury Visual Arts.

Yanaky, R., Tyler, D. and Guastavino, C. (2023) 'City ditty: An immersive soundscape sketchpad for professionals of the built environment', *Applied Sciences (Switzerland)*, 13(3), pp. 1–26. doi: 10.3390/app13031611.

Chapter Eight

Composing the soundscape in practice

The High Street Goodsyard, Glasgow

We concluded the site assessment and characterisation by defining the existing car park as a *non-place*. Yet, hidden below layers of tarmac flew the Molendinar burn, carrying with it past stories of the site. The proposed landscape narrative drew from these stories as a hook to embed the proposed neighbourhood in its historical context and confer a sense of place and belonging to it. The landscape narrative was accompanied by principles that sought to provide a legible, coherent, and varied public realm through a series of interconnected character areas (Figure 8.1).

We proposed a set of aural strategies to implement and reinforce the landscape narrative and principles for the site, as summarised in Figure 8.2, with key strategies highlighted in bold.

Narrative

Aural narratives

Early in the design process, we discovered that the Molendinar Burn flows culverted underneath the proposed central core of the development, dissecting the site in a north-south direction. The Molendinar was once instrumental to the development of medieval Glasgow, as it provided water for the mills and craft industry in the area and shaped the development of the local landscape and built environment around it.

While researching the history of the Molendinar, we came across hydrophone recordings of the burn by *Submerge Sounds* (2015), which drove the development of

DOI: 10.4324/9781003202981-11

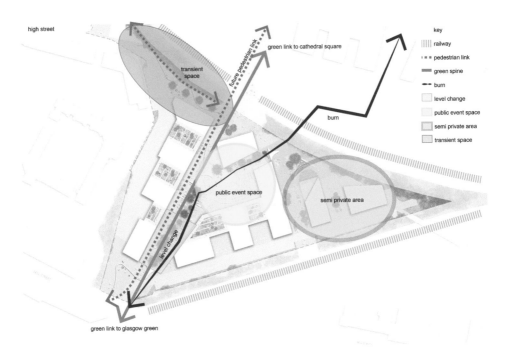

Figure 8.1 Proposed character areas and circulation, Credit: Oobe Ltd.

the narrative for the site: to uncover, through listening, the burn. Listening to the burn would enable new residents to connect with the historical layers of the site as new chapters for the site were starting to unfold. Sound and listening, therefore, would provide a connection between the past and the present, between hidden and exposed landscape layers.

Hide and reveal

Hide and reveal is an aural effect coined by Cerwén to describe the curation of an experience through a site where sounds are hidden and revealed as the listeners move through the site (2020). We proposed several listening pods alongside the length of the culverted river where residents and the wider community could listen, through hydrophones, to the water flowing underneath the site. These would become spots for focused listening to water, to invite the listener to imagine what the site once was and what it could become. The hidden sounds of the Molendinar would be revealed

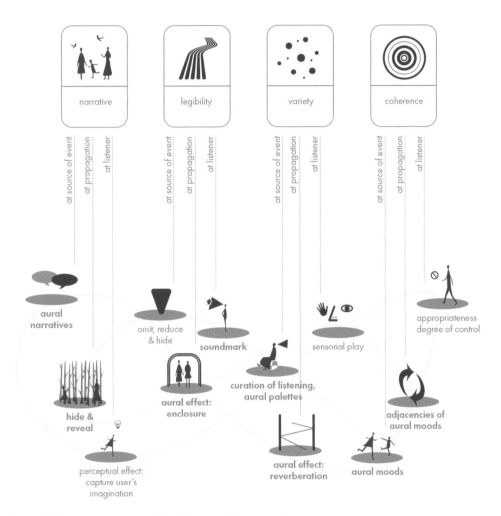

Figure 8.2 Aural principles and strategies drafted for the site.

at these listening pods and be hidden again as the listener traversed the central spine of the site (Figure 8.3).

Over ground drifts of planting were proposed to trace the flow of the burn in between the listening pods. The planting would subtly expose the Molendinar's course overground, where it could no longer be heard through hydrophones (Figure 8.4). By exposing the river through a myriad of ways, we argued, the rich history of the site would also be exposed. The aural narrative was thus integrated

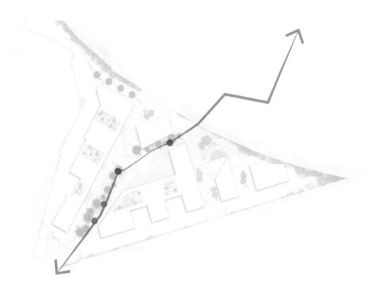

Figure 8.3 Proposed listening pods to trace culverted Molendinar burn, Credit: Oobe Ltd.

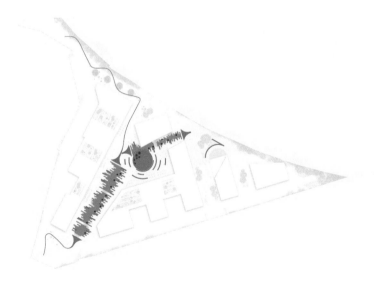

Figure 8.4 Proposed planting tracking flow of Molendinar burn over ground, sculptural trumpets and vibrant core, Credit: Oobe Ltd.

with other design principles to uncover the stories buried on the site and respond to the brief and the needs of the new communities that would inhabit the space.

Legibility and variety

Enclosure and reverberation

The public realm for the site was organised into a series of interconnected spaces for the community to come together: a main square at the centre of the development, a range of smaller and quieter activity spaces along the green spine, and key thresholds and transition spaces into the site. The square was enclosed by new residential buildings almost in its entirety, creating a secluded environment for residents to enjoy (Figure 8.5). The enclosure would help contain sound events within the site, with a degree of reverberation to add to its vibrancy, and prevent filtering sounds onto the site.

Figure 8.5 Proposed action plan, Credit: Oobe Ltd.

New listening experiences

New listening experiences were curated per the proposed aural moods described later. In developing these listening experiences, many factors were considered simultaneously. For example, the drifts of planting would increase biodiversity within the development, which in turn would sound and provide amenity value. Listening experiences were thus never considered in isolation.

Soundmarks: aural and visual

Sculptural trumpets were proposed at the gateways and key locations in the development to aid with wayfinding and circulation and express the site's history (Figure 8.6).

Coherence

Aural moods and adjacencies

The soundscape assessment concluded that the site was uneventful and unpleasant. The most pleasant character area of the site was the semi-natural boundary, and

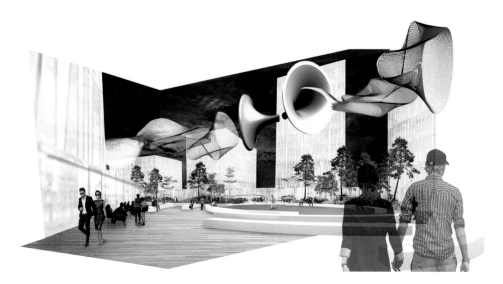

Figure 8.6 Sculptural trumpets in the public square, Credit: Oobe Ltd.

the proposed development sought to retain the most established vegetation within it.

In line with the landscape proposals, we sought to develop a series of aural moods to tie in with the character of the proposed spaces (Figure 8.7). These would be achieved by facilitating an appropriate variety of sound events for each space that could coexist, and through the enclosure created by the building layouts and landscape elements.

Vibrant core

The main public realm space of the scheme, a square at the centre of the development, was set to become its vibrant heart, with an amphitheatre and a variety of seating opportunities for everyday use. The enclosure of the space would mostly contain sound events within the site and prevent the existing traffic drone from adjacent roads from filtering into the site.

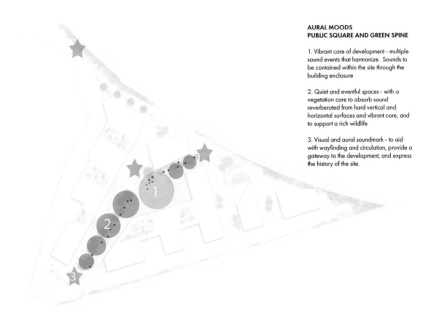

AURAL MOODS
PUBLIC SQUARE AND GREEN SPINE

1. Vibrant core of development - multiple sound events that harmonize. Sounds to be contained within the site through the building enclosure

2. Quiet and eventful spaces - with a vegetation core to absorb sound reverberated from hard vertical and horizontal surfaces and vibrant core, and to support a rich wildlife

3. Visual and aural soundmark - to aid with wayfinding and circulation, provide a gateway to the development, and express the history of the site.

Figure 8.7 Proposed aural moods.

Quiet and eventful spaces

Quieter spaces were developed, steaming from the square in both directions. These included quiet play, such as outdoor seesaws, to invite residents to slow down and engage with these spaces. To aid sound absorption, a low-mounded planted centre was proposed to absorb sound reverberated from hard vertical and horizontal surfaces and vibrant core and to tie in with the overall concept for the landscape design (e.g., to expose the Molendinar burn over ground). The vegetation would also be home to wildlife and connect with the retained semi-natural boundary of the site (Figure 8.8).

Auralisations

Oobe was invited for an interview to present the design, and I took the opportunity to develop an auralisation of the central spine of the development, to accompany the main site section.

Figure 8.8 Quieter streetscapes with mounding, Credit: Oobe Ltd.

Figure 8.9 Snapshot of video showcasing section through site (Soundtrack 8.1), Section credit: Oobe Ltd.

This auralisation was a loose realism auralisation: a simple soundscape composition and spatial imaginary created from hydrophone and field recordings in Glasgow and similar spaces in the north of the UK. The auralisation portrayed a walk through the site a morning in May, an aid the listener in imagining the spaces, habitats and inhabitants encountered along the way. Section and auralisation were combined into a video. The video starts with the section in black and white and gradually turns into colour as the auralisation plays, and the listener walks across the section from one end to another (Figure 8.9 and Soundtrack 8.1).

In conversation with Apex Acoustics

On 7 July 2022, I participated in an evening soundwalk along the Ouseburn Valley, Newcastle, organized by Apex Acoustics for the Yorkshire & NE Branch of the UK Institute of Acoustics (Figure 8.10). The Ouseburn Valley, known as Newcastle's cultural and creative quarter, is a vibrant post-industrial area that has undergone substantial development in the last three decades. The walk, thus, provided the opportunity to assess a rich and varied soundscape. We walked in silence for the duration of the walk, trailing the Ouseburn and listening and filling out a questionnaire (following ISO 12913-2 method A) at key points of the walk. The walk also provided the opportunity to engage with acousticians currently leading on soundscape assessment and design. Following a fascinating discussion with Jack Harvie-Clark, director of Apex Acoustics, on how they apply the *soundscape approach* in practice, I invited Jack

Figure 8.10 Participants filling in the questionnaire during the Ouseburn soundwalk, Credit: Jack Harvie-Clark, Apex Acoustics Ltd.

to my office to learn more about their innovative soundscape work. What follows is an edited version of our lengthy chat on all things soundscape.

Jack Harvie-Clark (JHC): Can we improve the acoustics of designs by employing a perceptual approach? This is the main question for me, which in turn raises a million other questions. Whose opinion? How do you measure what is good? How do you influence the design process and other consultants and clients involved? The ISO 12913 standards are slowly developing answers to these questions. Yet, they are heavily influenced by academics and have been applied mostly to urban public spaces rather than private or commercial buildings and spaces.

When the CoHUT project came along, a cohousing residential development in Newcastle, it was a great opportunity to apply a *soundscape approach* and work with future residents, which is very unusual [for a residential development]. Most of the residential developments we work on are led by big house builders or developers, the properties will be sold or rented, and residents are never involved at the start of the design process.

We engaged with residents, asking them about their concerns regarding acoustics on the site and in the buildings, and they had all sorts of concerns and questions. Such as, if the buildings were sealed from outside noise, would residents be able to hear their neighbours more? The question that I was most interested in, how would opening windows to mitigate overheating affect noise levels, was of no interest to them, even though the noise levels of the site are at the threshold of industry guidance that suggests you should not have to rely on opening windows to mitigate overheating.

We also led soundwalks on site and online (Figure 8.11). Although the site is small, it has a varied soundscape. On one side, the site overlooks Scotswood Road, which is 90 metres away and has heavy, steady traffic. Traffic noise is continuous. On the other side, the soundscape is dominated by traffic going up the hill, with a sharp bend just by the site. Therefore, traffic noise is intermittent and unpleasant, perceived as a danger because it approaches directly and comes very close. Perceived

Figure 8.11 CoHUT on-site soundwalk, February 2021, Jack Harvie-Clark, Apex Acoustics Ltd.

pleasantness did not correspond with average noise levels at these two ends of the site. But we didn't know how to use that information because plans had already been drawn for the site.

We couldn't go back in the design process, but we wanted residents to think about how the site might be perceived and how they might want to modify or use it. Interestingly, the architects had proposed a building layout with a courtyard. And because you have roads on both aspects, that would have been our suggestion too to create a protected aspect for all residents. Often, architects, through their proposals, carry out the most important aspects of acoustic design.

Do you think they consciously thought of sound on this site?

I asked, and they sought to create a protected place from the wind and a warmer place, with higher buildings at the back and lower at the front. They were partly thinking about the sound, but it was primarily for creating a protected thermal environment overall.

When they came on the soundwalk and stood at different places and listened for a few minutes, some of the residents were surprised at how much it helped them think about sound. Some concluded they didn't want to live on certain sides of the building. Others who had experience of living exposed to busy roads were not concerned by traffic noise.

Did you then propose any design solutions?

After the soundwalks, we did auralisations to demonstrate how it would sound inside different aspects of the building, daytime and nighttime, with the windows closed, partially open and fully open. We used the attenuation for the windows that we had calculated for the planning report, which provides more attenuation at high frequencies than low frequencies, and therefore traffic noise feels more dominant when you close the windows. We played the auralisations over Zoom, and people noticed they paid more attention to birdsong than during the in-situ soundwalks. People preferred the auralisations with open windows because they could hear more birdsong, which surprised me. That's different from how we have to design buildings for decibel levels!

Yes, because it also depends on the circumstances. Some residents complain of birdsong waking them up early in the morning. And not all bird calls are perceived as pleasant.

Seagulls, for example. This is a question that I've just come back to recently. I've been writing a guide for industry on what sources of noise should be included in building regulations for overheating. And I thought we should exclude all natural and meteorological sounds because building regulations shouldn't regulate those.

And all the epidemiological evidence on adverse effects of noise regards transportation noise, not natural sounds.

Other sources of noise that might cause anxiety are not captured currently in noise maps either, such as recreation or nightlife noise.

This is a concern in the city centre of Newcastle, as well. There's tension within the Council, on the one hand, wanting to encourage the nighttime economy and the adverse impact that might have on residents, on the other. Now that many offices in the city centre have been vacated, developers are trying to turn them into residential units. There is not enough guidance on how those buildings should be designed for residents to provide a suitable environment. For example, should you allow fixed windows [i.e., build them to be unopenable] or ensure the indoor environment can be managed with the windows closed but allow occupants to open them if they choose? At the minute, we are addressing these questions on a case-by-case basis, and the *soundscape approach* is a great way to manage them, as it involves residents.

A recent example we were involved with was a nightclub in the city centre, which was taken over and refurbished with a bigger sound system during the COVID-19 lockdown. The building is very poorly insulated for a nightclub. When the nightclub started operating again, it had been very quiet. Some residents are in a narrow lane to the south, which is all enclosed, with no big roads nearby. Residents raised complaints about music noise, and sometimes the complaints were on nights when the nightclub had not been operating. We did a test for the nightclub and were shocked at how much noise was coming out. They would have to carry out substantial work to address the noise, and they had just refurbished. Therefore, I suggested, why don't we ask the residents what sounds affect them to see whether we could improve their sound environment? We sent letters to all relevant residential addresses with a QR code to complete a questionnaire. We also held a public meeting on Zoom to explore the topic further, and only two people turned up. One person was distraught by the low-frequency noise, and another found it annoying. With the person who found the low-frequency noise intolerable, we agreed to do a test on their flat from the nightclub. We found they could hear low-frequency sounds way before anybody else because they had very high hearing acuity. DEFRA (Department for Environment, Food and Rural Affairs) published guidance on low-frequency noise identifies a threshold curve above which environmental health should investigate low-frequency noise problems. That resident could hear around 10 dB below that curve. It seemed like a reasonable balance to prevent the nightclub from exceeding that curve in their flat to reach a compromise.

This a fascinating example of trying to balance different users and priorities. What about the scheme in Durham that you are currently working on?

The former Durham Light Infantry Museum is located south of the Civic Centre, which is being refurbished as a cultural venue and art gallery. It is in the early stages of design (RIBA stage 2). I put a soundscape proposal together, which the client agreed to. We have primarily focused on internal spaces. We measured different art galleries and museums to understand what the client wanted to inform the acoustic design. For example, the Laing Art Gallery in Newcastle, a traditional gallery with big reverberant spaces and classical acoustics, sounds very imposing. When it's lightly occupied, it makes people be quiet. When it's busy, it gets very noisy because it doesn't have sound absorption at all. Other modern building examples included the Imperial War Museum in Manchester and the Sunderland Glass Centre. We measured and made binaural recordings in cafes, gallery spaces and entrance halls. We used the recordings to create aural mood boards and asked the client: are you looking for this sort of sound or this sort?

Were they surprised by that approach?

They were surprisingly not surprised, even though, to my knowledge, nobody had ever done this before. People do auralisations, of course, but much further down the design process because they take a lot of effort and are usually employed to approve the design. It was very useful to have the confirmation at the beginning of how the client wanted it to sound. For the cafe, we also talked about inclusion and how noisy places are difficult for some people. We suggested having acoustic refuges through booth seating where people could have some privacy and get out of the noise.

Have you used the approach of sound precedents with planners?

Not yet, as the *soundscape approach* does not replace planning requirements. In the legislation, the noise report for planning is about whether the living spaces can meet reasonable noise levels with windows closed, creating rooms that aren't exposed to too much noise, and detailing how to control that noise. The *Malings* residential development at the Ouseburn Valley is an interesting example of an alternative approach to noise control. The Tyne bar, next door to the development, has bands regularly playing outside. Yet, as far as we know, nobody in the *Malings* complains to the Council about that noise. I suspect it is partly because Fred, the landlord of the Tyne bar, is very good at liaising with people. When people express dissatisfaction with the music, he invites them to lunch with him at the Tyne Bar and is open about how he tries to minimize the noise impact. When it was first built, the developer gave new residents a voucher to spend at the Tyne bar, which meant they were actively introduced to him. I guess that the residents have a certain sympathy for how Fred runs the Tyne – he's very progressive, doesn't want the *wrong sort of people* drinking there, and is meticulous at keeping the street outside clean and tidy. We are investigating the relationship between Fred and the residents at the minute through a student project to better understand how the acoustic conflict is managed apparently so well. The music programme is published, so residents know when music will be on, and Fred keeps the music sets to limited and regular times.

That approach gives residents a degree of control. If you know there will be noise, you prepare yourself for it. Or you move to another part of the flat, to get away from the noise, if you can.

Control is absolutely key. If there is noise, and if you don't feel you have control, it is much more annoying. Control is even implied in the word noise, because it is sometimes described as sound you don't want to hear. Considering how much control people have over their sound environments should always be the starting point of soundscape assessments.

Old Pottery, Corbridge

We concluded the Old Pottery's soundscape assessment in Chapter 6 with a sound composition, *Murmuration I*, that expressed the aural identity of the site, as well as a summary of opportunities and constraints for the soundscape. From there, we developed a series of landscape design principles and accompanying aural strategies to inform the design of the site that also built on the initial themes developed by the architects.

Landscape design principles:

- To develop a narrative for the site, building on the historical remnants of the Pottery, and the existing identity and character of the site, and making use of the aural effects created by the architecture
- To enable a permanent home for the family, with a variety of spaces to enjoy, and a destination and temporary residence for visitors, again with varied spaces and activities.
- To enable a legible and coherent site, with clear separation of private, semi-private and public spaces, and logical circulation and wayfinding.
- To conserve and enhance existing habitats – working with the existing vegetation, we sought to provide a balance between preserving buildings and allowing a variety of (human) uses, and enabling natural and semi-natural habitats to thrive.

	strategies at source	strategies at propagation	strategies at listener
narrative	Development of an aural narrative to express the historic remnants of the Pottery and drive the design.	Facilitate focused listening at key points relating to historical and contemporary rhythms of the site (e.g., by pond)	Make use of perceptual effects related to the historic remnants (e.g., perceived mystery and absence)
variety	Facilitate a variety of new sound events (contemporary rhythms) & develop a varied & coherent aural palette.	Utilise existing aural effects (e.g., cut-out at kilns) to provide variety in listening & a listening journey	Multisensorial design: propose elements to target all senses
legibility & coherence	Increase positive and decreasing negative listening experiences. Facilitating aural moods appropriate to character.	Aural effects: increase absorption & filtration of low-frequency traffic sound throughout the site to improve legibility.	Consider the perceived appropriateness of sound events to character areas.
habitat conservation & enhancement	'Singing lines': increase bird habitats throughout site to increase bird calls and song & increase positive listening experiences.	Aural effects: as above, to reduce low-frequency traffic sound and improve health & well-being of all inhabitants.	Perceptual effects: playing with other senses to improve experience of place; encourage synedoche effect (focus on positive sounds).

Figure 8.12 Design principles and aural strategies.

The aural strategies proposed for the above principles are summarised in Figure 8.12, and key highlighted strategies are developed next.

Aural narrative to drive the landscape design: murmuration II

Mid–September (2021), I returned to the site to install a passive sound recorder on a hedgerow tree along the site's southern boundary. The recorder, an Audio-Moth, was programmed to record 5 minutes every other hour to find out how the soundscape of the site changes throughout the day and in time and to uncover other (non-human) inhabitants of the landscape that we might have missed on our first visit. The recorder was left on site for a month. Many listening hours followed, revealing a rich soundscape and a hedgerow full of bird life. In the midst of listening, we realised that the site was not only home to Mike and Cathy but also to many others that inhabit the site for short or long periods throughout the year. This realisation expanded the focus of our initial human-centred site analysis and characterisation based on historical and contemporary rhythms, such as the imagined repetitive bustle of the Pottery's production cycle that started with mixing water and clay and concluded in the kiln firing. Non–human rhythms were also present in our initial site visit. For example, the rhythmic stridulation of the crickets.

Yet listening to the recordings in time, made us realise up to what point the site was full of non-human others. Thus, through listening, conservation and enhancement of habitats became a key principle for the landscape design of the site.

Mark Whittingham, Professor of Applied Ecology at Newcastle University, kindly identified the bird species calling and singing in one of the recordings: chaffinches, robins, starlings, blackbirds, carrion crows and wrens, which gave us a sense of species present on site. Dan emailed me excited about another recording that he had listened to. The recording starts with heavy rain. Three minutes into it, some birds come to shelter close to the recorder and engage in a lively 'conversation', one that feels very human, one that seems to matter. That recording was the starting point for this second sound composition (Soundtrack 8.2).

🎵 Soundtrack 8.2 Murmuration II.

There are two superimposed narratives in the piece: the first centres on the birds and their habitats within the site and the tree as a place of shelter; the second on the historical and contemporary rhythms of the site. The composition interprets research on the bird species identified by Mark to form most of the musical motifs in the piece (trills, flourishes, arpeggios, rhythmic clicks from the Starlings, etc.), contributing to an overarching musical character for the piece that draws from the existing sonic identity and represents the future of the Pottery.

The piece opens with the distant bells of a local church resonating across the hills, chiming the hour as they have, no doubt, for many years. The timeless birdscape enters the foreground, and the listener is introduced to the site's two perennial sonic characters: building and birdsong. As the score progresses, the rain begins to fall, and a melancholic phrase enters from a distance, approaching slowly and carefully. As the vignette deepens, the Pottery is first fired, and human rhythms begin to impose themselves on the site, building and human work in tandem, ever-growing in ecoacoustic prevalence. The birdsong becomes drowned in the scene as industrial production increases until, following a sudden crescendo in motion, activity is diminished. Under the shelter of the branches, two birds return to the Pottery in the quietened shadow of its industrious past. They conduct an important meeting, speaking with brevity and cautiousness, as though fearful their sound may wake the kiln from its rest. The birds retreat, allowing the listener a moment to think about the Pottery's exclusion of some of the site's original inhabitants and what the potential reintroduction of human activity could mean. Informed of this critical conversation, the piece continues and the Pottery is once again enveloped in activity, yet now in knowing of its impact on the lives of non-human others. As the musical

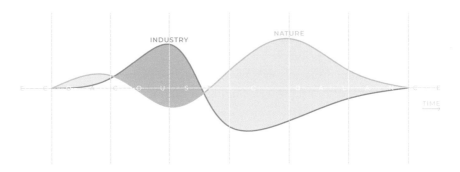

Figure 8.13 Murmuration II graphic score (Soundtrack 8.2), Credit: Dan Hill.

rhythms eventually fade, the birdscape once again establishes itself into the piece with optimism for a more sonically balanced future.

The piece attempted to highlight the entanglement and tension between human and non-human activity throughout the site's timeline and potential future and tries to engage the listener in thinking about how one impacts and could coexist with the other. The piece is accompanied by the following score (Figure 8.13).

These two interwoven narratives or rhythms – human and non-human, historical and contemporary – formed the overarching concept for the landscape design of the site. Existing rhythms and new rhythms were proposed to enhance the experience of the landscape by adding complexity and variation to it, animating it, and facilitating an engagement with it, while ensuring legibility and complexity through the aural strategies detailed next.

New sound events and aural moods for variety, legibility and complexity

With an emphasis on listening, therefore, the landscape strategy sought to

1. introduce aural moods or enhance existing ones that are appropriate to the overall identity and proposed character areas for the site,
2. to increase positive listening experiences (rhythms) and decrease negative listening experiences (drones) within each of the proposed aural moods.

These objectives were achieved by working in conjunction with existing and proposed aural and perceptual effects and with the overall mapped landscape strategy for the site, as summarized in the following diagrams (Figures 8.14 and 8.15).

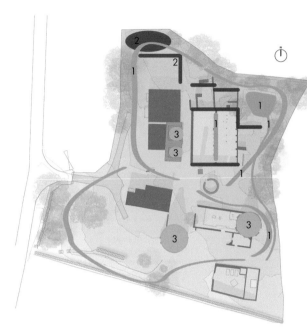

1. **SALIENCY**: bring attention to and increase - bird song, insects in meadows, water sounds - to punctuate drone of traffic and reference use of water in pugmill.
Visual component - additional vegetation to help mask (visually) traffic.

2. **ABSORPTION AND FILTRATION** of traffic drone through introduction of solid walls and earth berm

3. Utilise **CUT OUT** effect when entering spaces (in particular small kiln), **REVERBERATION** (mostly in southern kilns) and **AMPLIFICATION** when exiting spaces.

Proposed activities to reflect aural effects and character and increase positive listening experiences.
For example:
Small kiln - quiet art/community activities, contemplation/meditation, sensing the passing of the seasons and cyclical days.
Big kiln: performances, small scale concerts and other art activities. Horizontal kilns: accommodation, art studios, dining, semi-open.

Figure 8.14 Existing and proposed key aural effects diagram.

Aural Palette and landscape action plan

The action plan (Figure 8.17) emerged from the landscape strategy (Figure 8.16) and considered the three optional scenarios developed by the architects. These scenarios would, in time, bring temporal variation and animation to the site beyond what was detailed in the landscape action plan.

Aural palette

SOFT PALETTE: NON-HUMAN RHYTHMS THROUGH LANDSCAPE MANAGEMENT

We set out to increase the populations of invertebrates and birds within the site. This was a result of our engagement with the site and species encountered through listening and of a review of the main environmental priorities for the area identified in the UK Department for Environment Food and Rural Affair's MAGIC map (Natural England, 2022)

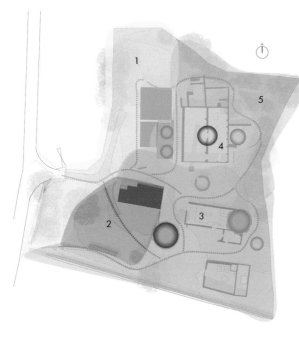

PROPOSED MOODS
○ Vibrant
○ Calm
CHARACTER AREAS
1. RURAL:
Aural mood - relatively calm and pleasant. Traffic drone dominates at first. Strengthen planting to increase sense of enclosure, ornamental planting next to drying rooms and former cottage. Increase non-human rhtyhms (bird activity).
2. DOMESTIC:
Aural mood - relatively calm and pleasant. Rhythmical domestic events, open views to countryside to be maintained.
3. PASTORAL/PRODUCTIVE: heart of pottery.
Aural mood - relatively calm and pleasant, with pockets of rhythmical vibrancy (temporal events at the big kiln, insects stridulation in meadow, bird activity) taking focus away from the traffic drone, and quiet areas (small kiln, terrace).
4. POST-INDUSTRIAL:
Aural mood - relatively vibrant, with calm pockets (horizontal kilns and proposed terrace to the east that provide opportunities to slow down and listen) and water flow.
5. WILDERNESS:
Aural mood - relatively vibrant, with rhythmical non-human events. Increase bird song, express water flow, provide opportunities to slow down and listen.

Figure 8.15 Proposed aural moods diagram.

Invertebrates

Sounding invertebrates, such as crickets, provide sonic saliency and moments of joy. The meadows within the site already support a wide range of invertebrates. The following interventions were proposed to increase invertebrate populations and, in turn, support birds and small mammals.

1. Grassland management for invertebrates (Suffolk Wildlife Trust, 2023):

   • Avoid sudden changes in management as this will affect the plants present at any time.
   • Preferable to have different height cuts across the site and different times for cutting (part of the site in early June and part of the site in mid-July onwards) to provide a continuous supply of nectar. Cutting from mid-July is also advisable for providing nesting habitats.

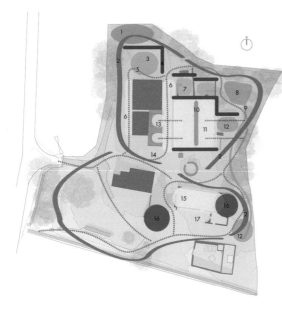

1. **EARTH BERM** to mitigate low frequency traffic sound.
2. **SINGING LINES** - strengthen vegetation to increase bird habitats. Manage grassland, increase lower planting - shrubs and herbaceous planting.
3. **CAR PARK** for increased private and by appointment use.
4. **BRICK WALLS** to define spaces, and absorb traffic sound.
5. **NETWORK OF INFORMAL PATHS**, partially surfaced (gravel)
6. **INSIDE-OUTSIDE THRESHOLDS** and circulation spaces.
7. **GARDEN ROOMS**, enclosed.
8. **POND** - part of former pottery. Emphasize flow of water & role in former pottery. Add seating to listen to underwater sounds.
9. **WATER RILL** - to aid with drainage, increase invertebrates and birds. Flowing water to punctuate traffic drone.
10. **ROOF WATER COLLECTION COLUMNS**. To express role of water in pottery industry and sound of flowing water.
11. **EVENT SPACE** partially covered.
12. **QUIET OUTDOOR TERRACES** to make use of quiet and sheltered spaces within the site.
13. **QUIET SEMI-COVERED SPACES**, artist studios.
14. **PRIVATE, BY INVITATION THRESHOLD** - first view into site.
15. **OUTDOOR TERRACE** - utilising long distance views to the south and the stridulation of crickets from meadows.
16. **KILNS** - potential for cultural and art community activities. West kiln: active, East kiln: passive, to match existing character.
17. **MEADOWS** - timber lounges to enjoy summer rhythms of the site - crickets, moving grass. Managed to increase invertebrates and ground nesting of birds.

Figure 8.16 Proposed landscape strategy (incorporating aural strategies).

- Keep some grassland areas uncut for at least a year – 'scattered islands or … strips at the edges' to accommodate the life cycle of invertebrates – rotating the uncut areas from year to year.
- Remove cuttings to avoid mulch development.

2. Planting of new hedgerows to the east and west of the site to connect with existing hedgerows, as they support the lifecycle of insects that takes place outside the grassland.
3. Addition of a water rill and potential pond, connecting to the existing puddling pond to the north.
4. New flowering shrubs and perennial planting to the west of the site,
5. Inclusion of 'bug hotels' in key brick walls of the site as part of their reinstatement.
6. Non-pesticide pest control methods such as hand removal of slugs, and encouragement of song thrushes for snail control.

A - **car park**, semi-private/by invitation, northern boundary lowered for accessibility & sound absorption; brick retaining walls to North & East boundary, loose gravel surfacing.
B- **boundary planting** - trees and hedgerow
C- **front gardens:** hard surfacing threshold between building & planting; reclaimed brick pavers or bricks on gravel/grass
D- **courtyard** with seating, sheltered, quiet - inside/outside paving as per C.
E - **path network**, loose gravel in places to facilitate circulation through site/increase commercial use. Crunching footsteps, rhythm.
F - **garden rooms**
G - **steel roof frame/water collection/feature**
H- **outdoor terrace**, quiet & intimate, long distance views, bound by existing walls, loose gravel surfacing
I - **proposed selected trees**, outside Schedule Monument designation
J - **outdoor seating terrace**, very quiet, long distance views, loose gravel surfacing
K - **contemplative kiln**, sky viewing seat/lounger
M - **mini pond**, connected to original pond - water at centre of pottery, increase invertebrates and drink for birds
N - **active kiln**
O - **resting pockets**, loose gravel surfacing
P - **semi-private/private outdoor terrace**
Q - **existing meadow**, managed to increase invertebrate and allow for ground nesting of birds.
R- **proposed hedgerow** - to fill in gaps and connect with existing hedgerow
T - **'by invitation' threshold**

scale 1:250 at A1

Figure 8.17 Proposed action plan.

Birds

Listening revealed many woodland and hedgerow birds on site. A review of DEFRA's *Magic Map* also revealed that farmland birds (both arable assemblage and grassland assemblage farmland birds) were an environmental priority for the area (Department for Environment Food and Rural Affiars, 2023). These included ground-nesting birds, such as skylarks and corn bunting, and hedgerow and tree-nesting birds, such as tree sparrows. Different bird species have different habitat needs. We proposed interventions conducive to an overall habitat enhancement for many of the bird species, as summarised below:

1. *Singing lines:* new hedgerows to the east and west of the site and additional trees proposed to complement the existing (outside the schedule monument designation) and provide tree cover continuity in time. These would increase birdsong within the site and, thus, positive listening experiences.

2. Grassland management for birds: meadows provide food for birds and nesting habitats for ground nesting birds (skylarks, lapwings, curlews and yellow wagtails). With regards to food, meadows support many invertebrates, as well as providing seeds during winter. To allow for nesting, meadows were proposed to be cut from mid-July onwards. To ensure food supply and provide refuge, uncut margins or islands were proposed to be kept all year round (RSPB, 2021)

3. Addition of damp areas and water supply for food (invertebrates) and drink.

The owners, Mike and Cathy, are currently implementing the landscape planting and management while they await planning permission for other architectural and landscape works to take place (Figure 8.18).

Figure 8.18 New planting by the Kilns (left), bird nests (top right), bee bricks (middle right) and log piles (bottom right), Credit: Mike Goodall.

HARD LANDSCAPE MATERIALITY

Hard landscape materials were selected:

- To alter sound propagation within the site – for example, the inclusion of new solid brick walls to absorb sound waves
- To increase positive listening experiences and provide saliency against the traffic drone – for example, loose gravel that crunches underfoot
- To fit in with the overall identity and character of the different areas, rural location and existing materiality of the site.
- To allow for sustainable drainage.

Key proposed materiality:

- Brick walls: selected to alter sound propagation within the site and reference the site's past use as a brick making Pottery.
- Loose gravel for road and car park: selected for permeable construction, to allow for plants to self-seed and grow, for the crunching of footsteps, and deemed in keeping with the identity of the site.
- Loose gravel paths: consisting of permeable construction, to facilitate crunching of footsteps, and with soft edges to planting.
- Brick pavers to front gardens and courtyard – reclaimed clay pavers on gravel or grass – in keeping with the brick making Pottery and character of the areas.
- Timber seats: chunky timber seats to the north of the site, timber loungers to the south of the site and inside the small kiln.

Conclusion

This project sought to develop a landscape design for the Old Pottery guided primarily by affective listening and sound making. Through listening, on and off site, we discovered what it is like to live at the Pottery, its aural identity and how it evolves in time. Sound making, or music making, enabled us to express the identity of the site with its many human rhythms. Music making also helped us to relate to non-human others that currently take shelter at the Pottery and their many rhythms. These two interwoven sets of rhythms – human and non-human, historical and contemporary – drove the landscape design for the site through aural strategies that attempted to celebrate the existing heritage of the site, the passing of time, and to provide shelter, food and joy to the many inhabitants that, at least for a while, call the Pottery home.

Listening and sounding exercises: from phonographs to aural speculations

Auralisations early in the design process can be used for many purposes in landscape architecture and urban design practice: from helping us capture and express the experience of an existing place to helping us envisage potential futures for a place. The two examples included here, *Audio Postcards Canada* and *Rewilding the Gardiner Expressway,* formed part of art installations developed as part of my creative practice Ph.D. thesis (Ruiz Arana, 2020) and devised while living in Toronto in 2015.

Audio postcards Canada[1]

Brief

In September 2015, I responded to a call for Audio Postcards curated by CASE (Canadian Association for Sound Ecology). My submission, Leslie Street Spit, was one of 16 soundtracks selected by jurors for the exhibition that launched online on World Listening Day 2016 (9th July) and can be accessed at the following link: audiopostcards.soundecology.ca

The brief for the postcards was to 'create or capture an aural image of a place, moment, or region of Canada' in up to two minutes (Randolph, 2015). Each postcard submission was accompanied by an artist statement and an image.

Concept

At the time of the call for audio postcards, I had been in the midst of listening to Hildegard Westerkamp *Kit's Beach Soundwalk* (1989), and I drew on several aspects of her piece for my own:

- The dissonance between the visual landscape that Westerkamp describes and the aural landscape that we listen to at the beginning of the piece, which corresponds with the dissonance that I wanted to transmit as experienced in the old part of the Spit. There, I was immersed in nature. However, sound extended far beyond what the eye could see, revealing the invisible, the soundscape of the city.

- The powerful narrative embedded in her composition that allows her to direct listeners to her response to the soundscape while enabling them to create their own response to the piece. In a short time, over nine minutes, she directs listeners' attention to an unbalanced soundscape and the joy that opening our ears up to tiny sounds, those of others, could bring. In an even shorter space of two minutes, I also wanted to lend my ears to the listeners, guiding them through the sounds of the Spit where the natural and artificial juxtapose. At times the natural and artificial juxtapose harmonically, at times stridently, revealing a truly entangled environment full of surprises.

Through my audiopostcard, I wanted to invite participants to listen and think critically about human and non-human agency at Leslie Street Spit, a man-made peninsula and accidental wilderness in Toronto. The piece brings to the forefront the wildness of the Spit and how it juxtaposes with its human origin and context. Human agency is also very palpable (and audible) at the Spit, at times taking a step back, at times filling all aural space. In the city, intrusive sounds seem inevitable, even unnoticeable. In this space, one questions them. And in doing so, one questions human agency. When one perceives this wildness as energizing and full of joy, why not allow more?

The Audio Postcard captures the experience of walking along a pedestrian trail through the oldest part of the Spit on a hot Sunday morning in August. The following extract from my artist statement for the exhibition captures the more-than-human experience of the Spit:

> …Here, I immersed myself in nature, and its sounds, but sound was also the reminder of where I was, within the realm of the city. Sound blurred the entangled natural and cultural boundary of the Spit. Footsteps, voices, the sound of planes taking off and landing, mixed with the chirping of the crickets, the birdsongs, and the waves, providing a rich and relaxing soundscape to listen to.
>
> (Ruiz Arana, 2016)

The making of the postcard

This audio postcard was created by combining three field recordings taken along the walk with a Zoom H5 recorder. I edited (minimally) the recordings in Audacity: amplifying the soundtracks first and cutting and pasting selected fragments of the recordings next to combine them into the final soundtrack (Ruiz-Arana, 2016).

Figure 8.19 Leslie Street Spit's shore, Toronto.

The piece starts with a harmonic juxtaposition and mixture of human and non-human sounds recorded inland within the old part of the Spit. As listeners accompany me towards the edge of the Spit, the harmonic relation turns to one of tension between the force of the laps of the water and the white noise around it, two voices juxtaposed without mixing (Figure 8.19).

Sound and image

Producing this piece and reviewing other artists' postcards led me to explore the relationship between the aural and the visual in more depth for practice. Sound and image can work together to extend and enrich information, providing insight into what happens in and around a place at a particular time. Sound and sight can also offer contrasting or dissonant information. For example, sound can add an element of surprise by extending the picture (sounding events out of view) or contradicting what is depicted within it. It is this relationship that I set out to explore further in the next multimedia art installation.

Rewilding the Gardiner Expressway[1]

In the summer and autumn of 2015, I created a multimedia exhibition for the Scotiabank CONTACT Photography Festival 2016. The work, entitled *Rewilding the Gardiner Expressway*, combined photographs, auralisations and videos and featured the spaces underneath the Gardiner Expressway. This municipal expressway runs parallel to the shore of Lake Ontario and serves traffic in downtown Toronto. The road, built in the 1950s and 1960s, is elevated as it passes the city's downtown core, leaving a network of roads and underused spaces underneath that disrupt the connection between the city and the lake. The Gardiner Expressway follows the 19th Century alignment of Lake Ontario along Front Street. Thus, in speculating a new future for the Gardiner, I imagined how these leftover spaces might rewild through the return of the water. The resulting piece aimed to immerse the viewer into the calm and chaos of nature as it took over the spaces under the Gardiner, bringing a lake experience closer to the city and a wild aesthetic to the urban realm.

The piece was exhibited at Evergreen Brick Works from the 1st to the 31st of May 2016. Evergreen Brick Works is a former brick factory and quarry recently transformed into a public open space and community and cultural hub that houses offices, temporary exhibitions, events, markets, outdoor learning and recreation. *Rewilding the Gardiner* was accepted for exhibition as it aligned with Evergreen's core themes of urban sustainability through nature, community connections and heritage. It aligned with the themes of nature and community as it sought to use wildness to connect the community to the underused, leftover spaces underneath the Gardiner, and, in doing so, it introduced a new aesthetic to the public realm and questioned the future of these spaces. And it aligned with the theme of industrial heritage as it used the spontaneous ecological succession of a former industrial site, Leslie Street Spit, as the precedent for rewilding (Figure 8.20).

The following section takes us through the concept of the work and the relation between images and auralisations for the making of the exhibition.

Concept

In mid-June 2015, Toronto City Council voted on the future of the Gardiner Expressway east of Jarvis Street for around 2 km. Here, the structure had deteriorated to the point of needing urgent attention. Three options had been the subject of a heated debate. The first option was a hybrid solution that kept the Gardiner elevated to the Don Valley Parkway, rebuilt the crumbling deck and replaced it with

Figure 8.20 Rewilding the Gardiner Expressway exhibited at Evergreen Brickworks, May 2016.

a ground-level boulevard east of the Don Valley. This solution would impact journey times of 10% of commuters and was the most expensive. The second option entailed the removal of the elevated road east of Jarvis Street and its replacement with a ground-level tree-lined boulevard. This option was the most economical, would result in the opening of new public spaces and would impact journey times of 26% of commuters. The third and final option entailed keeping the Gardiner as it was and repairing it as required. This option would have the least impact on current traffic and sat in the middle regarding cost (CBC, 2015). The first option described was approved 'based on a greater emphasis on the Environmental Assessment transportation and infrastructure study lens' (Toronto City Council, 2015).

I was surprised by a decision that favoured traffic flow in place of urban development and cohesion at a time when the lake shore was experienced as removed from the city. With this exhibition, I envisaged an alternative future for the Gardiner, one where the lake returned to its original alignment along Front Street, triggering a wilding process akin to the natural ecological succession that had taken place at Leslie Street Spit (Figure 8.21).

Figure 8.21 Location of Gardiner Expressway and Leslie Street Spit, Toronto.

The making of the exhibition: images and auralisations

Images, auralisations and videos were used in conjunction to present an experience of place. The images were compositions of photographs of the Gardiner and the Spit, using an overlaying technique to frame the time and space of the imagined wilderness. The pairing of the spaces underneath the Gardiner with those of Leslie Street Spit was inspired by the characteristics and atmosphere of the spaces. For example, standing on York Street looking towards the light filtering through the never-ending arches of the Gardiner, I was reminded of the feeling of infinity that one gets at the Spit when reaching the shore and looking towards the lake (see Figure 8.22).

I carried out several soundwalks along the Gardiner Expressway and Leslie Street Spit to explore and capture both spaces' aural and physical properties. I visited the Spit four times over three months (July to early October), as I wanted the viewer to experience seasonal change along this imagined walk. I visited the spaces underneath the Gardiner during working days mid-morning and early

🎵 Figure 8.22 York Street (Soundtrack 8.3).

afternoon in September, outside rush hours. The humming of traffic and sound reverberation from the elevated road structure were my constant companions on those visits. The volume of those sounds, however, varied considerably along the length of the structure, dissipating at the points where the structure was higher, or the surrounding urban layout was open. Over the visits, I learned to appreciate the architecture of the arches and the illusion of infinity created by the light filtering through. Over the visits, I was also stricken by the sense of desolation ingrained in the spaces.

Auralisations and images

The final images and videos reveal the Gardiner's architecture and the Spit's nature in snapshots, in a frozen moment and time. The auralisations that accompany the images, created from field recordings of the Spit, immerse the viewer into this new landscape. They expand the image, adding information and drawing the listener in, engaging them in these reimagined spaces. Through listening, the viewer becomes

Figure 8.23 Yonge Street (Soundtrack 8.4).

aware of time, the species that inhabit those spaces, and the materiality and uses of the spaces. Listening also reveals the unique acoustic quality of the spaces underneath the Gardiner, with the humming of the traffic and the reverberation of the structure (Figures 8.22 and 8.23).

Note
1. An earlier version of the making of Audiopostcards Canada and Rewilding the Gardiner was included in my Ph.D. Thesis (Ruiz Arana, 2020).

References

CBC. (2015). *Gardiner Expressway: What you need to know about the options*. CBC News. Available at: https://www.cbc.ca/news/canada/toronto/gardiner-expressway-what-you-need-to-know-about-the-options-1.3033963

Cerwén, G. (2020). Listening to Japanese gardens II: Expanding the soundscape action design tool. *Journal of Urban Design*, 25(5), pp. 607–628. https://doi.org/10.1080/13574809.2020.1782183

Department for Environment Food and Rural Affiars. (2023). *Magic map*. MAGIC. Available at: https://magic.defra.gov.uk/magicmap.aspx

Natural England. (2022). *MAGIC*. MAGIC. Available at: https://magic.defra.gov.uk/magicmap.aspx

RSPB. (2021). *Hay meadows*. The Royal Society for the Protection of Birds. Available at: https://www.rspb.org.uk/our-work/conservation/conservation-and-sustainability/farming/advice/managing-habitats/hay-meadows/

Ruiz Arana, U. (2016). *Leslie Street Spit, Audio Postcards Canada*. Available at: https://www.audiopostcards.soundecology.ca/

Ruiz Arana, U. (2020). *The enchantment of the wild: A journey into wildness through listening*. Newcastle University. Available at: http://theses.ncl.ac.uk/jspui/handle/10443/5178.

Submerge Sounds. (2015). *Submerge*. Submerge. Available at: http://www.submergedsounds.co.uk/submerge-workshops-2/

Suffolk Wildlife Trust. (2023). *Grassland management for invertebrates*. Suffolk Wildlife Trust. Available at: https://www.suffolkwildlifetrust.org/conservationadvice/meadows-and-grassland/grassland-management-invertebrates#:~:text=Many%20insects%20spend%20part%20of,the%20year%20could%20be%20disastrous.&text=To%20prevent%20scrub%20encroachment%2C%20rotate,leave%20uncut%20for%20even%20longer.

Toronto City Council. (2015). *Gardiner expressway and lake shore boulevard east reconfiguration environmental assessment (EA) and integrated urban design study - Updated evaluation of alternatives*. City of Toronto.

PART III

Performance

Chapter Nine

Listening to other voices

> *It all began with a blackbird.… The bird sang. But never before had song seemed so close to speech … and … never had song seemed further removed from language.*
>
> (Despret, 2022, pp. 3–4)

In 1988, musician and sound ecologist Bernie Krause started a long-term sound recording project at Lincoln Meadow, a commercial forest in the Sierra Nevada Mountains. Through his sound recordings, Krause sought to investigate the impact of selective logging on the environment. Selective logging was to be carried out with the premise that removing a few trees would not cause a detrimental impact. Krause was granted permission to record dawn choruses before the loggings, enabling him to establish a protocol and baseline for post-loggings recordings.

The baseline recordings, and associated spectrograms, showcased an environment full of bird life. On his return to Lincoln Meadow the following year, after selective loggings had taken place, Krause found a forest unaltered at first glance. However, his recordings told a different story. Most of the bird life was now gone. He returned to Lincoln Meadows 15 times over 25 years to record the soundscape. During that period, the biodiversity of the forest gradually recovered. However, it never reached its pre-logging abundance (Krause, 2013).

Krause's work at Lincoln Meadows demonstrates two aspects of relevance to urban soundscapes. First, it demonstrates how sound can be used to reveal the biodiversity and health of an ecosystem and thus be used to monitor changes in that ecosystem resulting from human activities or other stressors that might be hidden

DOI: 10.4324/9781003202981-13

from view. Second, it demonstrates the value of listening and expanding beyond the visual in assessing the environment to uncover those hidden environmental processes and changes. This alternative evaluation may invite less invasive interventions on the environment. This chapter turns to the fields of bio and ecoacoustics to unravel the first and returns to affective listening to affirm the second.

Bio and ecoacoustics

As discussed in Chapter 3, sound is integral to the behaviour and communication of many animal and plant species, including us. Animals defend their territories, attract mates and identify their offspring through vocalization. Animals rely on sound to navigate space, hunt and form communities. Plant species also listen, sound and are impacted by noise.

The soundscape, defined from an environmental perspective, is an expression of the landscape, the movement and interaction of its biological, geological and anthropological components. Often, the soundscape evolves with the landscape, but sometimes, the soundscape can 'reveal subtler environmental changes' (Ross *et al.*, 2018, p. 135). Lincoln Meadow is a great example of this last, as Krause's sound recordings revealed the loss of species in a seemingly untouched forest. Studying the soundscape can provide invaluable information on how a habitat develops or is impacted by human and natural processes.

The fields of bioacoustics and ecoacoustics investigate biological sound from an ecological perspective. Bioacoustics is concerned with the study of a single animal species and is sustained by the *Acoustic Niche Hypothesis* (ANH) introduced in Chapter 1 (Krause, 1987). As a reminder, the ANH proposes that a healthy habitat has an animal orchestra in tune, as animal species adapt their calls to avoid frequency and temporal overlaps with other species, thus finding their acoustic niches to communicate. In this manner, the soundscape is divided to avoid interference amongst different species. Therefore, the tuning of a habitat's orchestra can help determine its health, and the impact that interventions have on it. As per the Lincoln Meadows project, an ecosystem that is disrupted through tree logging for example, has an altered species make up, and thus an altered soundscape (Ruiz Arana, 2019). Animal orchestras require time to recover and retune following disruption (Krause and Hoffman, 2012).

Whereas bioacoustics is concerned with the study of a single species, ecoacoustics incorporates and extends its scope to entire ecosystems (Krause and Farina, 2016).

Thus, ecoacoustics differs from bioacoustics in that in ecoacoustics, sound is studied and regarded as an expression of 'ecological processes,' whereas, in bioacoustics, sound is studied 'as a signal that transfers information between individuals' (Fletcher, 2007 in Sueur and Farina, 2015, p. 494). Ecoacoustics operates at three acoustic levels: *species* (building on bioacoustics), *communities* and *soundscape* (Farina, 2018, p. 3). An *acoustic community* emerges from the combination of biophonies at a particular time and place and is subject to daily and seasonal changes and human impact. The *soundscape* results from the combination of geophonies, biophonies and anthrophonies of a particular landscape and is again affected by factors that influence the development and evolution of the landscape (ibid.).

Monitoring soundscapes can reveal information about a habitat's diversity, abundance and environmental dynamics and its evolution in time due to environmental changes and human impact (Sueur and Farina, 2015). Monitoring soundscapes in time also helps us understand the acoustic phenology of habitats, that is, 'the seasonal acoustic activity of animals' within it, and its threats, including anthropogenic noise and climate change (Sueur, Krause and Farina, 2019, p. 971). Climate change influences sound propagation, as it depends on atmospheric conditions such as temperature and moisture. Thus, climate change can affect acoustic phenology directly, through the effect on the propagation of vocalisations, and indirectly through affecting the habitat and food sources that sustain those vocalising species (ibid.). In turn, acoustic phenology changes could also affect human well-being by altering the 'natural soundscapes' that are the source of tranquillity and relaxation (ibid.). Therefore, the study of acoustic phenology can have wide-reaching applications and opportunities for further research.

Tools, protocols and applications

Ecoacoustics and bioacoustics use passive sound monitoring techniques to understand species' behaviour and makeup and how the diversity and abundance of a habitat evolve. Passive acoustic monitoring techniques use low-power, weatherproof sound recorders with in-built microphones attached to trees or other elements and left on site. Recordings can be analysed at a *species, community* or *soundscape* level.

At *species* and *community* levels, animal signals are studied to understand communication and behaviour in time. Recorded data are analysed through listening and visual analysis of spectrograms. A large amount of acoustic data is gathered through passive sound monitoring, and listening to data or visually analysing spectrograms is labour-intensive. To speed up data analysis, commercial and open-access artificial intelligence and machine learning bioacoustic analysis software has been developed (e.g., K.Lisa Yang Center for Conservation Bioacoustics, 2023; Wildlife Acoustics, 2023)

At a *soundscape* level, acoustic indices are calculated to quantify and summarize soundscapes in a snapshot (Ross *et al.*, 2021). Acoustic indices can be classified into 'intensity indices that measure sound amplitude, complexity indices that measure the level of complexity, and soundscape indices that investigate the importance of geophonies, biophonies, and technophonies' (Farina, 2018, p. 4). *Acoustic complexity indices* presume that the acoustic complexity of a habitat 'increases with the number of singing individuals and species' and thus provides a good indication of species diversity and phenology (ibid.) Frequently used indices include the *Acoustic Complexity Index* (ACI) and *Acoustic Richness*. *Soundscape indices* evaluate the prevalence and interaction of 'geophonies, biophonies and technophonies' (ibid., p. 6). Frequently used indices include the *Normalised Difference Soundscape Index*, which evaluates the proportion of biophonies and technophonies in an environment (ibid., p. 6). This index is particularly relevant for urban soundscapes as it evaluates the human impact on the environment and ranges from -1 (all technophonies) to $+1$ (all biophonies) (ibid.). Data analysis software for calculating soundscape indices includes *soundecology* (Villanueva-Rivera and Pijanowski, 2018) and *seewave* (Sueur, Aubin and Simonis, 2022) packages in R statistical software.

The efficacy of acoustic indices is still under debate, as acoustic diversity, as an expression of species richness, does not automatically reflect ecosystem quality or resilience (Bateman and Uzal, 2021). The performance of some acoustic indices is also compromised in the presence of certain sounds, including insect stridulations, geophony (wind or rain) or anthrophony, as they can mask biophonies (Ross *et al.*, 2018). This last results in some acoustic indices not performing well in urban environments dominated by anthropogenic noise and might need the removal of skewing anthropogenic sounds before calculation (Fairbrass *et al.*, 2017).

Despite these limitations, there are many advantages of passive sound monitoring techniques over traditional ecological survey methods, mainly:

- Passive sound monitoring techniques are non-invasive and can be deployed at a large scale (Sueur and Farina, 2015).
- Passive sound monitoring techniques are cost-effective (fewer human hours required).

- Batteries of recorders last a long time and allow for continuous monitoring and identification of long-term trends.
- They enable monitoring in sensitive and challenging sites (Ross *et al.,* 2018), including fresh and saline water habitats.

These advantages mean that the disciplines of bioacoustics and ecoacoustics are constantly being developed and protocols and best practice guidance produced. Recently published protocols that the reader might want to turn to plan their ecoacoustic monitoring study include the open-access *Good practice guidelines for long-term ecoacoustic monitoring in the UK* (Metcalf *et al.,* 2022). These guidelines provide in-depth information on choosing and deploying relevant hardware and collecting and analysing acoustic data for ecological purposes.

Many ecological research and practice projects are carried out through bioacoustics and ecoacoustics methods. Projects range from species studies (e.g., Abrahams, 2019) to soundscape studies (e.g., Bradfer-Lawrence *et al.,* 2019). Bio and ecoacoustic methods are not restricted to terrestrial animals but are also employed in aquatic environments. Research projects to date have concentrated on seawater environments to survey particular species (e.g., Picciulin *et al.,* 2021) or soundscapes (e.g., Nguyen Hong Duc *et al.,* 2021). Lately, attention has turned to ecoacoustics for freshwater environment monitoring, which has led to drafting a protocol for acoustic data collection in small waterbodies (Abrahams, Desjonquères and Greenhalgh, 2021). The case study in the next chapter draws from current freshwater ecoacoustics research and demonstrates applications for raising environmental awareness through community events.

Applications for landscape architecture and urban design

The theory and practice that sustains bioacoustics and ecoacoustics have applications for many aspects of our work. Bio and ecoacoustics theory and methods can be integrated throughout a design project's life and within a wide range of landscape research projects. For example, at the early stages of a project, ecoacoustic methods can be integrated alongside traditional ecological surveys to provide in-depth ecological surveys of sites at the species and community levels. Later, ecoacoustic methods can be employed to track the biodiversity impact, both positive and negative, of schemes in time (including subtle changes). Bio and ecoacoustic methods can also be integrated into citizen science projects to engage communities with the non-human world scientifically (in data analysis) and through listening (to recorded acoustic data).

Bio and ecoacoustics are up-and-coming fields with applications for the design and management of urban and periurban spaces. There are, however, challenges associated with these fields. First is the reliability of acoustic indices, which is still in development, and how recordings are affected by meteorological factors and human-made noise. Second, the volume of data obtained through ecoacoustics methods that requires AI analysis methods. The danger with this is that when studying the acoustic data, we no longer engage with the environment, and its inhabitants, through listening. With the turning of recorded sound into data, we lose listening as a way of relating to the environment. Last is the lack of integration of non-human-centred soundscape theory and methods (bio and ecoacoustics) and human-centred soundscape theory and methods (*soundscape approach*). Whereas human-centred methods prioritise the perception of sound over acoustic measurements, non-human-centred approaches rely on acoustic measurements. Whereas human-centred methods are primarily concerned with studying the quality of the soundscape, in non-human-centred approaches, sound is a vehicle to understand or diagnose an environment. Both fields of study are developing rapidly and finding ways of integrating human and non-human-centred aims and approaches is key for a holistic approach to multispecies urban soundscape research and design.

The next section, and the case study included after that, turns to practices and initiatives that seek to overcome these last two challenges of human and non-human centred approaches through the interweaving of affective listening, ecoacoustics and sound art.

Listening to other voices

Making space for other voices

For many people, 2020 marked the beginning of listening to other voices, of opening our ears and bodies to biophonic sound. Soundscapes worldwide changed radically as we worked from home and stayed local. With the reduction of anthrophonic noise (mainly from transport and industry), we started to notice the sounds of our immediate environments. Some of those sounds were welcome, such as a perceived increase in birdsong. Some other sounds were unwelcome, such as the sounds of noisy neighbours (Tong *et al.*, 2021). My neighbourhood's soundscape in

Newcastle was no different. The constant traffic hum that characterizes neighbourhood streets stopped radically and was replaced by birdsong at the beginning of spring. Neighbours commented that birds seemed to be singing louder, and there seemed to be more birds than in previous years.

The radical alteration of urban soundscapes during the pandemic initiated listening and sound monitoring initiatives worldwide for various purposes. For example, research projects documented the reduction of human noise through acoustic and perceptual measurements (e.g., Lecocq *et al.*, 2020; Lenzi, Sádaba and Lindborg, 2021) and its impact in human and non-human communities (Bates *et al.*, 2020; Derryberry *et al.*, 2020; Rutz *et al.*, 2020). Citizen-science projects (i.e., Challéat *et al.*, 2020; Alsina-Pages *et al.*, 2021) and arts-led participatory initiatives (Paisaje Sensorial, 2020; Cities and Memory, 2021; Stollery, 2021) also helped us try and make sense of the pandemic through listening.

Amongst this listening, what struck us that spring, was the realisation that the world was continuing without us and that we are only but a part of planetary life (Ruiz Arana, 2023). Whereas normal human activity had paused, it was business as usual for non-human life. This humbling realisation that we are only a part of planetary life was triggered in the pandemic by listening. Listening also connected us with the wildlife around us and with our own sounds. Thus, listening can help us uncover processes and changes hidden from view or masked by other sounds and actively engage with the voices of those we are finally starting to hear (ibid.).

Staying with the trouble through listening

Natural sounds are a conduit to tranquillity and human well-being. However, not all natural sounds are conducive to tranquillity, and in listening to others' voices, we need to welcome the chaotic and unpredictable as much as the pleasant and tranquil.

At a Landscape Institute roundtable in April 2021, I brought two bird soundtracks to listen to as a prompt to discuss soundscapes within landscape architecture practice. The first soundtrack was a recording on a Saturday afternoon in April 2021, shortly after pubs and restaurants were allowed to open for outdoor seating (Figure 9.1, Soundtrack 9.1).

Newcastle and Gateshead's quaysides were buzzing with life. Families, couples and friends wandered along the river, music spilled out of outdoor cafes and pubs, and a busker performed at the end of the Millennium Bridge that connects Newcastle

Figure 9.1 Kittiwakes calling by the Baltic, Gateshead (Soundtrack 9.1).

and Gateshead. The quaysides were buzzing not only with human life but also with the cries of a colony of kittiwakes on one side and a colony of large seagulls on the other. Newcastle-Gateshead is home to the furthest inland colony of kittiwakes in the world. Kittiwakes are nomadic seabirds that spend the winter in the arctic sea and return to Newcastle-Gateshead for the spring and summer. That Saturday afternoon, I took a recording for the roundtable underneath the Baltic, a former flour mill on the south bank of the River Tyne, now a centre for contemporary art and a prime nesting site for the kittiwakes. During the roundtable, on listening, participants described the soundtrack as *chaotic* and *not the bird song we usually think of when describing natural soundscapes.* One of the attendees, a parent, aptly described the soundtrack as *the sound of many children playing and shouting.* The soundtrack was undoubtedly chaotic, with a cacophony of kittiwakes' cries in the foreground and a mixture of human-made sounds in the background (music, traffic noise, voices).

The second soundtrack was recorded the following day at Gosforth Nature Reserve, a periurban nature reserve within a residential area of Newcastle comprising woodlands, wetlands and reedbeds. This is the type of spring bird soundtrack that we are more accustomed to. On listening, this soundtrack was described by all attendees as vibrant, yet calm and a *soundscape that I would welcome in the urban public realm* and one that would foster contact with nature (Figure 9.2, Soundtrack 9.2).

The above listening exercise demonstrates the need to retain listening as we monitor urban soundscapes, alongside the use of sound as a source for data. Ecoacoustics can monitor the health of habitats and become aware of the animals that we share our environments with. Listening, in turn, can help us relate to that wildlife, start to care for it and find ways of coexist with it. As discussed in Chapter 3, listening to non-humans benefits human health and well-being. Listening helps us establish a connection with the non-human world to be enchanted by it, and our schemes can promote this connection by incorporating habitats suitable for singing bird species.

Listening, however, also brings forward the chaos that comes alongside living entangled with non-humans, as the kittiwakes example demonstrates. When we think of biophilic design and the need to include nature to make our cities wilder, we seldom think of the chaos accompanying nature as we live entangled with it (Ruiz Arana, 2023). For residents of the quayside, the yearly return of the kittiwakes, with their chaotic soundscape, is conflicted, as it interferes with their sleep and downtime. Listening to the calls of the kittiwakes exemplifies the need to rethink how we live with wilder animals; nature is not all calm and balanced but chaotic and messy, and we cannot welcome nature into cities without welcoming the chaos that comes alongside it. Listening enables us to establish a connection with the non-human world but listening also forces us to welcome the chaos that comes

Figure 9.2 Gosforth nature reserve (Soundtrack 9.2).

with it, as we cannot close our ears at will. In the case of the kittiwakes, listening is chaotic, but listening also brings to the forefront how these birds, struggling for survival elsewhere, have once more successfully returned to their nests (ibid.). Listening reveals these aspects in a way that data do not.

In *Soundwalking in the Phonocene: Walking, listening, wilding,* I argued for listening as a conduit for understanding and embracing the kinship and difference embedded in the myriad of human-non-human relations that we live entangled with (2023), and the reader is encouraged to turn to that chapter for an in-depth exploration of the subject. Scholars such as Donna Haraway (1991, 2016), Plumwood (1993) and Wolch (1996) have long argued for the need to embrace chaos and difference in our lived entanglement with non-human others. Wolch, in a similar vein to Haraway (1991, 2016) and Plumwood (1993), foregrounds the need to recognise the similarities and differences of all animals. We need to recognise similarities between us and other species to establish a kinship with them, and we need to see them as different from us, as subjects, to acknowledge that they have distinctive needs (1996). Understanding difference is necessary to develop an ethical framework for urban planning, design and management that decentres human agency to consider all living organisms (Ruiz Arana, 2023). Interacting with urban animals brings many benefits to humans, but it also comes with a lack of control. Embracing lack of control in urban environments, what Haraway terms as *staying with the trouble (2016)*, is essential to understand that there are other urban agencies beyond us that we need to leave space for (Ruiz Arana, 2023). In soundscape terms, this calls for us to move beyond regarding birdsong as there to calm us. Moreover, in soundscape terms, it means leaving space for a cacophony of other voices besides our own (ibid.).

Listening, in our engagement with urban wilderness, brings comfort and familiarity. Through listening, we learn to identify sounds that we might have once perceived as anonymous, such as *a* birdcall (Ruiz Arana, 2020). The birdcall becomes the call of a kittiwake, for example, bringing with it a known story and a kinship with the non-human world. Listening also foregrounds differences. The cries of the kittiwakes are a stark contrast to other birdsong and cultural sounds. What this richness in listening advances in the city, with its familiarity and difference, is the potential for a new relationship with its non-human inhabitants, where the non-human and the human are intermingled at a variety of degrees and scales.

Having established the need to leave space for other voices and to recover listening as 'a way of relating' and *staying-with-the trouble*, we now touch on interdisciplinary collaborations that have sought to breach the objective and subjective in sound and listening to other voices.

Interdisciplinary collaborations: reclaiming listening in ecological conservation, management and design

Landscape architects and urban designers work with and alongside other disciplines in research and design projects from inception to completion. As we have seen throughout the past chapters, there are many advantages to working with other disciplines for sound and listening projects. However, it is here, in listening to others' voices, where interdisciplinary work comes to the forefront, as exemplified through the following pioneer projects. These projects have sought to incorporate objective and subjective approaches that interweave sound, listening and communities in environmental management and restoration. The projects rely on sound to monitor the health of ecosystems and assess change and on listening to communicate and engage communities in those dynamic ecosystems, drawing from many disciplines in the process.

Biosphere Soundscapes is a global initiative founded by Leah Barclay that demonstrates the interdisciplinary potential of ecoacoustics (Biosphere Soundscapes, 2022). *Biosphere Soundscapes* brings artists, scientists and local communities together to explore and understand UNESCO's dynamic biosphere reserves worldwide. The initiative was set up to work with sound to measure environmental health and a creative medium to engage communities in listening to the environment. Sound and listening become tools for environmental health assessment, environmental awareness and ultimately for positive environmental change. The work carried out in each biosphere changes in nature but always encompasses artists, the local community, the environment and sound. Each biosphere is explored through artistic residencies (BioScapes Residencies), scientific research (sound monitoring BioScapes Lab) and citizen science (BioScapes Community). Through *BioScapes Residencies*, artists, working alongside scientists, explore each biosphere through various formats, including soundwalks and field recordings, and outputs are geolocated on an interactive map. *BioScapes Lab* focuses on scientific research that engages the community. *BioScapes Community* provides a platform for the community to input content and engage with educational resources and other biospheres worldwide. The three approaches combine in a live Biosphere Soundscapes map (ibid.).

As well as interdisciplinary projects, many artists work in the interface of sound and listening, science and art. Artists engage with the environment through listening and work with various technologies and creative methods to bring awareness to aesthetic, political, environmental and social issues through listening (Bianchi and Manzo, 2016). Norwegian artist Jana Winderen, for example, through her spatial sound exhibitions and performances, brings awareness of difficult-to-reach environments (underwater, ice) and how human activity and climate impact the life within them (2023). Mhairi Killin is another multimedia artist engaged with human-impacted underwater environments, as exemplified by her project *On Sonorous Seas* (2022). Killin, who lives on the Scottish island of *Iona*, experienced a dead beaked whale being washed ashore in the summer of 2018, which prompted her to investigate whether military sonar was responsible for that and other similar recent whale deaths in Scottish and Irish shores (Barkham, 2022). Killin worked with scientists of the *Hebridean Whale and Dolphin Trust*, sailing with them and listening to hydrophones to the underwater soundscape. Her extended listening method was akin to ecoacoustic protocols, listening for 'one minute every 15 minutes over eight hours' and, in the process, being surprised by the amount of human noise that she heard (ibid.). The resulting artwork, *On Sonorous Seas*, included sound recordings, video, poetry and a six-episode podcast and sought to bring awareness to the complexity of human-non-human interactions in difficult-to-reach environments (2022). Although the research was inconclusive on whether the sonar activities were the cause of death, it did bring to the foreground that the frequency range of the sonar interferes with that of the whales' calls and the need for military exercises to consider the impact on others.

The connection through listening that Barclay, Winderen and Killin, amongst many others, seek to elicit has also been central to the work of composer Annea Lockwood since the 1980s. Lockwood has inspired many artists, and she credits *A Soundmap of the Hudson River* as the start of 'consciously working with sound, the body and the connection to and immersion in the environment' (Lockwood and Morrow, 2022). *A Soundmap of the Hudson River* was based on her extensive listening to moving river waters and wanted to elicit in listeners, in New Yorkers, a 'visceral sense of the river's power' and a contrast to the river as viewed, thus revealing a part of the environment hidden from view through listening (ibid.). In her most recent installation with Liz Phillips, *The River Feeds Back*, Lockwood takes the listener on a 135-mile aural journey through the Schuylkill River in Pennsylvania and its overwater and underwater sounds (Lockwood and Phillips, 2022). Through 'swirling currents … underwater lives of aquatic insects and fish … chirping birds, cheeping frogs, and the long, slow sweeps of toad calls,' this immersive aural journey connects and immerses people within their immediate waterways so that they care for them and seek to protect them (ibid.).

These examples are just, but a few of the many carried out globally and demonstrate the potential for ecoacoustics to have a wide-reaching impact through the interaction with other disciplines, particularly artists. Reclaiming listening through arts methods can make ecoacoustic data accessible and understandable for communities and can engage communities and designers with the biodiversity that is creating the data. The case study included in the following chapter features an interview with field recordist and sound artist David de la Haye, who seeks to engage communities with freshwater environments through listening.

These examples also show how to interweave non-human and human-centred aims and approaches to soundscape research. As both fields develop in years to come, finding ways to integrate aims, and approaches will facilitate successful multi-species urban soundscapes.

Affective listening to other voices

As we end our journey towards becoming *soundscape architects* (performers, composers and audience), we return to affective listening and its role for designers in engaging and designing with other voices. As we have argued, affective listening is the most simple, mundane and vital for the experience of the environment and can encompass listening as communication and an aesthetic practice.

In the design of the environment through affective listening, the designer appears twice.

First, through listening and soundmaking, the designer is an integral part of the environment, alternating between subject (experiencing) and object (for others to experience). It is in this interaction that affective bodily engagement is established and a kinship with human and non-human others. This kinship inevitably entails *staying with the trouble* and embracing chaos and the unknown. Through listening as communication, the designer uncovers processes hidden from view. Finally, through listening as aesthetic appraisal, the designer might also value environments that are not visually appealing yet rich in biodiversity, with eventful and vibrant soundscapes. Thus, affective listening and its kinship can encourage alternative site valuations.

Second, the designer starts to envisage alternative futures for the site from the affective and aesthetic engagement and knowledge acquired through listening. Through the resulting interventions, the designer sets the scene for new chapters in the landscape narrative to be co-produced by its inhabitants and natural processes, as landscapes are constantly changing and never finished. In thinking through those interventions and monitoring their evolution in time, a focus on affective listening might help us develop practices attuned to non-human others. From the kinship developed through affective engagement and the discovery of subtle environmental processes and changes hidden from view, we can develop an ethical framework for intervening in the environment that considers living beings other than humans as active co-makers of the environment and values more than visual.

Listening, as a conduit to emotion, can help us define what matters. Listening can help us establish a kinship with the world, which might encourage us to care for others. Reflecting on this engagement, we can develop a set of ethical values to guide ways of doing attuned to a myriad of non-human others. Feeling a kinship with more than human beings through listening does not guarantee that practices of care will follow; however, it does make it more likely to happen, encouraging the de-centring of humans in planning, design and management practices.

References

Abrahams, C. (2019) 'Comparison between lek counts and bioacoustic recording for monitoring Western Capercaillie (*Tetrao urogallus* L.)', *Journal of Ornithology*, 160(3), pp. 685–697. doi: 10.1007/s10336-019-01649-8.

Abrahams, C., Desjonquères, C. and Greenhalgh, J. (2021) 'Pond acoustic sampling scheme: A draft protocol for rapid acoustic data collection in small waterbodies', *Ecology and Evolution*, 11(12), pp. 7532–7543. doi: 10.1002/ece3.7585.

Alsina-Pages, R. M., *et al.* (2021) 'Soundscape of Catalonia during the first COVID-19 lockdown: Preliminary results from the Sons al Balco project', in *3rd International Electronic Conference on Environmental Research and Public Health*.

Barkham, P. (2022) 'Mhairi Killin: "Boat noise, seal detterrents, sonar – The sea is an industrialised soundscape"', *The Guardian*, 7 July. Available at: https://www.theguardian.com/artanddesign/2022/jul/07/mhairi-killin-artist-whales-sonar-interview.

Bateman, J. and Uzal, A. (2021) 'The relationship between the acoustic complexity index and avian species richness and diversity: A review', *Bioacoustics*, 00(00), pp. 1–14. doi: 10.1080/09524622.2021.2010598.

Bates, A. E., *et al.* (2020) 'COVID-19 pandemic and associated lockdown as a "Global human confinement experiment" to investigate biodiversity conservation', *Biological Conservation*, 248(May), p. 108665. doi: 10.1016/j.biocon.2020.108665.

Bianchi, F. W. and Manzo, V. (2016) *Environmental sound artists: In their own words*. Oxford: Oxford University Press.

Biosphere Soundscapes (2022) *About biosphere soundscapes, biosphere soundscapes*. Available at: http://www.biospheresoundscapes.org/about.html (Accessed: 10 April 2022).

Bradfer-Lawrence, T., *et al.* (2019) 'Guidelines for the use of acoustic indices in environmental research', *Methods in Ecology and Evolution*, 10(10), pp. 1796–1807. doi: 10.1111/2041-210X.13254.

Challéat, S., *et al.* (2020) *Silent cities, silent cities*. Available at: https://osf.io/h285u/

Cities and Memory (2021) *Sounds from the global Covid-19 lockdown, cities and memory*. Available at: https://citiesandmemory.com/covid19-sounds/ (Accessed: 27 June 2023).

Derryberry, E. P., *et al.* (2020) 'Singing in a silent spring: Birds respond to a half-century soundscape reversion during the COVID-19 shutdown', *Science*, 370(6516), pp. 575–579. doi: 10.1126/SCIENCE.ABD5777.

Despret, V. (2022) *Living as a bird*. Cambridge; Medford, MA: Polity Press.

Fairbrass, A. J., *et al.* (2017) 'Biases of acoustic indices measuring biodiversity in urban areas', *Ecological Indicators*, 83(February), pp. 169–177. doi: 10.1016/j.ecolind.2017.07.064.

Farina, A. (2018) 'Ecoacoustics: A quantitative approach to investigate the ecological role of environmental sounds', *Mathematics*, 7(1), pp. 1–16. doi: 10.3390/math7010021.

Haraway, D. J. (1991) *Simians, cyborgs, and women: The reinvention of nature*. New York: Routledge.

Haraway, D. J. (2016) *Staying with the trouble: Making Kin in the Chtulucene*. Durham and London: Duke University Press.

K.Lisa Yang Center for Conservation Bioacoustics (2023) *BirdNET Sound ID, The Cornell Lab*. Available at: https://birdnet.cornell.edu/ (Accessed: 26 June 2023).

Killin, M. (2022) *On Sonorous seas, on Sonorous seas*. Available at: https://www.onsonorousseas.com/ (Accessed: 27 June 2023).

Krause, B. (1987) 'Bioacoustics, habitat ambience in ecological balance', *Whole Earth Review*, 57 (Winter), pp. 14–18.

Krause, B. (2013) 'The voice of the natural world'. Available at: https://www.ted.com/talks/bernie_krause_the_voice_of_the_natural_world?language=en&subtitle=en.

Krause, B. L. and Farina, A. (2016) 'Using ecoacoustic methods to survey the impacts of climate change on biodiversity', *Biological Conservation*, 195(2016), pp. 245–254. doi: 10.1016/j.biocon.2016.01.013.

Krause, B. L. and Hoffman, J. (2012) 'Q & A Bernie Krause soundscape explorer', *Nature*, 485(May), p. 308. doi: 10.1038/485308a.

Lecocq, T., *et al.* (2020) 'Global quieting of high-frequency seismic noise due to COVID-19 pandemic lockdown measures', *Science*, 1343(September), pp. 1338–1343.

Lenzi, S., Sádaba, J. and Lindborg, P. M. (2021) 'Soundscape in times of change: Case study of a city neighbourhood during the COVID-19 lockdown', *Frontiers in Psychology*, 12(March), pp. 1–24. doi: 10.3389/fpsyg.2021.570741.

Lockwood, A. and Morrow, C. (2022) *Annea lockwood - From burning pianos to immersive sound [s] 2, immerse with Charlie Morrow* Available at: https://immersesoundlightspace.podbean.com/e/annea-lockwood-from-burning-pianos-to-immersive-sounds/.

Lockwood, A. and Phillips, L. (2022) *The river feeds back, The academy of natural sciences of Drexel University*. Available at: https://ansp.org/exhibits/past-exhibits/the-river-feeds-back/.

Metcalf, O., *et al.* (2022) *Good practice guidelines for long-term ecoacoustic monitoring in the UK*. UK Acoustics Network.

Nguyen Hong Duc, P., *et al.* (2021) 'Use of ecoacoustics to characterize the marine acoustic environment off the north atlantic french saint-pierre-et-miquelon archipelago', *Journal of Marine Science and Engineering*, 9(2), pp. 1–16. doi: 10.3390/jmse9020177.

Paisaje Sensorial (2020) *Sound stories of COVID19, Paisaje sensorial*. Available at: https://paisajesensorial.com/?project=sound-stories-of-covid19 (Accessed: 10 May 2021).

Picciulin, M., *et al.* (2021) 'Sound discrimination of two sympatric, threatened fish species allows for their in situ mapping', *Aquatic Conservation: Marine and Freshwater Ecosystems*, 31(8), pp. 2103–2118. doi: 10.1002/aqc.3581.

Plumwood, V. (1993) *Feminism and the mastery of nature, Feminism and the mastery of nature*. London and New York: Routledge.

Ross, S. R. P. J., *et al.* (2018) 'Listening to ecosystems: Data-rich acoustic monitoring through landscape-scale sensor networks', *Ecological Research*, 33(1), pp. 135–147. doi: 10.1007/s11284-017-1509-5.

Ross, S. R. P. J., *et al.* (2021) 'Utility of acoustic indices for ecological monitoring in complex sonic environments', *Ecological Indicators*, 121(July 2020), p. 107114. doi: 10.1016/j.ecolind.2020.107114.

Ruiz Arana, U. (2019) 'Thinking with my ears: Guidance on sound for landscape architects', Conference Proceedings of 48th International Congress and Exposition on Noise Control Engineering (Internoise 2019), Madrid: Spanish Acoustical Society, pp. 5968–5975.

Ruiz Arana, U. (2020) *The enchantment of the wild: A journey into wildness through listening*. Newcastle University. Available at: http://theses.ncl.ac.uk/jspui/handle/10443/5178.

Ruiz Arana, U. (2023) 'Soundwalking in the Phonocene: Walking, listening, wilding', in Smolicki, J. (ed.) *Soundwalking: Through time, space, and technologies*. New York: Focal Press, pp. 18–33. doi: 10.4324/9781003193135-2.

Rutz, C., *et al.* (2020) 'COVID-19 lockdown allows researchers to quantify the effects of human activity on wildlife', *Nature Ecology and Evolution*, 4(9), pp. 1156–1159. doi: 10.1038/s41559-020-1237-z.

Stollery, P. (2021) *COVID-19 sound map, Pete Stollery*. Available at: https://www.petestollery.com/covid (Accessed: 20 June 2022).

Sueur, J., Aubin, T. and Simonis, C. (2022) *Seewave v 2.2.0*. Available at: https://cran.r-project.org/web/packages/seewave/seewave.pdf.

Sueur, J. and Farina, A. (2015) 'Ecoacoustics: The ecological investigation and interpretation of environmental sound', *Biosemiotics*, 8(3), pp. 493–502. doi: 10.1007/s12304-015-9248-x.

Sueur, J., Krause, B. and Farina, A. (2019) 'Climate change is breaking earth's beat', *Trends in Ecology and Evolution*, 34(11), pp. 971–973. doi: 10.1016/j.tree.2019.07.014.

Tong, H., *et al.* (2021) 'Increases in noise complaints during the COVID-19 lockdown in Spring 2020: A case study in greater London, UK', *Science of the Total Environment*, 785(December 2019), p. 147213. doi: 10.1016/j.scitotenv.2021.147213.

Villanueva-Rivera, L. J. and Pijanowski, B. C. (2018) *Soundscape ecology v 1.3.3*. Available at: https://cran.r-project.org/web/packages/soundecology/soundecology.pdf.

Wildlife Acoustics (2023) *Kaleidoscope, wildlife acoustics*. Available at: https://www.wildlifeacoustics.com/products/kaleidoscope (Accessed: 26 June 2023).

Winderen, J. (2023) *Major exhibitions, Jana Winderen*. Available at: https://www.janawinderen.com/exhibitions (Accessed: 10 April 2022).

Wolch, J. (1996) 'Zoöpolis', *Capitalism Nature Socialism*, 7(2), pp. 21–47. doi: 10.1080/10455759609358677.

Chapter Ten

Performing the soundscape in practice

Freshwater soundscapes with David de la Haye

In February 2022, I took my children (aged ten, nine and four at the time) to a *Sonic Pond Dipping* event organised by David de la Haye in collaboration with Les Goodyer and Durham Wildlife Trust and with funding from Durham County Council. The event took place at *Low Barns Nature Reserve* (UK), a wetland reserve and designated *Site of Special Scientific Interest*, home to a rich wildlife that includes aquatic plants, amphibians and invertebrates. The wetlands had flooded over the weekend, and we arrived at the muddy reserve mid-morning, armed with waterproofs and wellies. More unusually for a family day out, we also brought headphones and a sound recorder, as, to my eldest disappointment, the purpose of the event was not to jump into the water but rather to use hydrophones to listen to underwater sounds. Her initial disappointment quickly faded as we engaged in the morning activities. We spent time at the visitor centre with David, Les, and Hannah (from Durham Wildlife Trust), listening to pre-recorded soundtracks of the wetland, learning how a hydrophone works, and observing some of the invertebrates we were about to encounter, such as boatmen and damselflies. As we listened to pre-recorded soundtracks, we struggled to find the words to describe the unusual biological sounds we heard. That which my youngest first identified as a 'crocodile', trying to imagine animals that might live in freshwater; she then refined it as an 'oven', perhaps a more apt description of the mechanical and rhythmical nature of the stridulating underwater sounds.

After our introductory session, we walked to the wetland and spent time amongst the tall reeds, immersing the hydrophones in the water and listening attentively.

DOI: 10.4324/9781003202981-14

Why can we hear overwater sounds underwater but not the other way around? – asked my son. This simple realisation – that the water surface acts as a sonic barrier allowing some transmission from air to water, but little the other way round – caught us all by surprise. Once we got used to listening underwater, my children had as much fun trying to see how far they could throw the hydrophone as seeking to identify the elusive underwater clicks and beeps. It was a windy morning, and the movement of the reeds dominated the soundscape, yet we got a chance to hear and record some water boatmen (Figure 10.1).

Since the event, my children have approached ponds differently, excited at what might lie hidden underneath nearby murky and green waters. They still compete to see how far they can throw the microphone and tiptoe around the water, aware of their own sounding within it.

Sonic Pond Dipping is a community engagement event devised by David de la Haye to raise awareness of ponds and their ecological and cultural values. David is a musician, field recordist, freshwater eco-artist and Ph.D. researcher who has been part of my journey to listening and sound-making from the start. I caught up with David before the event to learn more about his work in freshwater soundscapes, collaborations with a wide range of artists, communities and researchers, and the value artists bring to the growing field of ecoacoustics. We also exchanged e-mails afterwards to reflect on his most recent work.

From musician to freshwater eco-artist, could you tell us a little about your sound-making trajectory?

Figure 10.1 Sonic Pond Dipping at Low Barns Nature Reserve, Credit: Euan Preston.

I started playing bass aged 14 and spent all my time in the music block of our school, playing with the piano and early notation software as I had no access to such technologies at home. This musical trajectory led to my studying Jazz and Contemporary Music at Leeds Conservatoire (then College of Music), followed by postgraduate studies in Glitch Music and Aesthetics of Failure in Digital Composition at Newcastle University. At Newcastle, I focused on improvised music and microsound; on working with sound as a material object, rather than something 'just to play'; sound at a granular level, on the periphery of human experience. This was around 2003. I would purposely skip, or scratch CDs coaxing electronic equipment to have its own mind and direct the performance. However, this experimental scene seemed overtly masculine and noise-orientated, which I was uncomfortable with. I wanted to turn those unwanted sounds into something *listenable,* with its own sense of beauty; a sort of recycling and reusing of sound, as well as adopting a minimalist or frugal approach to music making – that is, working with a small amount of material to see how far I could take it.

As I completed my postgraduate studies, the Folk degree started at Newcastle University. This was an exciting time – I happened to live opposite a bunch of folk musicians and started going to *sessions* with them. The strong connection to place in Folk music encouraged me to investigate sound in the landscape. This in turn led me to field recording. I was working with Scottish Borders fiddle player Shona Mooney at the time, and we would go on to make some location-based recordings. I wore binaural microphones, standing in the middle of rural Northumberland or in the Scottish borders, while Shona would play, and we would incorporate environmental sounds.

Through Folk music, I realised the importance of place. Folk music can be tied to specific areas and, therefore, to animal species, which can be identified aurally and sonically. Landscapes and humans became connected sonically, which I found fascinating. Exploring hidden sounds in the landscape also became a big part of my work. An example is the sound installation that I made with James Davoll, *Bridges___*, exploring the internal resonances of the seven iconic bridges crossing the River Tyne in Newcastle upon Tyne.

Exploration and connection to place come across very strongly in your work. Lately, you have moved from recording terrestrial environments to recording and engaging communities almost exclusively in underwater environments. What triggered that shift?

Growing up on an island, it was inevitable that I'd develop a strong connection to water. In the Channel Islands, Jersey is nine miles by five; you cannot get away from the sea! Even where I live now, Durham in the Northeast of England, the sea is close (Figure 10.2).

Figure 10.2 David de la Haye field recording at Hetton Lyons Country Park, Durham, Credit: Joseph Truswell.

Over recent years, freshwater environments have taken over my work. This was in part due to the COVID-19 lockdowns. I could not travel far and realized I did not need to. I recorded four ponds around my home regularly: a small village pond, a pond on private farmland, another in a quarry and the large Brasside Pond in central Durham. You cannot tell what ponds will sound like by looking at them. Tiny puddles can be full of life and pristine reservoirs devoid of any. My practice led to studying inland waters, lakes and ponds and attending online seminars and lectures on the subject, encountering completely new terminology along the way! In these seminars and lectures, the soundscape of ponds was never discussed, despite their rich complexity. I realised that there was a knowledge gap to fill.

The field of ecoacoustics is developing rapidly. How do you see the field developing within freshwater environments?

Ecoacoustics has come along exponentially in the last few years. The global quietening experienced during the pandemic shifted public perception of sound in the environment. When it comes to aquatic listening, most emphasis has been on marine environments.

I joined the Hebridean Whale and Dolphin Trust in 2019. They have deployed their towed hydrophone for 15 years, creating an acoustic database of cetacean life in the region. I took my own equipment and managed to record some wonderful underwater seal vocalisations, which were intriguing even to staff aboard the vessel. These were subsequently added to the British Library collection.

The governance of freshwater environments is less stringent than marine ones, and there is currently little protection status for ponds and rivers. This may account for the gap in research and funding for deployable audio technologies in freshwater habitats instead of marine ones. When protections are in place, the technology might follow. There is a gap for people to develop more affordable, deployable setups for freshwater environments for both creative and monitoring purposes (Figure 10.3).

What is the purpose of your underwater recordings and community events, such as the 'Sonic Pond Dipping' I attended?

The main purpose is to widen people's knowledge about these rich and biodiverse environments. Simple technology can be used to engage communities with nature through attentive listening. An example is the family-orientated *Sonic Pond Dipping* sessions you attended. Another example is the work that I am doing with the *Durham Beach Rangers*, which focuses on rock-pool exploration and coastal soundwalks. It is about how listening positions us within the world, but also how we give a voice to unheard organisms around us.

The interdisciplinary angle that artists such as Leah Barclay pioneered is fascinating. It demonstrates the power of sound, and music, across scientists, artists and wider communities; the two are not mutually exclusive, and collaborations enrich each other's work. Understanding ecosystem health in freshwater through listening is something I am dedicated to pushing forward.

Figure 10.3 Underwater recording in County Durham, UK, Credit: David de la Haye.

The audio recordings support both scientific and creative outputs. For scientific purposes, the audio contributes to a database that could provide a baseline or be used to help identify underwater species using bioacoustics. The soundscapes of freshwater habitats are largely undocumented, presenting an emergent field of study. I try to expand this admittedly niche audience by making creative contributions to scientific events such as *Ecology Across Borders* (British Ecological Society, 2021), *INTECOL: Frontiers in Ecology* (Geneva, 2022) and the *Symposium for European Freshwater Sciences*, this time organised by Freshwater Biological Association (Newcastle, 2023). An approach that worked was an alternative to conference-style scientific posters: the *audio poster*. These short, sound-led videos convey a large amount of sonic information in a compact format. Once again, these works reflect my minimal approach; sonic miniatures that aim to spark curiosity and raise awareness of the soundscape of ponds.

Understandably, you place a high importance on sound quality for recordings for your creative work, which might not be a priority for environmental monitoring purposes. You have just discussed scientific and creative outputs. Where do you see the link between both in the recording and processing?

In both cases, much time is spent sifting through audio data! With my freshwater recordings, I try to inspire awe and wonder about these natural spaces, which might get lost in facts and figures. Finding sounds is simple; they are abundant. However, just like in the ecological monitoring situation, patience is required. This often-laborious searching is part of my creative process. I find some solace in the slow approach.

Data *proves* that these habitats are abundant with life, but it doesn't *feel* real because it's just data, numbers on a spreadsheet. The experience that listening embodies is an approach to fostering a caring relationship with our natural world.

As an artist, I am selective about what I present, especially as the sonic palette is quite unfamiliar to most. Many of the sounds in ponds are rhythmic rather than melodic, which I love as a bass player! I have begun to explore how selected fragments could be reinterpreted by musicians. Some spectrograms correlate closely to graphic scores of the 1960s, which can be used as a starting point for music-making. An example of this approach is a workshop I led in April 2022 at Sage Gateshead with the Young Sinfonia for a group of composers and performers from the Guildhall School of Music. In the workshop, I shared my underwater field recording practice, and together we experimented with graphic scores derived from these recordings. This allows musicians to get closer to underwater sounds and environments (Soundtrack 10.1).

♪ Soundtrack 10.1 The Pit Pond, Wildlife Sound Recording Society, restricted winner. Credit: David de la Haye

And it brings the listeners closer as well, interrogating what's happening, what the musicians are playing, where those sounds are coming from.

It creates a dialogue, a shared sonic space. When we walk past those ponds, sounds filter through; you can hear them under the water. But the reverse is not true.

We found that fascinating at your Sonic Pond Dipping Event – how, for example, human voices filtered through the water, which we did not think they would, by looking at the calm surface.

I have a lovely recording of a train passing on the rails beside one of the ponds I regularly visit, and as the train goes past, the soundscape on the pond notably changes. There are plants in the recording, too, not something you typically think of as responding sonically, but they do. It may be the substrate shifting as the ground rumbles. I do not know, and it does not matter because it is more about realizing that we all share a sonic space, and we should be more careful of our role in that sharing (Figure 10.4).

Figure 10.4 Easington Pit Pond (Soundtrack 10.2 Photosynthesis and trains), Credit: David de la Haye.

Annex

Scores for listening and sounding in landscape architecture and urban design

Introduction

> Why does the MOMA sculpture garden, for example, sound like any taxi stand in midtown NYC? Why is an expensive, quiet car quiet only when riding on the inside?
>
> (Odland and Auinger, 2010)

Environmental noise in cities is an aesthetic issue, as composers Bruce Odland and Sam Auinger suggest with their opening questions. Environmental noise can also impact the health and well-being of human and non-human communities. No less than 'one million healthy life years are lost every year from traffic-related noise in the western part of Europe' (WHO Regional Office for Europe, 2011, p. V). Sleep disturbance and annoyance are mainly responsible for this loss, followed by cardiovascular disease, cognitive impairment in children and tinnitus (ibid.). In non-human communities, exposure to environmental noise can interfere with animals' 'foraging behaviour, shifted temporal activity patterns, decreased abundance, reduced condition, and altered reproductive success' (Levenhagen *et al.*, 2021, p. 177).

Integrating listening and sound into built environment professions is essential to avoid the conflicts and health and well-being impacts that soundscapes can trigger and the domination of traffic noise in our urban soundscapes. Researchers and artists have called for built environment professionals to listen. Composer Pauline Oliveros, for example, invited us to become *deep listeners* to engage with and shape the urban soundscape (2015). Similarly, Bruce Odland and Sam Auinger invited us to *think with ears* and expand a culture that prioritises the eye when making decisions (2010).

Canadian composer and educator Raymond Murray Schafer also advocated *thinking with ears* when he proposed that we are all composers of the soundscape (1977). All landscape architecture and urban design interventions, no matter how small, sound. Everything vibrates, sounds or can be heard or sensed through bodies. Through our design and management interventions, we play a part in composing the *geophony* (geophysical sounds), *biophony* (biological sounds) and *anthrophony* (anthropogenic sounds) of the environment (Krause, 1987). Thus, could we think of ourselves as *soundscape architects*?

In the last 20 years, research on soundscapes across urban planning, acoustics, bio and ecoacoustics, acoustic ecology, and sound art, amongst others, has taken pace to improve acoustic environments beyond noise mitigation. With application to urban soundscapes and human health, this wave of research was triggered by the Environmental Noise Directive (END, Directive 2002/49/EC) and its implementation by member countries (European Parliament and Council, 2002). The END recognised noise's detrimental effect on human health and well-being. It required identifying and managing noise pollution and protecting quiet areas that reflected positive environmental soundscapes. The ISO 12913 publications emerged from the END and guided much of the current urban soundscape and practice (BSI, 2014, 2018, 2019). Despite the breadth of research on soundscapes, listening and active consideration of sound is yet to permeate everyday landscape architecture and urban design practice. In our training, drawing, sketching and manipulating visual space are key skills to develop and master, yet little attention is paid to listening, auralisations or aural space. In our practice, designs are conceptualised and presented through drawings and images, and landscape assessments largely focus on visual assessments to the detriment of aural assessments and aural ways of thinking and doing. Caught up in visual modes of thinking and doing, we are yet to fully embrace the possibilities of *thinking with our ears* as *soundscape architects*.

Listening to sound and soundscape

The soundscape is the aural expression of the physical environment, including its communities. It is the medium to perceive and interact with that environment, which depends on individual, social and cultural aspects and characteristics

(Thompson, 2012). Sound is also a material, creative and affective object in design, with applications to all project stages.

If we envisage sound as both a material object and mediator of a relation, listening, in turn, can have many interrelated functions and can be employed in interrelated modes to expand visual modes of thinking, knowing and doing in landscape architecture and urban design:

1. listening, as communication, can help us understand a place, and its communities, providing information about the character of a place and what is happening around it.
2. listening, as an aesthetic pursuit can contribute to how a space is used and valued
3. listening, as a source of affective engagement with the environment, conditions our actions within the environment and helps us determine our priorities (Figure 11.1).

Affective listening is the umbrella that can (but does not have to) encompass aesthetic listening and listening as communication. Affective listening enables designers to disrupt visual modes of doing. First and foremost, it embeds designers in an environment as part of fieldwork, interweaving experiential and objective site inquiries, thus interlinking the role of designers as active listeners and co-producers of a place and as planners, designers and managers. This mode of listening also helps designers to uncover the specificity of a place, its inhabitants and its aural affordances, which might contrast with visual affordances and invite other forms of practice (including more-than-human). This listening mode also helps designers relate to how current and future human and non-human communities might be affected by interventions and how they might interact with prospective spaces, refining conceptual designs.

Listening in those three interrelated modes can be threaded through all the stages of the life of a landscape architecture and urban design project, from site investigation to post-occupancy studies, as attested by the methodological tools and techniques outlined in this manual. The work of landscape architects and urban designers is concerned with reading, transforming and representing the environment (Jørgensen *et al.*, 2020) and monitoring sites post-completion, as landscapes are never finished and constantly evolving. Accordingly, this manual follows these stages in the design process to provide tools and techniques for listening and sounding as part of landscape architecture and urban design and enable planners, designers and managers

Figure 11.1 The three modes of listening in landscape architecture and urban design.

to become *soundscape architects*. The stages described below cross-refer to the stage classification detailed in the Landscape Institute's *The Landscape Consultant's Scope of Services* (2018) and the RIBA Plan of Work (2020).

Tuning in

RIBA and LI stage 0: strategic definition
To hear and to listen mean different things (Oliveros, 2015). To hear is an involuntary action whereby the body and mind perceive sonic vibrations. To listen is an intentional action whereby the mind pays attention to the sounds perceived (ibid.). We can train our listening; we cannot train our hearing. Training our listening to attune

to the environment is the starting point of our journey towards becoming *soundscape architects*. The following exercises and practices will help the reader to that end.

Ear cleaning and deep listening exercises

Ear cleaning

Murray Schafer considered *ear cleaning* a prerequisite to attuning to the environment through sound (Schafer, 1967a). Schafer devised several *ear cleaning* exercises for his experimental music students at Simon Fraser University. These included, for example, being silent for a day to focus on the sounds of others or keeping a diary of sounds encountered throughout the day (ibid.). Although these exercises would be better termed *listening* rather than ear cleaning, as hearing cannot be trained, the reader is encouraged to turn to them to start tuning into the environment.

Deep listening

Pauline Oliveros considered listening a 'lifetime practice that depends on accumulated experiences with sound' (2015). Therefore, with time, listening can be actively developed. *Deep listening* is an improvisation and meditation practice that Oliveros developed to integrate hearing (involuntary) with listening (intentional) (The Center for Deep Listening, 2021). *Deep listening* involves listening in 'as many ways as possible to everything that can possibly be heard all of the time' as a way to connect listeners with the environment and its inhabitants (ibid.). *Deep listening* comprises two intertwined 'modes of listening – focal and global' (Oliveros, 1999, p. 1). The first focuses on specific sounds and their detail, while the second on the entire soundscape (ibid.). In conjunction, both modes enable listening 'in every possible way to everything possible to hear no matter what you are doing' (ibid., p. 1). The reader is also encouraged to put into practice Oliveros's *deep listening* scores or exercises, to practice *focal* and *global* ways of listening (see, e.g., Oliveros, 2013).

Inspired by Oliveros's *deep listening,* in the autumn of 2022, I carried out a short-lived listening studio with 1st stage students of the Master of Landscape Architecture at Newcastle University to showcase how these early listening exercises can expand our practice. The studio entitled *Sounding Bodies, Sounding Space* helped students understand aural space, as a counterpart to physical and visual space, through listening. Aural space and visual space do not always correspond. Aural space is experiential and not defined by physical boundaries (Blesser and Salter, 2007). It is not defined by visual boundaries either: we can hear sounds out of sight, and sometimes the information we receive through listening and that received by looking do not correspond. Aural space is defined as much by 'virtual sonic boundaries', including background noise (ibid.), as it is by physical boundaries, atmospheric conditions, weather and listeners' abilities. In the first part of the studio, students were given a selection of scores (instructions) for *sounding* space to put into practice in their own time. For example, one of the scores asked students *to pick any sound in a public space and draw its acoustic arena (how far out from the source the sound can be heard). Follow the sound in all directions to determine its acoustic arena.* Figure 11.2 shows this score put into practice by one of the students, Kazusa Hayashi.

In the second part of the studio, students were tasked with developing their own scores for sounding space or sounding bodies in space, which were collated in a booklet for distribution. The booklet included instructions for calibrating listening

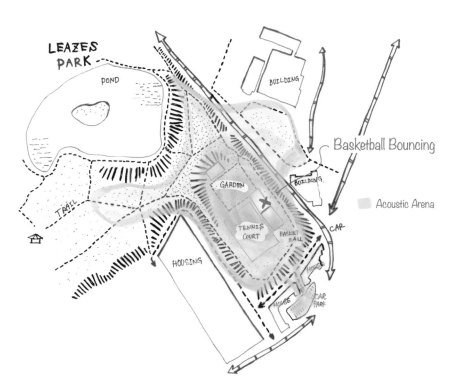

Figure 11.2 Sounding bodies, sounding space studio: Score 02 in practice. Credit: Hazusa Hayashi

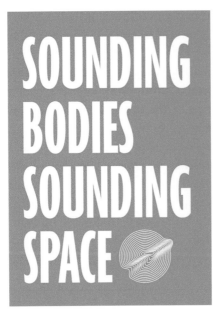

Following these tips will help you focus your listening[2]:

▸ Be silent, and turn your phone or other devices to silent too

▸ Start by paying attention to your own soundmaking – the sounds that your body makes while interacting with the environment – your movements, your footsteps, your breathing... Then focus your attention on nearby sounds, and finally those in the distance.

▸ To focus on the detail, select a continuous sound and follow it until you can no longer hear it.

▸ Closing your eyes, where you can, also focuses your listening (but not whilst walking!)

▸ Try not to get frustrated with any unwanted sounds, as to listen is to be open to all sounds.

[2] Tips adapted from BSI (The British Standards Institution) (2018) 'PD ISO/TS 12913-2 Acoustics - Soundscape Part 2 : Data collection and reporting requirements'

Calibrate you listening   12

Figure 11.3 Extract from sounding bodies, sounding space booklet, with instructions for calibrating listening, Credit: Usue Ruiz Arana and Stef Leach.

that might be helpful to the reader (Figure 11.3). Further project details are included as a case study in Chapter 6.

Soundwalking

Organising or participating in soundwalks is also useful for training our listening. Soundwalks are guided walks, usually carried out in silence, to pay attention to the environment through listening. The guide takes participants through several interesting soundscapes, and the walk can include stops along the way to discuss experiences. Artists, practitioners, activists and researchers organise soundwalks for various purposes. For some, soundwalks actively engage with the environment and social, ecological, cultural and political issues within it. For others, soundwalks are a way of assessing the soundscape itself, its aesthetic and affective qualities and how these contribute to the perception of the environment. Both purposes feed into our work, as we must engage with an environment to assess and transform it.

Soundwalks for engagement

In the early 1970s, members of the *World Soundscape Project* (WSP), led by Schafer, carried out soundwalks to bring awareness to the soundscape of Vancouver that the group felt was getting increasingly noisier. For the WSP, as the noise in citizens' lives increased, their listening ability decreased (Schafer, 1967b). These were silent soundwalks where participants came together at the end to discuss the experience. Today soundwalks are employed to bring attention to the soundscape through active listening and to the inhabitants, spaces and relations of the environment listened to. For Hildegard Westerkamp, a member of the WSP, a soundwalk is 'an ear-environment relationship … it is an exploration of what the naked ear hears and how we relate and react to it' (1974). Thus, soundwalks are a way of affectively relating to the environment through listening and can be successfully integrated into the fieldwork of any project to understand, engage with and assess an environment through listening.

Soundwalks for soundscape (affective) assessment

Within the ISO 12913 methodology, soundwalks are used to collect data on the perception of the soundscape. These are guided soundwalks where participants fill in standard questionnaires at key spaces along the walks. These soundwalks and questionnaires are intended to gather information on sound sources and the perceived affective quality of the soundscape and to assess the surrounding sound environment and its appropriateness (BSI, 2018). Along these soundwalks, binaural sound recordings are also used to extract noise indicators, such as sound pressure level, and psychoacoustic indicators, such as sharpness and tonality (ibid.).

In the soundwalks I have led with a wide range of participants, I have adapted the method according to the walk's purpose and the participants' makeup. For example, the soundwalk I led for the *Walking Festival of Sound* in October 2019 was a pure listening walk. The walk was open to anyone, and the purpose was to trigger participants' imagination through the timing and route, an initial prompt and the listening along the walk. The soundwalk took along Newcastle's medieval Quayside through low frequented paths and uneven stairs sporadically maintained as the day turns into night. The initial prompt was the story of a folklore creature once thought to have inhabited the Quayside, terrorising residents through his presence. We came together at the end to discuss thoughts and impressions of the walk, and the discussion was very open to any thoughts. Further information on the *Walking Festival of Sound* is provided in Chapter 4.

Other examples include my many walks with landscape architecture students and practitioners. In these soundwalks, we usually follow the ISO 12913 methodology, primarily without sound recordings, to gather perceptual data only to inform designs and encourage participants to incorporate soundscape assessments in their projects. In these soundwalks, participants are given a questionnaire to complete, instructions for the walk and recommendations for calibrating their listening at the beginning. The questionnaire is usually based on method A, ISO 12913 part 2 (2018), expanded with additional open ended questions to get participants thinking about potential interventions at each of the spaces we stop at. Chapter 6's listening and sounding exercises include details of a typical soundwalk with landscape architects.

Reading the soundscape

RIBA and LI stage 1: Preparation and brief

Listening helps us understand the stories embedded within landscapes, allowing us to bring attention to them through our interventions and setting the stage for communities and natural processes to start new chapters in those stories. Listening in its three interrelated modes – affect, communication and aesthetic evaluation – is integral to reading the landscape. It provides an affective engagement with the environment, helps understand a place's communities, culture, materiality and geometry, and contributes to its aesthetic valuation. The purpose of reading the landscape through listening is to determine the qualities and character of a site, identify opportunities for transformation and determine the existing aural character and identity. This stage of the design process, known as the *soundscape inventory and analysis*, informs site-wide conceptual design responses and strategies to improve or conserve the existing soundscape (Figure 11.4).

The scope of the *inventory and analysis* will vary according to the brief and scale of the project. At a masterplanning scale, we can employ the methodology recommended by ISO 12913 (BSI, 2018, 2019), expanding it to incorporate ecoacoustic methods such as soundscape indices to consider other living organisms. At this scale, reviewing existing noise and quiet area maps is also a useful starting point for understanding noise levels from major airports, railways and roads. Through this review, we can identify areas where unwanted sound might be an issue, and the involvement of an acoustician would be beneficial, and potential quiet spaces. At a detailed design scale, a more nuanced understanding of the soundscape and its context is required

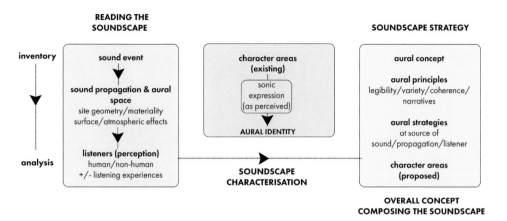

Figure 11.4 From reading to composing the soundscape.

to develop aural strategies that can be integrated into the overall design concept and principles for the site.

Deciphering a place through listening can be integrated into the following stages of the *site inventory and analysis* process: (1) site inventory, (2) landscape characterization and (3) identification of constraints and opportunities.

Site inventory

The perception of the environment through listening depends on physical, environmental and individual and species variables. Those variables can be grouped into three parameters to be captured in the soundscape inventory and analysis of a site: (1a) sound events, (1b) environment and (1c) listeners.

Sound events

Sound events are the sources of sound. There are three aspects to record as part of the site inventory concerning sound events:

- Origin of sound event (whether natural or cultural, biological or non-biological).
- Acoustic properties (including temporality and rhythm) and type of sound in relation to its ambiance (background, foreground and salient).
- Cultural, symbolic or functional relevance of those sounds and how they contribute to the character and navigation of space (Figure 11.5).

LISTENING STATION 1

SOURCES OF SOUND

1. Source (most to least noticeable) + origin
2. Duration, rhythm, peridiocity
3. Loudness & pitch
4. Background (B), foreground (F) or salient (S)
5. Quality of listening experience: +/-

Insects (bees buzzing)
1. Biophonic
2. Intermittent, monotonous, frequent
3. High pitch, relatively quiet
4. F
5. +

Rustling of vegetation
1. Biophonic + geophonic
2. Intermittent with wind, rhythmical, frequent
3. Medium pitch, quiet-medium (gush of wind)
4. F
5. +

Voices & footsteps
1. Biophonic + geophonic
2. Intermittent, rhythmical, occassional
3. Medium to high pitch, quiet to moderate
4. F with attentive listening, B otherwise
5. +

Seagulls
1. Biophonic
2. Intermittent, monotonous, occassional
3. Low-medium pitch, loud
4. F
5. +

Traffic
1. Anthrophonic
2. Constant (outside site), intermittent (inside)
3. Low pitch, medium to high loudness
4. B (outside site), F (inside site)
5. Negative to neutral

ENVIRONMENT

1. Spatial definition & microclimate;
2. Existing aural effects

1. Low to medium shrubs provide definition to the vehicular approaches to the car park and might provide small grade of sound absorption (vegetated soil). Trees to the northern boundary partially obscure views into the railway and further along. Open aspect, susceptible to wind.

2. Cocktail party effect (able to focus on biophonic sounds and discard traffic); Traffic drone; Rapid dispersion of sounds due to openness of site.

CHARACTER

1. Character area description
2. Soundscape character

1. A car park entrance with no provision for pedestrian, poor legibility due to lack of signage and pedestrian friendly features, ornamental planting framing entrance roads and softening an otherwise hard environment. Bees buzzing, rustling of vegetation, voices and footsteps are appropriate to this time of year and contribute positively to this mainly 'characterless' entrance and enliven the space. The buzzing and rustling of vegetation distract from the traffic (some cocktail party effect) and enliven the space. Seagulls also contribute to the character of the place as they link the site to its context in close proximity to the river Clyde.

2. Uneventful and unpleasant, illegible and uncoherent.

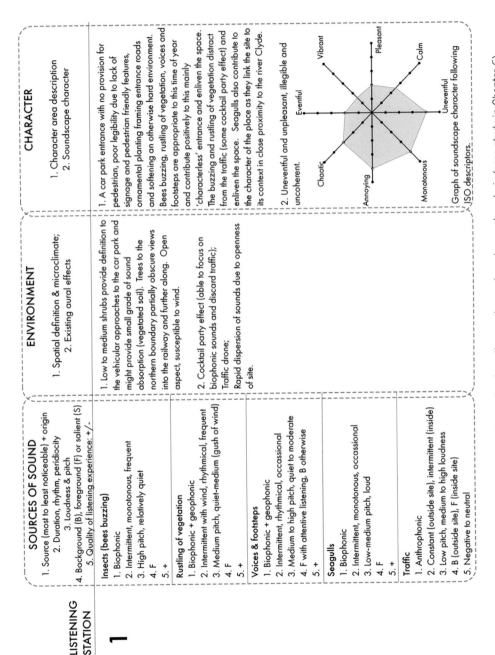

Graph of soundscape character following ISO descriptors.

Figure 11.5 Custom table to capture The High Street Goodsyard's soundscape inventory and analysis (case study in Chapter 6).

Environment

Sound waves are transformed as they travel through the environment. Therefore, the acoustic properties of the environment, determined by its geometry and materiality, as well as weather conditions, influence what we hear. Thus, listening in space can tell us invaluable information regarding the geometry and materiality of a place and help us understand aural space. With regards to the environment during the soundscape inventory and analysis, we can record:

- *Acoustic arena* of key sound events and *acoustic horizon* of listeners at key each character area, if relevant (Figure 11.6).

    Acoustic horizon is 'the farthest distance in every direction from [a source of sound] from which [the] sound may be heard' (Truax, 1999). The acoustic horizon, therefore, denotes the longest distance between the listener and the sonic event.

    An acoustic arena is an area 'where listeners can hear a sonic event because it has sufficient loudness to overcome the background noise' (Blesser and Salter, 2007, p. 27). The acoustic arena is centred on the sound event and delineates the area or space inside which listeners can hear the sound event.

    Auditory channel refers to the connection established between a sound event and a listener (ibid.).

    Sound, in the environment, does not propagate as uniformly as shown in Figure 11.6, as it is affected by atmospheric conditions, physical features and background sounds. Listeners' acoustic horizons also vary among individuals and are affected by a dynamic soundscape.
- *Surface* and *aural effects* caused by the materiality and geometry of a place

    Surface effects include absorption, reflection and diffraction, which depend on the materiality of objects and surfaces (Truax, 1999). Hard surfaces reflect sound waves, whereas soft surfaces, such as dense grass, absorb them (ibid.). High-frequency sounds tend to be either absorbed or reflected. In contrast, low-frequency sounds 'have wavelengths that are much longer than most objects and barriers' and can therefore diffract around those larger objects and barriers (ibid.)

    Sonic effect refers to the discernible sound effects that result from the interaction of 'the physical sound environment, the sound milieu of a socio-cultural community, and the *internal soundscape* of every individual' (Augoyard and Torgue, 2005, p. 9). This manual employs the term *aural effect* instead of sonic to shift the emphasis from the sound effect to its perception through listening. Some *aural effects*, such as reverberation, are linked to the morphology and materiality of

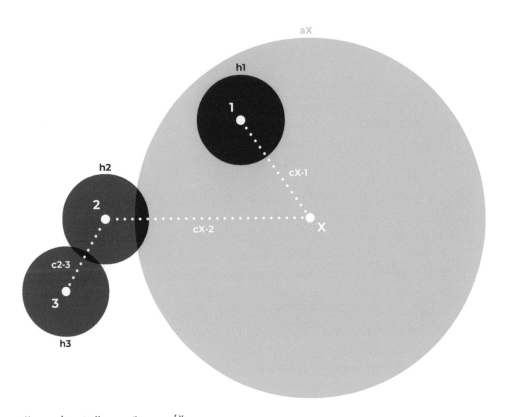

X = sound event; aX = acoustic arena of X
1, 2, 3 = listeners; h1, h2, h3 = acoustic horizons for 1, 2, 3
cX-1 = auditory channel that enables 1 to hear X; cX-2 = auditory channel that enables 2 to partially hear X
c2-3 = auditory channel that enables 2 and 3 to communicate

Figure 11.6 Theoretical diagram of acoustic horizons, acoustic arena and auditory channels, Credit: Dan Hill.

space; others are dependent on the listener or community, including semantic effects and those that relate to memory (ibid.). Key *aural effects* that the reader might encounter on their site include (Figure 11.7):

a) *Drone* refers to a continuous sound with 'no noticeable variation in intensity or pitch' (ibid., p. 40). The constant flow of traffic typically causes it.

b) *Cut-out* occurs when sound intensity falls suddenly when moving from one space to another due to material features or passing from a reverberant space to a dull one.

c) *Filtration* is the flowing of sound from one space to another and is caused by 'features of the environment separating the source and listener' (ibid., p. 49)

Figure 11.7 Key aural effects.

d) *Reverberation and echo* are caused by the reflection of sound waves in surfaces that add indirect signals to the direct signal, resulting in an environment perceived as louder than the original signal (ibid., p. 111). Reverberation results from multiple reflections, whereas echo results from a 'single reflection delayed long enough to be perceived as a separate acoustic event' (Truax, 1999).

e) *Ubiquity* refers to the inability to locate the source of the sound as the sound seems to come from all directions simultaneously.

f) The *cocktail party* effect refers to our ability to be selective in what we listen to, focusing on a sound and disregarding others.

g) *Phonomnesis* is the ability of a particular context and situation to trigger a sound memory.

h) *Anamnesis* is the instinctive recall of a memory through listening and can bring back a past atmosphere to the current experience of place (ibid.).

i) *Remanence* refers to the perceptual listening effect of perceiving a sound that can no longer be heard, just as the sound event disappears, and it is therefore an aural illusion that can provide spatial connection (ibid.).

All the above effects are derived from and described in detail in *Sonic Experience: A Guide to Everyday Sounds* (Augoyard and Torgue, 2005).

- *Atmospheric effects*, which might relate to the specific timing of the assessment.

Atmospheric effects include absorption, scattering or reflection of sound waves (Truax, 1999). Absorption depends on temperature and humidity, with higher absorption in low-humid, high-temperature places, due to water reflecting sound (Trikootam and Hornikx, 2019). Scattering depends on wind speed and direction, with sound levels increasing when sound waves travel downwind towards the receptor (Hannah, 2006). Reflection depends on temperature gradients, with sound waves refracted upwards when the temperature is higher closer to the ground and colder away from it (e.g., daytime) and refracted downwards at nighttime, causing multiple ground reflections. (ibid.).

Listeners

Through listening, we are affected by the sounds of the environment. This affection conditions how we interact and act within that environment. According to prevailing theoretical models of soundscape perception, how we are affected by sound depends on two dimensions: *pleasantness* and *eventfulness* (BSI, 2019). Positive soundscapes include *vibrant* soundscapes on one end that are *pleasant* and *eventful* and calm soundscapes on the other that are *pleasant* and *uneventful*.

During the *site inventory and analysis*, human affection can be recorded through:

- *Descriptors.* The descriptors advanced by the ISO 12913 include: 'pleasant, chaotic, vibrant, uneventful, calm, annoying, eventful, monotonous' (BSI, 2018). It is also important to record the *degree of control* over the soundscape and the *appropriateness* of the soundscape to the existing character, as these influence the affective response to the soundscape (Axelsson, 2015). Descriptors captured can then be related to the character of the space (Figure 11.8).
- *Experiential aural effects* can also capture human affective responses. Examples are included in Figure 11.9 and in the aural strategy section of the manual.

We are yet to find ways of recording non-human affection; however, the behavioural response to sound can be recorded through ecoacoustic methods.

Landscape characterisation

Establishing a site's character areas helps us intervene in it. Through the soundscape assessment, we seek to identify the aural qualities of an area that contribute to its distinctiveness and how listening contributes to the aesthetic and perceptual appraisal of the landscape. Aural qualities are the aural expression of a place's natural and cultural elements and events. These aural qualities can be identified in the site inventory and assessed with the broader elements that contribute to the character.

To determine how the perception of sound events contributes to the character of a place, classifying them into *background, foreground* and *unique* sounds is an useful exercise. In any given place, there will be unique sounds, either in how they interact or are perceived. Another evaluation that can be useful to determine how sound events contribute to the character of a place is thinking about how appropriate those sounds are to the overall character of the place and the events and interactions that occur there.

The overall identity of a place or *genius loci* has an aural expression, an *aural identity*. The *aural identity* refers not only to the characteristic sounds themselves but also to the characteristics of a place that determine how those sounds interact, propagate and are perceived.

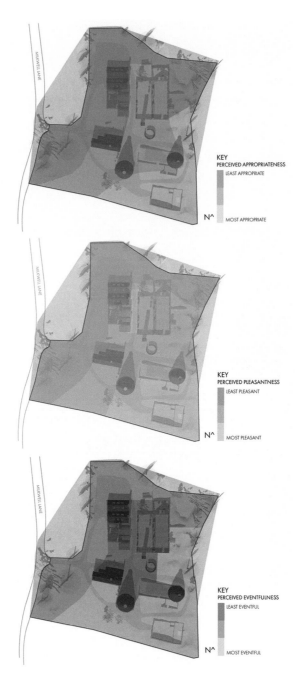

Figure 11.8 Perceived appropriateness, pleasantness and eventfulness at the Old Pottery, Corbridge (case study in Chapter 6), Base drawing credit: EDable Architecture.

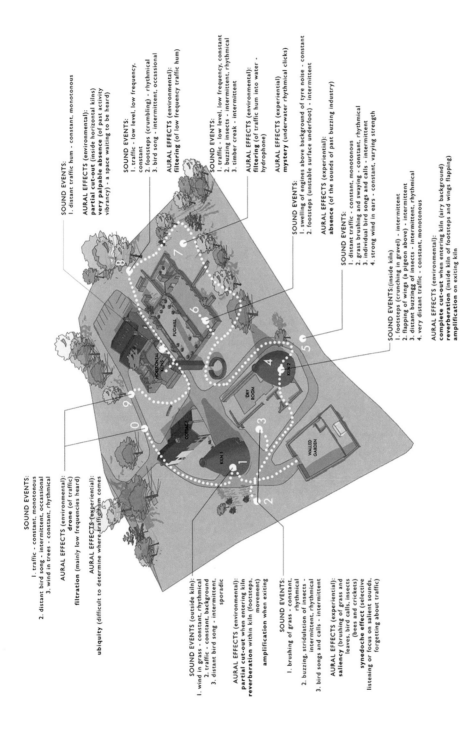

SOUND EVENTS:
1. distant traffic hum - constant, monotonous

AURAL EFFECTS (environmental):
partial cut-out (inside horizontal kilns)
very palpable absence (of past activity
vibrancy) - a space waiting to be heard)

SOUND EVENTS:
1. traffic - low level, low frequency,
   constant
2. footsteps (crumbling) - rhythmical
3. bird song - intermittent, occassional

AURAL EFFECTS (environmental):
filtering (of low frequency traffic hum)

SOUND EVENTS:
1. traffic - low level, low frequency, constant
2. buzzing insects - intermittent, rhythmical
3. timber creak - intermittent

AURAL EFFECTS (environmental):
filtering (of traffic hum into water -
hydrophone)

AURAL EFFECTS (experiential)
mystery (underwater rhythmical clicks)

SOUND EVENTS:
1. swelling of engines above background of tyre noise - constant
2. footsteps (unstable surface underfoot) - intermittent

AURAL EFFECTS (experiential):
absence (of the sounds of past buzzing industry)

SOUND EVENTS:
1. distant traffic - constant, monotonous
2. grass brushing and swaying - constant, rhythmical
3. individual bird songs and calls - intermittent
4. strong wind in ears - constant, varying strength

SOUND EVENTS:(inside kiln)
1. footsteps (crunching in gravel) - intermittent
2. flapping of wings (a pigeon above) - intermittent
3. distant buzzing of insects - intermittent, rhythmical
4. very distant traffic - constant, monotonous

AURAL EFFECTS (environmental):
complete cut-out when entering kiln (airy background)
reverberation (inside kiln of footsteps and wings flapping)
amplification on exiting kiln

SOUND EVENTS:
1. traffic - constant, monotonous
2. distant bird song - intermittent, occassional
3. wind in trees - constant, rhythmical

AURAL EFFECTS (environmental):
drone (of traffic)
filtration (mainly low frequencies heard)

AURAL EFFECTS (experiential):
ubiquity (difficult to determine where traffic hum comes

SOUND EVENTS (outside kiln):
1. wind in grass - constant, rhythmical
2. traffic - constant, background
3. distant bird song - intermittent,
   sporadic

AURAL EFFECTS (environmental):
partial cut-out when entering kiln
reverberation within kiln (footsteps,
movement)
amplification when exiting

SOUND EVENTS:
1. brushing of grass - constant,
   rhythmical
2. buzzing stridulation of insects -
   intermittent, rhythmical
3. bird songs and calls - intermittent

AURAL EFFECTS (experiential):
saliency (brushing of grass and
leaves, bird calls, insects
(bees and crickets)
synedoche effect (selective
listening or focus on salient sounds,
forgetting about traffic)

Figure 11.9 Sound events and aural effects for the Old Pottery, Corbridge, Base axonometric credit: EDable Architecture.

Identification of constraints and opportunities

Once the site inventory is complete, all information is assessed in line with the brief for the site to determine a place's *aural opportunities* and *constraints*. These can be summarised in a diagram or map (Figure 11.10).

Aural opportunities might include retaining or bringing attention to positive listening experiences or the chance to introduce new listening experiences that can contribute to the design principles and strategies for the site.

Aural constraints might derive from a place's geometry and materiality, which causes aural effects that impede communication. Alternatively, they might be negative listening experiences that originate outside the site and might prevent the enjoyment or legibility of a place.

Composing the soundscape

RIBA and LI stages 2–4: concept design, developed design and technical design
We read the landscape to intervene in it. Reading the landscape enables us to identify opportunities for change and conceptualise ideas to inform the design interventions that follow. Conceptual ideas might spring from a place's identity or *genius loci*, the existing narratives uncovered during the reading stage or other sources of inspiration. Conceptual ideas are turned into themes or principles to drive the outline design. Once the outline design has been agreed upon with the client and end users, we develop proposals into a final design and detail materials. We produce a set of technical drawings and specifications and visualisations or other forms of representation, such as models, that help us represent and sell the proposed scheme. We use visualisations for various purposes, including planning applications, community engagements, client engagements and marketing.

Through listening, we decipher stories embedded in the landscape and seek opportunities to intervene in it; thus, we play a part in its composition. However, listening requires time, as we cannot instantly grasp landscapes. Thus, listening can help us uncover qualities and processes in the landscape that are otherwise missed and design from or with what is already there instead of starting anew.

Sound, in turn, can be a creative element in the concept and detailed design process, expressing or emphasizing the overall concept and thus engaging existing and future listeners with a site's stories. Sound plays an important role in how a site functions, aiding with legibility and navigation, supporting context-based activities and adding complexity, where needed, to enrich the multisensorial experience and

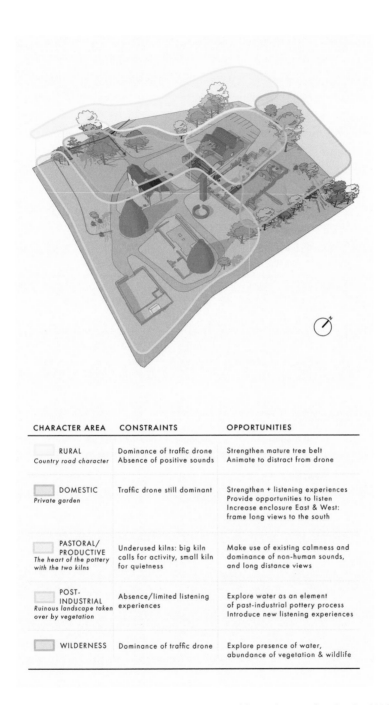

CHARACTER AREA	CONSTRAINTS	OPPORTUNITIES
RURAL *Country road character*	Dominance of traffic drone Absence of positive sounds	Strengthen mature tree belt Animate to distract from drone
DOMESTIC *Private garden*	Traffic drone still dominant	Strengthen + listening experiences Provide opportunities to listen Increase enclosure East & West: frame long views to the south
PASTORAL/ PRODUCTIVE *The heart of the pottery with the two kilns*	Underused kilns: big kiln calls for activity, small kiln for quietness	Make use of existing calmness and dominance of non-human sounds, and long distance views
POST- INDUSTRIAL *Ruinous landscape taken over by vegetation*	Absence/limited listening experiences	Explore water as an element of past-industrial pottery process Introduce new listening experiences
WILDERNESS	Dominance of traffic drone	Explore presence of water, abundance of vegetation & wildlife

Figure 11.10 Landscape character areas with aural opportunities and constraints for the Old Pottery, Corbridge, Base axonometric credit: EDable Architecture.

quality of the place. Finally, auralisations, as a counterpart to visualisations, can also be used for a variety of purposes, together with visualisations or on their own: from aiding the designer in the creative processes through helping designers and communities envisage how proposals will sound, to supporting planning applications, client presentations and marketing. In this last, we can use the affective engagement that listening elicits to engage listeners with a potential project or site.

At this stage, we can develop a *soundscape strategy* with a set of aural *principles* and *strategies* to strengthen the layered concept for the site, work with each of the character areas and uses proposed and, in the process, increase positive listening experiences and reduce negative listening experiences identified through reading the soundscape. In doing so, the *soundscape strategy* is integrated within the overall *design principles* and *strategies* for the site and, thus, concerned not only with the experience of the soundscape but also with the experience of the landscape.

Aural principles

The four core principles for successful landscape and urban design schemes are *legibility, variety, coherence* and *narrative*. These core principles emerge from Kaplan and Kaplan's (1989) environmental behaviour research, as highlighted by Dee (2001),

	strategies at source	strategies at propagation	strategies at listener	
legibility	omit, reduce, hide / distract / reveal, reinforce, amplify	aural effects / landscape elements	soundmarks / sensorial distraction	
variety	curation of listening experiences: active passive natural/other sounds	form / materiality	sensorial play	
coherence	aural moods	adjacencies of aural moods	appropriateness / degree of control	
narrative	aural narratives	aural effects	perceptual aural effects	

Figure 11.11 Core design principles and corresponding aural strategies at the source of sound, propagation and listener.

acoustic design principles proposed by Truax (1984), placemaking and placekeeping literature and practice (Project for Public Spaces, 2022; Hickey, 2023), and my project experience as a landscape architect and educator. *Legibility* and *coherence* are linked to understanding the environment and *variety* and *narrative* to explore the environment (Kaplan and Kaplan, 1989).

In aural terms, we can envisage these principles applied to places as:

Legible places are aurally accessible and connected. They can be understood aurally, and listening aids in navigating through them.

Varied places have sufficient sound events to keep our listening active, enabling users to receive information to understand and engage with the environment.

Coherent places come together as a whole, aurally. That is, they have sound events that are appropriate to each character area and the activities that each will hold and are appropriate to the overall identity of the place and its context.

Finally, places with a *narrative* are embedded in their physical and cultural context, in the aural stories that the landscape already holds or in new stories to be held in the landscape. These places encourage social interaction and invite visitors to return and explore them.

Aural strategies: modification of listening experiences to implement aural (and design) principles.

There are three points of intervention where listener experiences can be modified: at the source of a sound event, at the propagation of sound and at the perceiving end (the listener). For each design principle introduced above, we can propose a corresponding set of aural strategies to implement those principles at each point of intervention, as summarised in Figure 11.11.

Key strategies for each design principle are introduced next, and the reader is encouraged to turn to Chapter 7 for further detail.

Aural strategies for legibility

STRATEGIES AT THE SOURCE OF SOUND EVENT

Omit, reduce, hide
The soundscape assessment would have identified a series of negative listening experiences that might be detrimental to legibility. Those negative listening experiences

could be linked to specific sound events within the site that we can *omit, reduce* or *hide*. We can also predict future negative listening experiences that can be omitted or reduced at this stage.

Distract

If we cannot omit or reduce the source of a sound, we can introduce positive sounds to *distract* from the negative ones through a *masking* effect. For example, adding fountains is a common strategy to *distract* from traffic noise, particularly when constant (Coensel, Vanwetswinkel and Botteldooren, 2011).

Reveal, reinforce, amplify

This is a simple case of revealing what is already there, choreographing a listening experience across a site that encourages users to listen at a particular place to particular sounds. This could be achieved by re-routing a path or adding seating that brings listeners closer to the source of the sound. This approach aligns with the origin of the word design as to 'mark out' (OED online, 2023). All a site might need might already be there, and listening might encourage us to keep and reveal it.

STRATEGIES AT PROPAGATION

Aural effects

At the design stage, we can remove or amend *aural effects* that reduce legibility, such as *ubiquity*, and introduce aural effects that might contribute positively to the experience of place and navigation through it, for example, through reverberation of *soundmarks*.

Landscape elements

Shallow planted earth berms, or noise walls close to sound events can reduce the propagation of sound waves (Figure 11.12). Deep tree belts (15–30 m) close to the source of sound can also help, as tree trunks scatter sound waves and planted soil absorbs them (Van Renterghem, De Coensel and Botteldooren, 2013). Enclosing a space partially or fully through soft or hard landscaping can also limit other sounds filtering into the space and accentuate positive sound sources already there.

STRATEGIES AT LISTENER

Soundmarks

Soundmarks are the aural counterpart to landmarks and can help with legibility. *Soundmarks* are the salient aural features of a place and can be introduced to help

Figure 11.12 Inside the earth berm ridges at Buitenschot Park, Schipholf Airport, Amsterdam, designed to reduce low-frequency ground-level noise caused by airplanes taking off through absorption and dispersion, Paul de Kort.

the listener orientate themselves and navigate a place. Examples include the church bells of a town or a characteristic foghorn of coastal communities.

Sensorial distraction

Each sense provides information about the environment differently, which is useful in the design process. The sight of vegetation, for example, can *distract* from traffic noise and contribute to a more positive evaluation of the environment (Van Renterghem and Botteldooren, 2016; Aletta, Oberman and Kang, 2018). This can help with the legibility and use of that environment.

Aural strategies for variety

STRATEGIES AT THE SOURCE OF SOUND EVENT

Curation of listening experiences

Aural variety in a place might be actively sought or a byproduct of the wider variety sought through the design proposals. In both instances, to prevent soundscapes from becoming monotonous, sounds within them should balance a degree of *regularity* and *variation* (Truax, 1984, p. 101).

Aural variety could be introduced by facilitating natural sounds that are associated with health and well-being benefits (Levenhagen *et al.*, 2021) and contribute to evaluating an environment as pleasant. Natural sounds can be introduced in design by establishing new habitats that will increase the biophony of the place, new trees, vegetation planting and the introduction of flowing water.

Aural variety can also be introduced by facilitating a wide range of activities appropriate to the character of a place. For example, designing a streetscape to facilitate informal play and socialisation that will result in a vibrant soundscape of voices.

STRATEGIES AT PROPAGATION

Form
The *forms* we create in the landscape and how those forms are surfaced and enclosed in all dimensions will give rise to one or several aural effects that contribute to variety and legibility. For example, a *cut-out* effect could add variety to a string of interconnected spaces.

Materiality
How a material sounds should be a consideration when curating a materials palette for a scheme. Materials, whether hard or soft, will alter the absorption, reflection and diffraction of sound waves travelling through space. Materials also sound through interaction with atmospheric and biotic agents. For example, footsteps vary depending on the surfacing walked: from the crunching of gravel surfaces to the sharpness of smooth granite paving.

STRATEGIES AT LISTENER

Sensorial play
The richness of the senses can also be employed to add variety through the design of spaces that provide diverse sensorial stimuli to create a varied environment. Listening can provide engagement with the environment as a complement to other sensorial stimuli or in the absence of other sensorial stimuli, thus adding variety to an otherwise monotonous space. For example, a post-industrial landscape might not have much to look at but could have a rich biodiversity and, thus, plenty to listen to.

Aural strategies for coherence

STRATEGIES AT THE SOURCE OF SOUND EVENT

Aural moods

Outline design proposals for a site are often drafted as conceptual diagrams and spatial diagrams that indicate the character or functional areas proposed for a site, with the array of activities each will host. Character areas have key characteristics that make them distinctive to those experiencing and perceiving the place. In turn, character areas have distinctive soundscapes that express the physical characteristics of the environment, the communities living within them and their interactions and activities. An aural character can be actively designed or composed through *aural moods* or indirectly result from those characteristics and interactions.

We should consider activities, interactions and uses as sound events in composing *aural moods*. Sound events are altered by the acoustic properties (physical characteristics) of the spaces proposed, affecting the behaviour and activities of the people experiencing those spaces. Theoretical models of soundscape affective perception can help us develop aural moods. These models follow prevailing theories of affect and focus on two orthogonal dimensions: *pleasantness* and *eventfulness* (BSI, 2019) and are primarily focused on calm and vibrant moods. According to these affective models, a *vibrant* soundscape would include a suitable number of sound events (varied), perceived to harmonise with one another (coherent and pleasant), appropriate to the setting (legible), and with a degree of variation over time. A *calm* soundscape could be described very similarly, but with quieter or fewer events that still provide a degree of engagement and are audible against the ambient noise.

STRATEGIES AT PROPAGATION

Adjacencies of aural moods

All elements and activities should come together for a site to be coherent, including their aural expression. Accordingly, we need to think that some activities can share an acoustic space, and it might be beneficial to do so, for example, to create vibrancy, as detailed above. Others, however, might need isolation. Equally, we need to consider how the aural expression of activities of one space might impact the activities of nearby others and whether we might want to apply strategies to contain them or whether filtering one to another provides a degree of connection and, therefore, coherence.

STRATEGIES AT LISTENER

Appropriateness and degree of control
The *appropriateness* of sound events to a place and the perceived *degree of control* over those sounds add to the affective quality of the soundscape (Axelsson, 2015).

With regard to *appropriateness,* as designers, we can consider how the proposed aural environment might influence the behaviour of its users within the space. With regard to the *perceived degree of control*, as designers, we can provide *clarity* within a space. *Clarity* refers to the ability of a listener to distinguish sounds clearly within a space. *Clarity* might be achieved by avoiding the design of constant hums, for example, by keeping car circulation and car parking to the perimeter of a masterplan and encouraging pedestrian-priority streetscapes.

Aural strategies for narrative

STRATEGIES AT THE SOURCE OF SOUND EVENT

Aural narratives
Aural narratives can drive the design of a site and link to the existing or proposed character, ecology or communities within a site. The case study *The High Street Goodsyard* in Chapter 8 provides an example of an *aural narrative* to guide the design. In this case, sound was used to reveal a buried history of *a non-place,* that of the culverted Molendinar Burn. The aural concept sought to expose the burn through sound in the landscape to expose the site's rich history and was accompanied by other design principles that, in conjunction, drove the site's design.

STRATEGIES AT PROPAGATION

Aural effects
Aural effects that are both environmental (propagation) and experiential (listener) can invite exploration of a place, thus adding mystery. Landscape architect Gunnar Cerwén has coined a set of soundscape actions (2019, 2020), three of which are applicable at this stage:

- *Tranquillity by contrast*: linked to the cut-out effect, it refers to an aural spatial contrast that can induce tranquillity
- *Shrouded sounds* refer to sources of sound that can be heard but not seen and can add mystery to a place, inviting further exploration.
- *Hide and revel* is an example of an aural walking narrative, where sounds are hidden and revealed as the user moves along a path (ibid.).

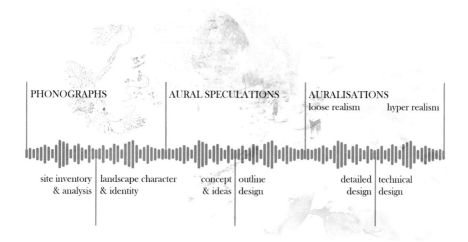

Figure 11.13 Three-stage sequence of auralisations mapped to design stages.

STRATEGIES AT LISTENER

Perceptual *aural effects* can also invite further explorations of a place, including *anamnesis* and *remanence*, introduced earlier.

Auralisations

Auralisations as a counterpart to visualisations for landscape and urban design can be envisaged following a three-stage sequence (Figure 11.13):

1. *Phonographs*, as projections from the ground and documentation. These are the aural counterparts of photographs, and can be simple field recordings taken during the site inventory to document the existing soundscape.
2. *Aural speculations*, as spatial speculations that emerge from the context and are situated between the real and imaginary. Aural speculations can vary in degree of abstraction. They can start from site field recordings, manipulated through software such as Audacity (free), Reaper and Adobe Audition (part of Adobe creative suite). Designers might also seek to collaborate with sound artists and musicians for more elaborated sonic outputs.
3. *Auralisations*, as aural projections onto the ground. These can range from *loose realism* auralisations that help the designer think and communicate draft ideas and

plans to *hyperreal* auralisations that seek to represent proposals aurally as accurately as possible. The first can vary in degree of abstraction and can start from field recordings of sites. The second requires specialist simulation software and might require input from acousticians.

Performing the soundscape

RIBA and LI stages 5–7: Construction, handover, and close and in use

During the construction and post-construction stages of a project, sound can be used to monitor the health and changes in a habitat, but also on our journey towards becoming *soundscape architects*. Monitoring and recording how the soundscape of a site and our designs evolve throughout the day and in time will help us predict future soundscapes with applications at all project stages.

Bio and ecoacoustic for sound monitoring

Sound is integral to the behaviour and communication of many animal and plant species, including us. Animals defend their territories, attract mates and identify their offspring through vocalization. Animals rely on sound to navigate space, hunt and form communities. Plant species also listen, sound and are impacted by noise. The soundscape, defined from an environmental perspective, expresses the landscape, the movement and the interaction of biological, geological and anthropological components. Often, the soundscape evolves with the landscape, but sometimes, the soundscape can 'reveal subtler environmental changes' (Ross *et al.*, 2018, p. 135). Studying the soundscape can provide invaluable information on how a habitat develops or is impacted by human and natural processes.

The fields of bioacoustics and ecoacoustics investigate biological sound from an ecological perspective. Bioacoustics is concerned with the study of a single animal species and is sustained by the *Acoustic Niche Hypothesis* (ANH) (Krause, 1987). The ANH proposes that a healthy habitat has an animal orchestra in tune, as animal species adapt their calls to avoid frequency and temporal overlaps with other species, thus finding their acoustic niches to communicate. In this manner, the soundscape is divided to avoid interference amongst different species and the tuning of the resulting animal orchestra can be a sign of the ecosystem's health, as species need time to find their acoustic niches. Consequently, temporary or permanent habitat disruptions, such as tree removal and subsequent replanting, could have considerable soundscape implications (Krause and Hoffman, 2012).

Ecoacoustics differs from bioacoustics in that in ecoacoustics, sound is studied and regarded as an expression of 'ecological processes,' whereas, in bioacoustics, sound is studied 'as a signal that transfers information between individuals' (Fletcher, 2007 in Sueur and Farina, 2015, p. 494). Ecoacoustics operates at three acoustic levels: *species* (building on bioacoustics), *communities* and *soundscape* (Farina, 2018, p. 3). An *acoustic community* emerges from the combination of biophonies at a particular time and place and is subject to daily and seasonal changes and human impact. The *soundscape* results from the combination of geophonies, biophonies and anthrophonies of a particular landscape and is again affected by factors that influence the development and evolution of the landscape (ibid.).

Ecoacoustics tools, protocols and applications

Ecoacoustics and bioacoustics use passive sound monitoring techniques to understand species' behaviour and makeup and how the diversity and abundance of a habitat evolve. Passive acoustic monitoring techniques use low-power, weatherproof sound recorders with in-built microphones attached to trees or other elements and left on site. Recordings can be analysed at a *species*, *community* or *soundscape* level.

At *species* and *community* levels, animal signals are studied to understand communication and behaviour in time. Recorded data are analysed through listening and visual analysis of spectrograms. To speed up data analysis, commercial and open-access artificial intelligence and machine learning bioacoustic analysis software has been developed (e.g., K.Lisa Yang Center for Conservation Bioacoustics, 2023; Wildlife Acoustics, 2023). For example, in April 2022, I installed a passive sound monitor (AudioMoth) on a small tree in our terraced house small front garden to track the evolution and composition of the Dawn Chorus. The AudioMoth was programmed to record from 3 am to 7 am at regular intervals every day. Initial recordings were analysed with BirdNet first to identify bird species make-up and change in time and annotate spectrograms (Figure 11.14, Soundtrack 11.1). These annotations facilitated the visual analysis of spectrograms of later recordings.

At a *soundscape* level, acoustic indices are calculated to quantify and summarize soundscapes in a snapshot (Ross *et al.*, 2021). Frequently used indices include the *Acoustic Complexity Index* (ACI), *Acoustic Richness* and *Normalised Difference Soundscape Index* (NDSI). The latter evaluates the proportion of biophonies and technophonies

Figure 11.14 Annotated spectrogram of a section of a dawn chorus monitoring soundtrack at the author's home; 15 April 2022, 5 am (UTC) (Soundtrack 11.1,50 to 115 seconds).

in an environment (ibid., p. 6). This index is particularly relevant for urban sound-scapes as it evaluates the human impact on the environment and ranges from −1 (all technophonies) to +1 (all biophonies) (ibid.). Data analysis software for calculating soundscape indices includes *soundecology* (Villanueva-Rivera and Pijanowski, 2018) and *seewave* (Sueur, Aubin, and Simonis, 2022) packages in R statistical software.

There are many advantages of passive sound monitoring techniques over tradi-tional ecological survey methods, including that passive sound monitoring tech-niques are non-invasive and can be deployed at a large scale (Sueur and Farina, 2015), and they enable monitoring in sensitive and challenging sites (Ross *et al.,* 2018), including fresh and saline water habitats.

These advantages mean that the disciplines of bioacoustics and ecoacoustics are constantly being developed and protocols and best practice guidance produced. Recently published protocols that the reader might want to turn to plan their ecoa-coustic monitoring study include the open-access *Good practice guidelines for long-term ecoacoustic monitoring in the UK* (Metcalf *et al.*, 2022). These guidelines provide in-depth information on choosing and deploying relevant hardware and collecting and analysing acoustic data for ecological purposes.

Bio and ecoacoustics are up-and-coming fields with applications for designing and managing urban and periurban spaces. For example, at the early stages of a pro-ject, ecoacoustic methods can be integrated alongside traditional ecological surveys to provide in-depth ecological surveys of sites at the *species* and *community* levels. Later, ecoacoustic methods can be employed to track the biodiversity impact, both positive and negative, of our schemes in time (including subtle changes). Bio and ecoacoustic methods can also be integrated into citizen science projects to engage communities with the non-human world scientifically (in data analysis) and through listening (to recorded acoustic data).

Bio and ecoacostics challenges include that the large amount of data obtained requires AI analysis methods. The danger with this is that when studying the acous-tic data, we no longer engage with the environment, and its inhabitants, through listening. Various interdisciplinary projects have sought to interweave objective and subjective approaches to environmental management through sound to overcome this shortfall. Projects such as *Biosphere Soundscapes* (2022) rely on sound to monitor the health of ecosystems and assess change and on listening to communicate and engage communities in those dynamic ecosystems through arts and citizen science methods.

Conclusion

Becoming *soundscape architects* will require time, the development of new tools, skills and knowledge, and collaboration with other disciplines. All landscape architects and urban designers involved in designing and managing meaningful environments would benefit from being exposed to those tools, skills and knowledge as part of their training and development. A standard approach that can be integrated into existing pedagogical and working practices, such as that introduced in the preceding manual, is also required to accompany landscape architects and urban designers on their journey.[1]

Note
1. An early version of this manual was presented at the Inter. Noise conference in Madrid (Ruiz Arana, 2019) included in my Ph.D. thesis (Ruiz Arana, 2020) and published in the Landscape Journal (Ruiz Arana, 2021). The draft guide was also granted the 2020 Landscape Institute's Innovation Award.

References

Aletta, F., Oberman, T. and Kang, J. (2018) 'Associations between positive health-related effects and soundscapes perceptual constructs: A systematic review', *International Journal of Environmental Research and Public Health*, 15(11), pp. 1–15. doi: 10.3390/ijerph15112392.

Augoyard, J.-F. and Torgue, H. (2005) *Sonic experience: A guide to everyday sounds.* 1st englis. Montreal, Ithaca: McGill-Queen's University Press.

Axelsson, Ö. (2015) 'How to measure soundscape quality', *Proceedings of Euronoise 2015*, Mastricht, pp. 1477–1481. Available at: https://www.conforg.fr/euronoise2015/proceedings/data/articles/000067.pdf.

Biosphere Soundscapes (2022) *About biosphere soundscapes, biosphere soundscapes.* Available at: http://www.biospheresoundscapes.org/about.html (Accessed: 10 April 2022).

Blesser, B. and Salter, L. (2007) *Spaces speak, are you listening? experiencing aural architecture*. Cambridge, MA: MIT Press.

BSI (The British Standards Institution) (2014) 'ISO 12913-1: 2014 acoustics — Soundscape Part 1 : Definition and conceptual framework'.

BSI (The British Standards Institution) (2018) 'ISO / TS 12913 - 2 : 2018 BSI Standards Publication Acoustics — Soundscape', *BSI Standards Publication*.

BSI (The British Standards Institution) (2019) 'ISO / TS 12913 - 3:2019 BSI Standards Publication Acoustics — Soundscape - Part 3: Data analysis', pp. 1–30.

Cerwén, G. (2019) 'Listening to Japanese gardens: An autoethnographic study on the soundscape action design tool', *International Journal of Environmental Research and Public Health*, 16(23), pp. 1–30. doi: 10.3390/ijerph16234648.

Cerwén, G. (2020) 'Listening to Japanese gardens II: Expanding the soundscape action design tool', *Journal of Urban Design*, 25(5), pp. 607–628. doi: 10.1080/13574809.2020.1782183.

Coensel, B. De, Vanwetswinkel, S. and Botteldooren, D. (2011) 'Effects of natural sounds on the perception of road traffic noise', *The Journal of the Acoustical Society of America*, 129(4), pp. EL148–EL153. doi: 10.1121/1.3567073.

Dee, C. (2001) *Form and fabric in landscape architecture: A visual introduction*. online. London: Spon Press.

European Parliament and Council (2002) 'Directive 2002/49/EC of the European Parliament and of the Council of the 25th June 2002, relating to the assessment and management of environmental noise', *Official Journal of the European Communities*, L189, pp. 12–25.

Farina, A. (2018) 'Ecoacoustics: A quantitative approach to investigate the ecological role of environmental sounds', *Mathematics*, 7(1), pp. 1–16. doi: 10.3390/math7010021.

Hannah, L. (2006) 'Wind and temperature effects on sound propagation', *New Zealand Acoustics*, 20(2), pp. 22–29.

Hickey, M. (2023) *Through an indigenous lens: A shift from placemaking to placekeeping, evergreen*. Available at: https://www.evergreen.ca/blog/entry/through-an-indigenous-lens-a-shift-from-placemaking-to-placekeeping/ (Accessed: 23 June 2023).

Jørgensen, K. *et al.* (2020) 'Teaching landscape architecture: A discipline comes of age', *Landscape Research*, 00(00), pp. 1–12. doi: 10.1080/01426397.2020.1849588.

Kaplan, R. and Kaplan, S. (1989) *The experience of nature: A psychological perspective*. Cambridge: Cambridge University Press.

K.Lisa Yang Center for Conservation Bioacoustics (2023) *BirdNET Sound ID, The Cornell Lab*. Available at: https://birdnet.cornell.edu/ (Accessed: 26 June 2023).

Krause, B. (1987) 'Bioacoustics, habitat ambience in ecological balance', *Whole Earth Review*, 57 (Winter), pp. 14–18.

Krause, B. L. and Hoffman, J. (2012) 'Q & A Bernie Krause soundscape explorer', *Nature*, 485(May), p. 308. doi: 10.1038/485308a.

Landscape Institute (2018) *Landscape consultant's scope of services S1: Landscape design & administrative/post contract services.* London: Landscape Institute.

Levenhagen, M. J. *et al.* (2021) 'Ecosystem services enhanced through soundscape management link people and wildlife', *People and Nature*, 3(1), pp. 176–189. doi: 10.1002/pan3.10156.

Metcalf, O. *et al.* (2022) *Good practice guidelines for long-term ecoacoustic monitoring in the UK.*UK Acoustics Network.

Odland, B. and Auinger, S. (2010) *Hearing perspective (Think with Your Ear), O + A.* Available at: http://www.o-a.info/background/hearperspec.htm (Accessed: 21 July 2015).

OED online (2023) *design, v., Oxford University Press.* Available at: https://www. oed.com/view/Entry/50841?rskey=16BETF&result=2&isAdvanced=false#eid (Accessed: 23 June 2023).

Oliveros, P. (1999) 'Quantum listening: From practice to theory (To practice practice) ', *Sound Art Archive*, pp. 1–22. Available at: https://s3.amazonaws.com/aren a-attachments/736945/19af465bc3fcf3c8d5249713cd586b28.pdf.

Oliveros, P. (2013) *Anthology of text scores, women & music.* Edited by S. Golter and L. Hall. Kingston, NY: Deep Listening Publications.

Oliveros, P. (2015) *The difference between hearing and listening, TEDx talks.* Available at: https://www.youtube.com/watch?v=_QHfOuRrJB8 (Accessed: 27 March 2023).

Project for Public Spaces (2022) *PLACEMAKING what If we built our cities around places ? A Placemaking primer.* Available at: http://www.pps.org/wp-content/uploads/ 2016/10/Oct-2016-placemaking-booklet.pdf.

RIBA (2020) *RIBA Plan of Work 2020, Contract administration.* doi: 10.4324/ 9780429347177-2.

Ross, S. R. P. J. *et al.* (2018) 'Listening to ecosystems: Data–rich acoustic monitoring through landscape-scale sensor networks', *Ecological Research*, 33(1), pp. 135–147. doi: 10.1007/s11284-017-1509-5.

Ross, S. R. P. J. *et al.* (2021) 'Utility of acoustic indices for ecological monitoring in complex sonic environments', *Ecological Indicators*, 121(July 2020), p. 107114. doi: 10.1016/j.ecolind.2020.107114.

Ruiz Arana, U. (2019) 'Thinking with my ears: Guidance on sound for landscape architects', Conference Proceedings of 48th International Congress and

Exposition on Noise Control Engineering (Internoise 2019), Madrid: Spanish Acoustical Society, pp. 5968–5975.

Ruiz Arana, U. (2020) *The enchantment of the wild: A journey into wildness through listening.* Newcastle University. Available at: http://theses.ncl.ac.uk/jspui/handle/10443/5178

Ruiz Arana, U. (2021) 'Thinking with my ears', *Landscape Journal*, 21(2), pp. 29–32.

Schafer, R. M. (1967a) *Ear cleaning.* Toronto: Berandol Music Limited.

Schafer, R. M. (1967b) *The book of noise.* Wellington, New Zealand: Price Milburn & Co.

Schafer, R. M. (1977) *The soundscape: Our sonic environment and the tuning of the world.* New York: Knopf.

Sueur, J., Aubin, T. and Simonis, C. (2022) *Seewave v 2.2.0.* Available at: https://cran.r-project.org/web/packages/seewave/seewave.pdf.

Sueur, J. and Farina, A. (2015) 'Ecoacoustics: The ecological investigation and interpretation of environmental sound', *Biosemiotics*, 8(3), pp. 493–502. doi: 10.1007/s12304-015-9248-x.

The Center for Deep Listening (2021) *About deep listening, the center for deep listening.* Available at: https://www.deeplistening.rpi.edu/deep-listening/.

Thompson, E. (2012) 'Sound, modernity and history', in Sterne, J. (ed.) *The sound studies reader.* Oxon and New York: Routledge, pp. 117–129.

Trikootam, S. C. and Hornikx, M. (2019) 'The wind effect on sound propagation over urban areas: Experimental approach with an uncontrolled sound source', *Building and Environment*, 149(November 2018), pp. 561–570. doi: 10.1016/j.buildenv.2018.11.037.

Truax, B. (1984) *Acoustic communication, Springer handbook of Ocean engineering.* Norwood, NJ: Ablex Publishing Corporation. doi: 10.1007/978-3-319-16649-0_15.

Truax, B. (1999) *Handbook for acoustic ecology.* Second ed. Vancouver: Cambridge Street Publishing.

Van Renterghem, T. and Botteldooren, D. (2016) 'View on outdoor vegetation reduces noise annoyance for dwellers near busy roads', *Landscape and Urban Planning*, 148 (April), pp. 203–215. doi: 10.1016/j.landurbplan.2015.12.018.

Van Renterghem, T., De Coensel, B. and Botteldooren, D. (2013) 'Loudness evaluation of road traffic noise abatement by tree belts', Proceedings of the 42nd International Congress and Exposition on Noise Control Engineering (Internoise 2013), Innsbruck, Austria.

Villanueva-Rivera, L. J. and Pijanowski, B. C. (2018) *Soundscape ecology v 1.3.3.* Available at: https://cran.r-project.org/web/packages/soundecology/soundecology.pdf.

Westerkamp, H. (1974) 'Soundwalking', *Sound Heritage*, III(4), pp. 18–27.

WHO Regional Office for Europe (2011) *Burden of disease from environmental noise*, World Health Organization.

Wildlife Acoustics (2023) *Kaleidoscope*, Wildlife Acoustics. Available at: https://www.wildlifeacoustics.com/products/kaleidoscope (Accessed: 26 June 2023).

Index

absorption 104–106, 169–170, 263, 266
acoustemology 18
acoustic(s) 17–18, 20; *arena* 103–104, 257,
 263; communication 6, 20, 73; *community*
 21, 26, 229, 281; ecology 17–18, 26, 85;
 environment 6, 23–24; *horizon* 103–104,
 263; *indicators* 24, 40, 58, 101, 108; indices
 100, 107, 230, 281–282; psychoacoustics
 17; *see also* Apex Acoustics
action plan *see* masterplan
affective: affordances 37–39; *intentionality*
 37–39
affectivity *see* embodied affectivity
amplify 167–168, 170, 274
amplitude 52, 230
anthrophony 4, 100, 253
Apex Acoustics 199–204
appropriateness 106–107, 176–178,
 267–278
attunement 7, 10, 45, 59; *see also* tuning in
Audio Postcards Canada 215–217
auditory: *channel* 103–104, 148,
 263–264; effects 49–50; *sensation*
 23, 34
Auinger, S. 3, 252–253

Augoyard, J.-F. 110–111, 115, 168, 180,
 263, 266
aural: character 96, 101–102, 175, 260; *diversity* 33; effects (*see* sonic effects); identity 101–102, 109, 141, 146, 267; mood
 175–177, 277; palette 173–174, 209;
 principles 160, 272–273; space 102–104,
 263; speculations 182, 215, 279
auralisations 181–186, 279–280; aural
 speculations 182–186, 279; phonographs
 182–186, 279

Barclay, L. 18, 26, 238–239, 249
binaural 24, 33, 58, 137, 204, 259
bioacoustics 17–18, 228–231, 280–282
Biodiversity Net Gain 125
biophony 4, 100, 253
bodily: feedback 38, 40–41; *resonance* 37–42
Building with Nature 124–125

cacophony 1, 235, 237; *cacophony-hubbub*
 22, 176
Cerwén 168, 180, 192, 278
Chion, M. 32, 35–36
climate 9, 99, 104, 229